THE ROLE OF AN
EDUCATION ASSISTANT

THE ROLE OF AN EDUCATION ASSISTANT

Supporting Inclusion

EDITED BY

Mary Harber
and Asha Rao

CANADIAN
SCHOLARS
Toronto | Vancouver

The Role of an Education Assistant: Supporting Inclusion
Edited by Mary Harber and Asha Rao

First published in 2019 by
Canadian Scholars, an imprint of CSP Books Inc.
425 Adelaide Street West, Suite 200
Toronto, Ontario
M5V 3C1

www.canadianscholars.ca

Library and Archives Canada Cataloguing in Publication

Title: The role of an education assistant : supporting inclusion / edited by Mary Harber and Asha Rao.
Names: Harber, Mary, 1961- editor. | Rao, Asha, 1974- editor.
Identifiers: Canadiana (print) 20190119691 | Canadiana (ebook) 20190119705 | ISBN 9781773381121 (softcover) | ISBN 9781773381138 (PDF) | ISBN 9781773381145 (EPUB)
Subjects: LCSH: Teachers' assistants—Canada. | LCSH: Inclusive education—Canada.
Classification: LCC LB2844.1.A8 R65 2019 | DDC 371.14/1240971—dc23

Page layout by S4Carlisle Publishing Services
Cover design by Michel Vrana
Cover image by iStock.com/ivanastar

Printed and bound in Ontario, Canada

Canada

CONTENTS

Intercultural

SECTION IV – SUPPORTING ALL STUDENTS   213

Classroom Inclusion

Academics

FOREWORD

When my son Asher, who is funny and smart, autistic and has an intellectual disability, was in grade 5, his education assistant Ms. Kinard taught him how to do double- and triple-digit multiplication. I was shocked … and so were his teacher and my mathematician husband. We had tried to teach him how to "carry the …" but no one had succeeded, and so we had given up, believing that single-digit multiplication was as much as he could do.

Asher is now a young man, and I could tell you many similar stories of education assistants who were involved in our lives over the years— *our* lives, because the best years we had in the early intervention and education systems were those in which we worked in teams: teachers, parents, education assistants. Not all of the education assistants were so exceptional and not all of the school years great, of course, but our interactions with outstanding teachers and education assistants showed us the possibilities of inclusive education. Those good years taught us to resist the pressure toward self-contained "resource rooms" and to advocate for an educational environment with high expectations, well-qualified and -trained education professionals, and a culture of belonging. Often it was Asher's education assistants that brought those classroom characteristics to life, supporting him academically in the classroom, recognizing his behaviours as communication, and helping him form social connections in the classroom, on the playground, and in the cafeteria.

At each stage of Asher's schooling, creative education assistants provided him with access to a rich general education curriculum. His inclusion in our neighbourhood schools and in typical classrooms continued through high school, when most students like him were being placed in "life skills" programs. His teachers and education assistants supported access to biology, English, and history classes, and he learned food science alongside students interested in becoming professional chefs. In grade 10, Asher's interest in the television series *Dora the Explorer* resulted in two years of Spanish classes and in grade 12 he elected to take a social justice class that explored disability rights alongside the rights of women, LGTBQ+, Indigenous Peoples, and racial minorities. None of this was expected. All the classes were heavily modified, and these learning opportunities would not have been accessible without the support of very determined education assistants who knew Asher well.

That's why I am so excited about this collection. Its themes— inclusion, professionalism, social and emotional well-being, social justice, culture, and intersectionality—are timely. In many provinces chronic underfunding of education has had a direct effect on the quality of inclusive education, impacting both students with disabilities and education assistants. This collection of essays focuses on the role of the education assistant and highlights practices that enhance education for every student. Of equal importance, this book is a Canadian collection, something that has been missing for far too long. To date, the professional and academic literature in the field has been dominated by American publications that don't quite work in Canadian colleges and university programs nor in the diverse schools and communities across Canada in which education assistants work. Given the stark and nuanced differences in the two countries' education systems, Canadian research and writing in the field is essential.

As a reader who is preparing to become or is already a practicing education assistant, the essays included here will both validate and challenge you. This book, which reflects the complexity of the work done by education assistants, will expand your thinking and motivate you to become more creative in your work with students of all abilities. It will help you make a difference in the lives of children and youth and their families.

Asher can still do double- and triple-digit multiplication ... and he can hold a social conversation, tell a joke, make change for customers at work, and ride the bus independently. He has a good life. He is included in his community as he was included in his school classes—thanks in large part to education assistants who believed in his capabilities and used their skills to help him develop his own.

—Catriona Johnson, MSc, Research and Innovation Lead,
Community Living BC

PREFACE

The education assistant (EA) provides a wide range of both academic and social support for students in school. This role, frequently viewed as that of a "paid friend" who was "velcroed" to the student and was responsible for making sure that they maintained appropriate behaviour has now evolved. Brown, Farrington, Knight, Ross, and Ziegler (1991) suggest that students with the most complex challenges to learning "are in dire need of continuous exposure to the most ingenious, creative, powerful, competent, interpersonally effective, and informed professionals" (p. 252). In contrast to this, EAs often have limited education and receive minimal support within the job yet are supporting more and more students with complex needs in the classroom (Malcolmson, 2009). Hoyano (2012) and Blatchford et al. (2012) identify common concerns over how EAs are supported and used within the education system. These relate to a lack of preparation time, ongoing training, and education; lack of recognition of the role as critical to the overall team; and expectations of working more hours than allotted to support students with higher and more complex needs. In addition, we know that use of EAs has increased over the last two decades and that role expectations have become increasingly instructional in nature (Breton, 2010).

Blatchford et al. (2012) also identify positive impacts of EAs within the system. They are seen by teachers as an important addition to the classroom and contribute to the work of classroom teachers, although EAs sometimes see themselves as providing alternative support as opposed to additional support as they often spend much more time than the teacher with students individually. This can have a positive impact on the student in terms of reducing distractibility and disruption, and improving relationships with peers as a result of direct facilitation. Unfortunately, this negatively impacts student-teacher relationships and growth in academic learning as a result of being focused on task completion rather than learning and understanding (Blatchford et al., 2012).

Recommendations in both Hoyano (2012) and Blatchford et al. (2012) consistently focus on the need for EA standards of practice, access to ongoing learning and professional development, supportive and collaborative relationships within the school community, and systemic examination and recognition of the complexity of the role. Research confirms that when EAs are prepared and trained for specific curricula, receive guidance from the teacher and school about practice, and are included as team members their involvement shows positive effects around student progress (Farrell, Alborz, Howes, & Pearson, 2010). Individuals working as EAs need to develop critical thinking skills and have a clear understanding about how their role and interactions with students either support or hinder learning, and consider social capital and interdependence within the school community. This need (in a Canadian context) is the basis on which this book was conceived of and written.

This book is framed within the context of both what EAs need in the field and the understanding that what they do with students has great influence on how the system responds to students with additional learning needs. Increasingly, EAs are providing a range of supports to students, including, but not limited to, instruction in academic, social, communication, and life skills, behaviour support, and delivery of personal care (Giangreco, Edelman, Broer, & Doyle, 2001). Education assistants must understand the power they hold and use critical thinking and systems thinking skills to support an inclusive school climate that is safe, positive, and welcoming. This book bridges the needs of EAs and the experiences of those in the field within a Canadian context. The intent is to situate EAs as an important part of a collaborative team that supports students who need to feel mastery, personal agency, and belonging.

Although we acknowledge varied practice across the country this book is primarily British Columbia referenced. We understand that terms and policies around practice may differ across provinces and hope that those using this book as a learning tool will accommodate and adjust to specific provincial guidelines. We invited authors from across the country to contribute and included authors from Ontario, Alberta, and Nova Scotia. In addition, please note that for the purpose of this text the term *education assistant* is used, but we are aware that a number of terms are used to describe the role; these include, but are not limited to, *paraprofessional, special education aide, paraeducator, teacher aide, teacher associate, assistant teacher, teacher assistant, teaching assistant, special education assistant, program assistant, staff assistant, classroom assistant, certified education assistant, learning support teacher, auxiliary personnel,* and *support personnel.*

The four sections of this book reflect the complex and important nature of work as an EA. Section I provides an overview of the role of the EA, highlighting the diversity of the position within the school team. Section II highlights issues related to mental health and wellness. Section III reflects the intersectionality of culture and diversity within the classroom, and, finally, section IV reviews the larger context of relationships within the system.

Each section contains several themed chapters, organized to highlight key concepts in practice. We felt it was important for each chapter to clearly articulate and address three key ideas and to finish by hearing from those who are in direct practice. This section, Voices from the Field, informs the reader about how key concepts directly link to practice. Critical thinking questions are included with the intent to invite the learner to explore how the content may influence their own professional development.

We know that the field is ever changing, and our hope is that this book will inspire further conversation to influence change and growth in both individual and systemic practice. We know that relationship building is one of the most important aspects of inclusion and belonging. When an inclusion lens motivates the work of EAs and the education system, cultural norms around issues of vulnerability and disability are impacted. This highlights the potential to develop all kinds of relationships and supports difference and diversity (Lord & Hutchison, 2011, p. 17). The work of authors from across Canada shines a light on how influential and dynamic EAs are in the shared vision and action of inclusive communities.

REFERENCES

Blatchford, P., Bassett, P., Brown, P., Martin, C., Russell, A., & Webster, R. (2012). *Deployment and impact of support staff project.* London: Institute of Education, University of London.

Breton, W. (2010). Special education paraprofessionals: Perceptions of preservice preparation, supervision, and ongoing developmental training. *International Journal of Special Education, 25*(1), 34–45.

Brown, L., Farrington, K., Knight, T., Ross, C., & Ziegler, M. (1991). Fewer paraprofessionals and more teachers and therapists in educational programs for students with significant disabilities. *Journal of the Association for Persons with Severe Handicaps, 24*(4), 250–253.

Farrell, P., Alborz, A., Howes, A., & Pearson, D. (2010). The impact of teaching assistants on improving pupils' academic achievement in mainstream schools: A review of the literature. *Educational Review, 62*(4), 435–448.

Giangreco, M. F., Edelman, S. W., Broer, S. M., & Doyle, M. B. (2001). Paraprofessional support of students with disabilities: Literature from the past decade. *Exceptional Children, 68*(1), 45–63.

Hoyano, N. (2012). *White paper: Call for standards of practice for education assistants in BC.* Burnaby, BC: Langara College.

Lord, J., & Hutchison, P. (2011). *Pathways to inclusion: Building a new story with people and communities.* Concord, ON: Captus Press.

Malcolmson, J. (2009). *Education assistants in British Columbia: An educational profile and agenda.* N.p.: CUPE BC. Retrieved from http://d3n8a8pro7vhmx.cloudfront.net/cupebcvotes2014/legacy_url/1137/ea_education_report_final_version_apr-09.pdf?1460990591

SECTION I

THE EDUCATION ASSISTANT

In this section, the authors explore various elements of the role and activities of an education assistant. Major activities for education assistants in the school environment include being an advocate for students and ensuring that opportunities for inclusion are recognized and facilitated. Education assistants encourage independence and interdependence in order to help students develop skills that will best prepare them for life beyond the school system.

As members of an education team, relationships that education assistants have with others in the system are important, but none more critical than the foundational relationship with the classroom teacher. Chapter 1 provides specific information regarding the various roles of the education assistant; later in the book, chapters 13, 14, and 15 discuss not only best practice in a general context, but also collaborative working strategies. This serves to reiterate the importance of this working partnership in terms of the impact not only on the students in the classroom but also as a working environment for the school community. Although this section by no means covers all aspects of practice, it is a good starting place for the student who is exploring becoming a professional in this field.

Role of an Education Assistant

CHAPTER 1

From the Margins to the Centre: Education Assistants as Inclusion Facilitators

Cornelia Schneider

THREE KEY IDEAS

1. Education assistants often find themselves in a liminal position (that is, in the margins) if their role in the classroom is not well defined.
2. Inclusive education demands the shift of the role of education assistants toward a new model.
3. Education assistants in a well-functioning team can become key players in the facilitation of the inclusion of children with disabilities.

For a long time and in many industrialized countries, public school systems have considered education assistants (EAs) an essential paraprofessional group to support the integration of children with disabilities into mainstream schools. However, unfortunately, while this position seems to have evolved into a pillar of inclusive education, the status of the EA has often been precarious, as they have not been well trained nor well paid for the important task of helping children with disabilities to be part of the classroom community and supporting their learning.

As schools are supposed to shift from an integrative to an inclusive setting, the role and status of EAs also needs to change: first, to address the aforementioned issues, and second, to serve a system that no longer focuses on the individual child with a disability but on the classroom as a whole. Instead of being assigned to one particular child in the classroom, an EA should be a resource for the entire classroom, as a go-between for those in need of support, access, and inclusion and the teachers and other students. For this to occur, education and enhanced status of the EA role is required, as many EAs are often acting in a liminal space inside the classroom and the school community. This chapter addresses this issue by using the theoretical framework of liminality, as well as pieces of empirical research on inclusive classrooms in different industrialized countries. Resources such as the Index for Inclusion highlight the richness that an EA could bring to a fully inclusive classroom, if we address the need for professionalization and status recognition of EAs, who have been identified as "key players" (Abbott, McConkey, & Dobbins, 2011) in inclusive education.

LIMINALITY AND EDUCATION ASSISTANTS

In a study using the theory of liminality, Schneider (2002) analyzed the situation of EAs in France. Even though this study dates back almost two decades, some of the structural problems identified around the very existence of the professional role of an EA continue to exist—not only in France, but also in many industrialized countries around the world. The study uses the framework of liminality developed in the field of disability studies by Murphy (1990), which recognizes that people with disabilities are continually "betwixt and between" (Turner, 1969), neither excluded from nor included in society. The imagery used to convey this concept shows people standing at the threshold of a house, allowed to look inside, but never really able or allowed to take the step inside.

Schneider (2002) applied this theory to the analysis of the professional situation of EAs supporting children with disabilities, who, frequently, encounter a similar situation when it comes to their professional status and inclusion within the school staff. As a result of precariousness, lack of training, questions of volatility (staff turnover and absenteeism), frequently changing student assignments, and lack of debriefing, EAs are without the status and role clarification that are important to defining one's sense of belonging to an educational institution (Basford, Butt, & Newton, 2017). Frequently, EAs do not benefit from a professional network (such as a union or professional association) to address issues such as work conditions and professional development, and to exchange information about their professional practices (see, for example, Abbott et al., 2011). More often than not, in terms of whether they will have a satisfying and productive work environment at the service of the child they are assigned to, EAs are at the mercy of the school in which they work or the principal or teacher they work with.

Schneider (2002) interviewed six EAs in the Paris region about their professional and personal situations. At that time, EAs were often funded by a national youth employment program, which certainly added to their liminal situation. The EAs, who were mostly in their early 20s, arrived in the schools because they did not have alternative employment. Through the interviews, the EAs learned about the model of liminality and were then asked if they thought it applied (1) to the lives of the children with disabilities who they were serving and (2) to themselves. They all found that it applied to the children with whom they were working, and half expressed that they saw their current professional and personal situation as liminal, often because they saw themselves in a waiting position they knew they did not want to be in forever and that they hoped would improve. They felt that being an EA was not a "real job." Most of them also cited a lack of recognition in the schools they were working in as a reason for not being able to develop a sense of belonging and job satisfaction. Often, the school community considered them to be the only ones who would take care of the children with disabilities, and so they had little additional support from teachers and other staff. In all cases, there was a lack of adequate training. In the classrooms, the EAs would often do activities with the child with a disability separately from the rest of the class, which put them, together with the child with a disability, in a liminal position:

not totally excluded, but not veritably included either, on the margins of the community. We need to ask how EAs who are experiencing their professional reality in this way, as outside the school community, can support the inclusion of children. This is highly problematic for the children that they are supposedly supporting in their educational path in the inclusive school system. Doyle and Giangreco (2013) address this issue when they describe a teenage girl with a disability:

> As high school graduation approached, Sarah's educational team realized that while the lives of students without disabilities were opening up to new opportunities for work, school, activities, and re-lationships[,] Sarah's world was becoming smaller. The majority of her segregated secondary school experiences had been facilitated by paid service providers (e.g., special educators, paraprofessionals, ther-apists) and now it was likely that her adult life would be similar. The school team members began to ask themselves, "Why did we think segregated experiences would prepare her for an interesting life in an inclusive community?" "Without relationships with her nondisabled peers, how can she access their support and friendship now or de-velop new relationships in the future?" "How might the lives of her classmates have been enriched by long-term friendships and shared experiences with Sarah?" (p. 58)

MOVING FROM THE MARGINS TO THE CENTRE: ASKING THE RIGHT QUESTIONS

To move from the margins and situations of liminality to a stronger sense of participation and belonging, this section will move toward a more positive outlook for this profession, with the goal of improving the professional situation of EAs.

There has been an increasing number of studies that attempt to research and address the issues raised in the previous section. The first issue examined is the frequency of interaction between EAs and children with disabilities. The Deployment and Impact of Support

Staff (DISS) study (Blatchford, Russell, & Webster, 2012) found that EAs had a direct pedagogical role, usually interacting with pupils (predominantly those with special education needs [SEN]) in one-to-one and group contexts. The more severe a student's needs, the more their interaction with an EA increased, and their interaction with a teacher decreased. This corresponds to the observations made by Doyle and Giangreco (2013). Students' interactions with EAs were much more sustained and engaged than their interactions with teachers. This might seem pedagogically valuable, but it also meant that EA-supported students became separated from the teacher, missing out on everyday teacher-student interactions and mainstream curriculum coverage. In the classroom, one can observe this in the child with a disability and their "appendix," as the EA almost turns into an extension of the child, which impedes interaction with teachers and other peers.

The second issue is the nature of the interactions between EAs and pupils or what the DISS project referred to as "practice." Detailed analysis of audio transcripts showed that, in comparison to teachers' interactions with students, EAs' interactions were less academically demanding, had a greater stress on completing tasks, and tended to "close down" rather than "open up" talk, linguistically and cognitively (Blatchford, Russell, & Webster, 2012; Radford, Blatchford, & Webster, 2011; Rubie-Davies, Blatchford, Webster, Koutsoubou, & Bassett, 2010).

The third issue, preparedness, concerns the widespread lack of both training and professional development of EAs and teachers. It also addresses day-to-day aspects of planning and preparation before lessons and feedback afterwards, which, the DISS study found, are highly likely to have a bearing on learning (Webster et al., 2011).

Giangreco, Yuan, Mackensie, Cameron, and Fialka (2005) have argued that an implicit form of discrimination has developed as a result of the commonplace model of EA usage, as "the least qualified staff members are teaching students with the most complex learning characteristics" (p. 29). Inclusive education has struggled with this paradox for the longest time, as EAs were often used as a cheap means to replace the special teacher presence available in a school or classroom. In a provincial context in Canada, Aylward, Farmer, and MacDonald (2007) wrote the following in a review of Nova Scotia Student Services:

> Many parents of students with disabilities expressed their concerns about support for their children in school in terms of "fighting for" teacher assistant time, communicating to the review committee that the teacher assistant position has become synonymous with individualized programming for many families. Although the provincial Teacher Assistant Guidelines point out that teacher assistants are assigned to teachers in order to meet the needs of their students, it appears that in practice many teacher assistants are de facto assigned to specific students. (p. 22)

Aside from those findings, there is also concern about how EAs might impact the development of peer relationships between children with and without disabilities in the school setting. Studies involving children with disabilities in the field of sociology of childhood also touch on the role of EAs and other adults in peer relationships; this is especially evident in Shakespeare's Life as a Disabled Child study (1999), which took the perspectives of children with exceptionalities into account by conducting in-depth interviews with them about their social situations inside both special and mainstream schools. The outcomes of these studies show that this neglected perspective of children offers surprising insights into the lives of children with disabilities that adult specialists often have not been able to consider. The children expressed the concern that they could not "misbehave" when the EA spent too much time with them. Peer interactions, which normally may include transgression of rules and trying new things despite adult concerns, were thus often impossible, as the students were "watched over" by an EA who discouraged those types of behaviours, even though transgression is essential to the experience of growing up for any child. Pitt and Curtin (2004) took the same approach in order to explore the perspective of adolescents with disabilities about inclusive and segregated schooling. These studies have shown that there are a number of children with disabilities who actually feel that, at times, the adult presence—often an EA—in their lives is too great, as it turns into a barrier to creating peer relationships with other children in the class. Schneider (2011, 2015) has pointed out that, formal learning outcomes aside, social participation and peer interaction of children and youth with disabilities are crucial parts of inclusive education. Thus, this aspect needs to be taken into account when reconceptualizing the professional status and role of EAs in the inclusive education system.

SHIFTING GEARS AND RETHINKING INCLUSION AND THE ROLE OF THE EA

There is one particular underlying issue when it comes to thinking through inclusive practice and the role of the EA in the classroom: even though we have been using the terms *inclusion* and *inclusive education* since the Salamanca Statement (UNESCO, 1994), we are actually mostly still functioning in a system of *integrative practice* or *integration*. This has impacted severely not only the entire practice of inclusion but also the way EAs continue to be deployed. Hinz (2002) has extrapolated the differences between these two ideas and what they mean for schooling. First, inclusion requires a particular thinking about diversity and heterogeneity, which we often do not employ when we are loosely using the term *inclusion* or *inclusive education*. We often think about the child with a disability being "added on" to a homogeneous group of learners, and not in terms of how to open up classroom teaching and learning to a broad recognition of diversity. We are still teaching in schools under the illusion that all children at the same age learn at the same pace and have the same interests. Second, and this is one of the most important observations for the practice of an EA, in a truly inclusive system resources are not allocated to one particular child who has received the label of being disabled or having diverse learning needs, but rather to the system as a whole, for example, the classroom, the grade level, or the school. Thus, the EA is one resource in the school and not the "appendix" of the child with diverse learning needs, and can, from this perspective, fulfill a role that is at the service of all children, and facilitate inclusion by working with different children at different times, including the children with disabilities. In Schneider's work on EAs in France (2002), one EA was deployed in her school in that way, and her job satisfaction and engagement with the whole school community was very high (and, as a consequence, the status and participation of the children with disabilities in that particular school, and their interactions with their peers, were heightened). Inclusive education requires working as a team, where all members receive recognition and participate in making it a success.

A UK-based research team (Blatchford, Russell, & Webster, 2012; Blatchford, Webster, & Russell, 2012) has been working for some time on the issue of the effective deployment of EAs. This team's DISS project and subsequent EDTA (Effective Deployment of Teaching Assistants) project have more systematically shown the benefits of working strategies that EAs have reported have proven to be effective in inclusive education. Many of the strategies counter the criticism that EAs often encounter in their workplace on a daily basis. In their final report for the EDTA project, Blatchford, Webster, and Russell (2012) organized their results in three major categories of preparedness, deployment, and practices. First, they insisted on the importance of giving teachers and EAs the necessary time in their schedules to meet and prepare upcoming lessons and units, in which the role of the EA was laid out clearly.

Second, in regard to deployment, the role of the EA became more flexible inside the classroom, where

> there were marked and productive changes to the deployment of TAs [teaching assistants] at the classroom level. TAs worked more often with middle and high attaining pupils, and teachers spent more time with low attaining and SEN pupils. This greatly improved and enriched teachers' understanding of these pupils and their needs. Careful thought had been given to less unproductive uses of TAs; for example, teachers reduced the proportion of time in which TAs were

passive during lessons, and TAs more often remained in the classroom, thus reducing pupil-teacher/pupil-peer separation. (Blatchford, Webster, & Russell, 2012, p. 3)

Lastly, the practices of EAs and outcomes for children with disabilities improved when EAs were encouraged to be more reflective of the way in which they were interacting with these students, for example, speaking less and using other methods to encourage students to engage with the learning contents. As Blatchford, Webster, and Russell (2012) report, "At the classroom level, there were two key developments: firstly, questioning frameworks to help pupils remain in charge of and responsible for their own learning; and secondly, strategies to help pupils become independent learners, thereby reducing dependency on adult support" (p. 3).

When thinking about how to make inclusive education work, one angle certainly points toward the better education and training of EAs, but we also need to give the entire school community the tools to be successful in this work, and educate other staff about how to improve the entire team's effectiveness. After all, when we attempt to create an inclusive system, it cannot be at the expense of any one professional group; all staff need to be included in what happens in the school and in the classroom. The Index for Inclusion (Booth & Ainscow, 2011) addresses this issue; this tool contains self-assessment indicators to help schools improve their inclusive culture, policies, and practices. Similar to the outcomes of the EDTA project (Blatchford, Webster, & Russell, 2012), the findings of the research on EAs in Paris (Schneider, 2002), and the principles noted by Causton-Theoharis, Giangreco, Doyle, and Vadasy (2007), the Index for Inclusion emphasizes developing a collaborative and welcoming culture for EAs, so that they are included, experience a sense of belonging, and are better prepared to work together with the classroom teacher. The Index for Inclusion sets particular indicators for these goals, such as "staff co-operate" (indicator A1.2), or "all new staff are helped to settle into the school" (indicator B1.5). There is also one indicator that even more explicitly refers to the work of EAs: "Teaching assistants support the learning and participation of all children" (indicator C2.11), which is a move away from the model of EAs being in charge of only those children with disabilities in the classroom. A tool such as the Index for Inclusion can encourage the whole system to be reflective of its practices, rather than leaving this task up to the EA and their professional training. Teachers have pointed out that they also do not possess much knowledge or skills related to working with an EA in the classroom (see Basford et al., 2017) and, as a result, reflexive practices need improvement.

RECOGNITION OF EDUCATION ASSISTANTS

Education assistants, in recognition of their role, have been referred to as "sous-chefs" (Causton-Theoharis et al., 2007), "key players," (Abbott et al., 2011), or "pillars" of inclusive education. Rather than dwelling on the negative situations that early practice in the profession of EAs created, it appears there are many ways forward to better recognition and effectiveness of this group, which has an essential role in the system of inclusive education. If inclusive education is to be successful in the future, we need to work hard to make sure that nobody—not children or staff—is left on the margins or in a liminal state. The whole school community needs to be able to celebrate its members, be they students, teachers, EAs, parents/families, or other staff in the school, and give them ways to participate meaningfully.

Research has demonstrated that when EAs are well trained and meaningfully included in educational processes, they can become pillars of inclusive education; however, it must also be clear that everyone is responsible for every child in the school. In the words of French EA Patricia (Schneider, 2002),

> There are … no barriers between the teachers and me, that means, I was a part of the meetings … like all the teachers, I participated in discussions, so, this was very, very important.… And then, there is also something else, which is, that here, the teachers, which means, the teachers and all the other adults in the school know all the children. (p. xvi)

Voices from the Field

Schneider, 2002, translated from French by C. Schneider

Views of EAs on Liminality

Patricia: Yes, so, I think that you are putting people in situations where you are leaving them ... on the threshold. Yes, on the threshold. On your own threshold. Because ... after ... I think that they are making ... I am thinking of persons ... with disabilities who are in groups, in centres etc.

Evelyne: Because I, I don't know, I am not in a real job, I would prefer to be a teacher. I am a bit in-between, to say it like this, I am also not a student, I am not ... it's true, I am on the threshold, of course! I feel like I am in the middle, so, I am trying to clear the threshold, but it is true, it is not easy. So, I do not think that I am turning back, but [laughs] I hope not ... and yes, it's true, I am a bit on the threshold right in this moment.

Evelyne: Oh, at the last team meeting for K. [little boy with disability] where the usual people were attending ..., there was this guy who needed photocopies and he tells me: "oh, could you go and make some pho-tocopies?" Ok, fine, the first time, why not? I go downstairs ... and I come back, and then, he says: "oh, I will need two more, please." And there, I start wondering, I go downstairs, I return ... and then, we start to discuss, and then, he still needs another photocopy and he asks me again. At that point, I tell him: "wait a second, I am not here for making photocopies! Ok? I am the education assistant, for you, maybe that's nothing, but I am here for K., to talk about K., how to help him progress, I am not here for making photocopies."

CRITICAL THINKING QUESTIONS

1. The idea of liminality means that people feel betwixt and between different roles and role expectations. How might this apply to a situation involving a child with a disability and an EA?

2. What is the difference between an integrative and an inclusive education system?

3. If you were a teacher, and you were to work with an EA, how would you go about it? Create an action plan that outlines how you would welcome the EA in the classroom, and what you would put into place to make this collaboration work.

REFERENCES

Abbott, L., McConkey, R., & Dobbins, M. (2011). Key players in inclusion: Are we meeting the professional needs of learning support assistants for pupils with complex needs? *European Journal of Special Needs Education, 26*(2), 215–231. doi:10.1080/08856257.2011.563608

Aylward, L., Farmer, W., & MacDonald, M. (2007). *Minister's review of services for students with special needs: Review committee report and recommendations.* Halifax: Province of Nova Scotia.

Basford, E., Butt, G., & Newton, R. (2017). To what extent are teaching assistants really managed? "I was thrown in the deep end, really; I just had to more or less get on with it." *School Leadership and Management, 37*(3), 288–310. doi:10.1080/ 13632434.2017.1324842

Blatchford, P., Russell, A., & Webster, R. (2012). *Reassessing the impact of teaching assistants: How research challenges practice and policy.* Abingdon, UK: Routledge.

Blatchford, P., Webster, R., & Russell, A. (2012). *Challenging the role and deployment of teaching assistants in mainstream schools: The impact on schools. Final report on findings from the Effective Deployment of Teaching Assistants (EDTA) project.* London: Institute of Education, University of London. Retrieved from http:// maximisingtas.co.uk/assets/content/edtareport-2.pdf

Booth, T., & Ainscow, M. (2011). *Index for Inclusion: Developing learning and participation in schools* (3rd ed.). Bristol, UK: Centre for Studies on Inclusive Education.

Causton-Theoharis, J. N., Giangreco, M. F., Doyle, M. B., & Vadasy, P. F. (2007). Paraprofessionals: The sous-chefs of literacy instruction. *Teaching Exceptional Children, 40*(1), 56–62.

Doyle, B., & Giangreco, M. F. (2013). Guiding principles for including high school students with intellectual disabilities in general education classes. *American Secondary Education, 42*(1), 57–72.

Giangreco, M. F., Yuan, S., Mackensie, B., Cameron, B., & Fialka, J. (2005). "Be careful what you wish for …": Five reasons to be concerned about the assignment of individual paraprofessionals. *Exceptional Children, 37*(5), 28–34.

Hinz, A. (2002). Von der Integration zur Inklusion: terminologisches Spiel oder konzeptionelle Weiterentwicklung? [From integration to inclusion: Terminological play or conceptual development?]. *Zeitschrift für Heilpädagogik, 53*(9), 354–361.

Murphy, R. F. (1990). *The body silent.* New York: W. W. Norton.

Pitt, V., & Curtin, M. (2004). Integration versus segregation: The experiences of a group of disabled students moving from mainstream school into special needs further education. *Disability and Society, 19*(4), 387–401.

Radford, J., Blatchford, P., & Webster, R. (2011). Opening up and closing down: How teachers and TAs manage turn-taking, topic and repair in mathematics lessons. *Learning and Instruction, 21*(5), 625–635.

Rubie-Davies, C., Blatchford, P., Webster, R., Koutsoubou, M., & Bassett, P. (2010). Enhancing learning? A comparison of teacher and teaching assistant interaction with pupils. *School Effectiveness and School Improvement, 21*(4), 429–450.

Schneider, C. (2002). *L'intégration scolaire des enfants handicapés: Liminalité, la reconnaissance de la différence et les "gens du seuil"* [School integration of children with disabilities: Liminality, recognition of difference, and "people of the threshold"]. Mémoire de Diplôme d'Etudes Approfondies, Université René Descartes, Paris, France.

Schneider, C. (2011). *Une étude comparative de l'éducation inclusive des enfants avec besoins particuliers en France et en Allemagne: Recherches dans onze salles de classe* [*A comparative study of the inclusion of children with special needs in mainstream schools in France and Germany: Case studies of eleven classrooms*]. Lewiston, NY: Edwin Mellen Press.

Schneider, C. (2015). Social participation of children and youth with disabilities in Canada, France and Germany. *International Journal of Inclusive Education, 19*(10), 1068–1079. doi:10.1080/13603116.2015.1037867

Shakespeare, T. (1999). *Life as a disabled child: A qualitative study of young peoples experiences and perspectives.* Economic and Social Research Council Full Research Report, L129251047. Swindon, UK: ESRC. Retrieved from https://www .researchcatalogue.esrc.ac.uk/grants/L129251047/outputs/read/96fce713- c2fb-4352-8d59-270ecacf3ec2

Turner, V. W. (1969). *The ritual process: Structure and anti-structure.* Ithaca, NY: Cornell University Press.

UNESCO. (1994). *The Salamanca statement and framework for action on special needs education.* Salamanca, Spain: UNESCO and the Ministry of Education and Science, Spain. Retrieved from http://www.unesco.org/education/pdf/SALAMA_E.PDF

Webster, R., Blatchford, P., Bassett, P., Brown, P., Martin, C., & Russell, A. (2011). The wider pedagogical role of teaching assistants. *School Leadership and Management, 31*(1), 3–20. doi:10.1080/13632434.2010.540562

CHAPTER 2

Education Assistants as Advocates

Alison Taplay and Joanie Chestnut

THREE KEY IDEAS

1. Advocacy is a critical role for education assistants.
2. Continuous development of communication skills is essential in this role.
3. As advocates, education assistants lead positive change in schools especially in the areas of human rights, universal design for learning, and full inclusion.

Education assistants (EAs) work within a complex system to which they bring knowledge critical to the creation of an inclusive environment and awareness of the broader disability rights movement. They work with others who may not share this knowledge and skill set and alongside students in a unique role that provides an invaluable perspective. As part of their role, EAs may find themselves advocating for individual students and sometimes even for broader systems change to increase both individual success and inclusion; therefore, an understanding of advocacy is essential for EA practice. After defining each type of advocacy, this chapter explains how to advocate, with a focus on self- and individual advocacy. The suggested steps in the advocacy process are contextualized within the requirement for communication skills. Arising from these topics is a discussion of the importance of leadership; as Covey (2013) asserted, "Leadership is a choice not a position" (para. 7). In this chapter, the reader is invited to consider the pivotal role EAs can play in leading positive change in the school and community.

ADVOCACY

The formal definition of advocacy is "the act of pleading for, supporting, or recommending; active espousal" ("Advocacy," n.d.). The objective of advocacy is to remove barriers and/or enhance quality of life. To accomplish this end, advocacy often addresses social injustice and seeks to improve our social policy framework. There are four types of advocacy: self-advocacy, individual or natural advocacy, group advocacy, and strategic or systems advocacy.

Types of Advocacy

Self-advocacy is the first level of advocacy and typically the most powerful. When individuals tell their own stories, the outcome can move hearts and minds; therefore, best practice for an EA begins by encouraging students and/or families to speak for themselves. In this situation, the EA's role is to provide a listening and affirming ear, resource information, and, if asked, suggestions for steps the student/family can take to advocate on their own behalf.

Individual or natural advocacy is the second level of advocacy; at this level, an EA might decide to speak on behalf of another person. According to Meeker (2013), the seven steps one can take in this role are the same as those that can be recommended to a self-advocate:

1. Identify the issue(s)
2. Identify others who care about this issue
3. Identify who can help solve this problem. Develop partnerships, alliances, and coalitions

4. Explore the question, What is getting in the way of solving this problem? Become informed and knowledgeable
5. Develop the messages needed to get the point across
6. Problem solve and identify some possible solutions
7. Then … make appointments and pursue your objective

It is most effective to resolve issues at the most direct level possible. In practice, if, for example, the EA's goal is a specific practice change within the classroom, this would mean meeting with the teacher before meeting with the principal. Other tips for advocates include the following: show respect and be compassionate toward others, even those who seem to be on the opposite side of a situation/issue; develop relationships with people who can help; be prepared, informed, and realistic; stay calm, focused, and relaxed, which will allow for effective listening; ask someone to attend meetings as a support whenever possible; take notes; and send a follow-up email to restate one's understanding of the outcome of the meeting or the agreements made.

Group advocacy occurs when a number of people come together to achieve a common goal. This goal is often broader and involves a strategy to create social or system-wide change rather than improvement for one individual or family. Because issues addressed using group advocacy are generally more complex, a multi-pronged approach may be required and greater attention given to establishing alliances, being aware of politics, identifying leverage points, and adhering to process.

An example drawn from practice distinguishes individual advocacy from group and strategic advocacy. EAs often support children whose behaviour is hard to understand and more difficult to support. They are specifically trained to provide this support from a person-centred frame within an inclusive environment and are positioned alongside the student. When a student is struggling to regulate emotions and focus on work, the EA may advocate for specific changes. The EA might say, "I notice Tish focuses on her work best when the classroom is quiet or when we are working alone. Could we create a quiet spot within the classroom for her to work so she won't leave the room so frequently, or can we find another way to meet her needs?"

Bringing this information to the teacher is helpful and may lead to an improvement for the student, such as the use of headphones or the creation of a quiet space at the back of the room. The EA might advocate further by suggesting that these options be available for all students in the class rather than just one, thus advancing the use of universal design for learning (UDL) principles; however, if the EA or the team has an interest in making these kinds of changes consistently throughout the school or the school district, then group and strategic advocacy are required. These types of advocacy build on the same skill set but require more advanced critical thinking and systems thinking skills, discussion of which is beyond the scope of this chapter.

Why Do We Need to Advocate?

Despite a plethora of legal frameworks established to uphold human rights in Canada, quality of life for children and adults with disabilities is lower than that of citizens without disabilities. An awareness of both the legal frameworks in place and the lived experiences of children and adults with disabilities provides a compelling case for an individual to advocate in their role as an EA.

As an EA it is important to be familiar with the Canadian Human Rights Act, the Canadian Charter of Rights and Freedoms, and the Canadian Bill of Rights. In addition, each province has its own human rights legislation. Canada ratified the Convention on the Rights of Persons with Disabilities (CRPD) on March 11, 2010. Of note, Canada has not signed the Optional Protocol that would allow individuals to lodge complaints related to violations of the CRPD. Though the anticipated Canadians with Disabilities Act provides some hope, Canadians who live with disabilities continue to experience discrimination in areas such as education, employment, and decision making. Without advocacy, there are serious consequences for quality of life.

In British Columbia, public school policies include a commitment to inclusion and special education programs and services. While the purpose of the policies is to enable students with exceptionalities to have equitable access to learning and opportunities to achieve their educational goals, the policy does not guarantee inclusion:

> BC promotes an inclusive education system in which students with special needs are fully participating members of a community of learners.… The practice of inclusion is not necessarily synonymous with full integration in regular classrooms.… The emphasis on educating students with special needs in neighbourhood school classrooms with their age and grade peers, however, does not preclude the appropriate use of resource rooms, self-contained classes, community-based settings or specialized settings. Students with special needs may be placed in settings other than a neighbourhood school classroom with age and grade peers. (BC Ministry of Education and Training, 2006)

The policy requires that reasonable efforts be made to integrate students prior to looking toward segregated options; however, this is where the difficulty lies. Each individual involved with a student may have a different view of their strengths and needs, a different level of expertise with UDL, and a different interpretation of reasonable effort. Opinions are informed by each person's values and beliefs. Perceptions of disability are often based on stereotypes, misinformation, and limited exposure. Alongside budget and other resource constraints, it is easy to see how opportunities for full inclusion can be missed.

Although decades of research show that an inclusive education benefits all students and best prepares them for post-secondary education, a career, and an adult life of quality, the Canadian public school system is a long way from achieving this standard. The Canadian Association for Community Living (CACL; 2017) found that two-thirds of school-aged children with intellectual disabilities are segregated in special classes or schools or are not attending school at all, and that adequate in-class supports, preparation time, and teacher training are lacking. Inclusion BC's position statement on inclusive education states the following:

> After many years of eroding supports for diverse learners, many are finding their needs unmet in BC's public schools. Too many are no

longer welcomed at their local schools, excluded from regular classes, sent home due to a lack of staffing or support or traumatized by restraint or seclusion. Too many families are forced to pay for their child's education in segregated private "special education" programs with sometimes questionable standards and oversight. (n.d., para. 3)

Importantly, education is closely tied to employment outcomes after graduation. The employment rate for working-age adults with an intellectual disability is half that of people with other disabilities and one-third the rate of people without a disability. The main approach to daytime support for thousands of people with intellectual disabilities remains sheltered workshops and segregated day programs (CACL, 2013b, p. 6). Adults with intellectual disabilities are three times more likely than non-disabled citizens to live in poverty (CACL, 2013a, p. 1).

These facts inform practice and galvanize the need for advocacy. The good news is that when EAs advocate for the children who are the most complicated to support in the classroom, they create learning environments that are better for all children.

CHARACTERISTICS OF EFFECTIVE ADVOCATES

There are numerous advocacy guides and handbooks available; many are specific to education, inclusion, and disability rights issues. Two examples are the Representative for Children and Youth's *Champions for Change: A Guide to Effective Advocacy for Youth and the Adults Who Support Them* (2011) and Inclusion BC's *Everyone Belongs in Our Schools: A Parent's Handbook on Inclusive Education* (2014). To advocate effectively, one needs to cultivate certain skills and develop high ethical standards for practice. Moore (2016) explains the characteristics of an effective advocate in an online video about transforming inclusive education.

The requisite skills include being focused, informed, articulate, committed, assertive, respectful, and self-confident, and showing perseverance. Advocates must speak and act with honesty and integrity. They must be organized, aware of the facts relating to a particular matter, able to think clearly about problems and issues, and aware of the decision-making processes within their own environment. They must cultivate a respectful and assertive communication style and have the self-awareness and self-monitoring ability to know when they need help. They must also consistently operate from a place of strong ethical standards.

These ethical standards go beyond core ethics such as confidentiality, consent, and conflict of interest. They include maintaining awareness of current advocacy resources; always placing the interests, preferences, and decisions of the individual above their own; avoiding any false, misleading, or unfair statements or claims about the advocacy process; and consistently advising individuals to be honest and realistic. In the advocacy role, it is a priority to behave in ways that respect and understand cultural, social, and individual diversity. Advocates must maintain their skills and knowledge about advocacy issues and withdraw or refer onward when their involvement is no longer appropriate or useful (Penticton Advocacy Network, 1997).

All of these skills and ethical considerations rely on communication skills for both in-person and written interactions. Most EA training programs emphasize these interpersonal skills; a discussion of these within the context of self-confidence, a reflective practice, and teamwork follows.

Communication

Clear, confident communication has the potential to inspire new ideas, build awareness among co-workers, and promote inclusion. An EA's communications are important in daily interactions at school and essential in order to advocate effectively, whether for a simple change to a classroom routine or for a student's inclusion in a setting where resistance is encountered; however, the various levels of authority and roles within our school system impose a challenge for communication. Teachers, learning support teachers (LSTs), and administrators have extensive post-secondary education and broad teaching experience, whereas EAs—with comparatively little post-secondary education—have often obtained specialized training and valuable on-the-job experience, including a solid understanding of UDL and inclusion theory and the implementation of both in the classroom. Importantly, EAs usually know the student they support more personally than most staff and have valuable observations to communicate about strengths, needs, and behaviour.

Despite this unique skill set and knowledge, many EAs report reluctance to voice their ideas or concerns even though their approach can reflect valuable insights, creative problem solving, strong abilities, and current best practices. Each province typically has a set of established guidelines for EAs; it is important to be aware of these protocols to establish clarity of roles and responsibilities (see, for example, British Columbia Teachers' Federation/CUPE British Columbia's *Roles and Responsibilities of Teachers and Teaching Assistants*, 2009), so that with good communication skills, concerns and ideas can be voiced appropriately at the right time to the right person. Within the busy school environment, this means choosing the right time for a conversation with other staff members. It is best for an advocate to have prepared what they want to say so they can be clear, succinct, factual, and focused on finding a positive outcome in collaboration with co-workers. Coming prepared to be fully present with one's emotions well in hand will enable active listening. An advocate should be genuinely curious about the other person's viewpoint. This style of communication demonstrates respect for the very real time constraints the education team works within and is best practice for any potentially difficult conversation (Kippist & Duarte, 2015). Despite having a set of guidelines and information on interpersonal communication skills, EAs often lack the confidence to express concerns and possible solutions.

Confidence and Positive Mindset

Behavioural psychologist Galinsky points to a possible source of this low confidence, stating that those who feel they have less power in a situation feel less credible and less self-assured (2017, 5:00). Self-confidence leads us to feel more powerful, which gives us increased options for how to behave including, importantly, how we communicate (6:08).

Intentionally being empathetic to another's view, building allies, offering choices, and modelling humbleness by authentically seeking advice can balance power. Galinsky further suggests that while our expertise gives us some credibility, we can tap into passion by advocating for others and gain a sense of increased power and confidence in what he describes as "mama bear behaviour" (7:08).

As Adler, Rolls, and Proctor II (2015) state, "It may sound simple but research confirms positive expectations can lead to positive communication which can lead to positive results" (p. 56). This insight offers a strong reminder that positive thinking is an overarching goal for all EAs; a goal that can be applied to all workplace interactions and can propel advocacy forward.

Practice (Fake It 'Til You Make It)

Greater confidence in both receptive and expressive communication is linked with increased practice. Adler et al. (2015) remind us that there are four levels of communication skill acquisition one must navigate. Initially, one simply learns about communication skills such as "I" statements, curiosity, open-ended questions, paraphrasing, and summarizing. Then, when faced with a situation an individual cares strongly about, they will take their first awkward steps using these skills. If they persevere, they will go on to develop fluid skills and see positive results. Finally, they will successfully integrate the skills into their daily interactions (p. 19), so a well-developed "I" statement like the one provided in our example of individual advocacy ("I notice Tish focuses on her work best when the classroom is quiet or when we are working alone") flows naturally. This process requires acceptance: the EA is a learner on a continuum who will make mistakes and perseverance is required to make excellent communications skills second nature.

Reflection

Simply making mistakes and moving on does not make a competent communicator. Reflective practice—the mindful application of theory, self-awareness, and reflection—allows us to gauge our effectiveness as communicators and the response of others. For instance, in the example provided, a first awkward effort may be something like this: "I see Tish gets upset when the classroom is noisy. She needs a quiet space to work." While this might achieve a positive outcome, taking time for reflection provides the advocate with the chance to consider where there is room for improvement. With reflection, they may remember that asking for what one wants is more powerful than stating what is wrong, and using a question better engages the listener while conveying one's desire to work toward a collaborative solution. Applying these communication theories to the statement can result in something more akin to the aforementioned example: "I notice Tish focuses on her work best when the classroom is quiet or when we are working alone. Could we create a quiet spot within the classroom for her to work so she won't leave the room so frequently, or find another way to meet her need?"

A reflective practice helps individuals develop a strong sense of self including a comprehensive identification and understanding of their own beliefs, values, attitudes, bias, and motivations, combined with a dedication to continuous learning and curiosity about disability theory that is integrated with a commitment to practice in a way that contributes to the full inclusion of all students. As EAs grow in their reflective practice, they gain greater ability to provide effective situationally defined responses rather than formulated ones. Thompson (2002) described this as "cutting the cloth to suit the specific circumstances, rather than looking for ready-made solutions" (p. 235).

Reflective practitioners aren't satisfied simply with understanding *what* they do, but seek to understand *why* they do certain things. When individuals use a model of reflective practice, they can listen mindfully to others' points of view and take time to craft an appropriate response. They can be observant of non-verbal and para-verbal communication and shape their behaviour to show respect to co-workers, support staff, and students at all times. Ruiz (1997) reminded us to be impeccable with words; he called all forms of gossip destructive. He urged us to speak with integrity at all times: "The word is not just a sound or a written symbol. The word is a force; it is the power you have to express and communicate.… The word is so powerful that it can change a life or destroy" (pp. 26–27).

Workplace Communications and Team

There are strong similarities between interpersonal and work-related communication skills (Schweitzer & Wood, 2017). Considering others' perspectives, listening mindfully, avoiding destructive versus constructive communication behaviours, and self-monitoring relate back to reflective practice. Schweitzer and Wood suggest that in work situations we should celebrate accomplishments and use humour; consider not only the task at hand, but also the needs of team members; and recognize the whole person—body, mind, and heart—which they refer to as "bringing soul to the workplace" (p. 355).

The need for EAs to possess communication competence goes beyond successful one-to-one interactions. Education assistants are called upon to participate in team meetings, document observations, and, at times, write memos or emails. Bringing mindful listening skills and the elements of a reflective practice to team meetings allows them to actually hear the concerns of others and better express their own ideas. It is important to remember that written communication is a permanent record that can be forwarded to and read by others for whom it was not intended; therefore, discretion, a respectful tone, and objective language are essential. It is also important to keep written communication brief and clear (Levine, O'Hara, & Weber, 2016).

Supporting students is a team effort and rebuilding the team every year because of staffing changes and new assignments is an ongoing challenge. An EA's dedication to clear and honest communication will help with this task. Trust provides the foundation of a team's function and cohesion (Lencioni, 2002, p. 195), so it's important to reach out with intention and make connections with allies who share a common vision. An EA's work can at times feel isolating. Having a team to draw upon when they need help and with whom they can celebrate successes brings joy and energy to their work. In addition to connecting with teachers, LSTs, and the principal, it's important for EAs to get to know the librarian, administrative assistants, facility services employees, and other EAs as they may play an important role in the experiences of the student(s) they work with.

When one acknowledges the contributions of these important players, as well as the specific efforts of traditional team members, they expand interprofessional trust as well as the student's support network. Education assistants may also empower and enable others to act in ways that promote inclusion and student success. Kouzes and Posner (2012) found that advocating for change and sparking a passion in the hearts of others that enables them to act in new ways are among the most effective leadership traits (p. 29). Other key leadership traits are modelling positive interaction and inspiring a shared vision. We often think of leadership quite narrowly, believing it is tied to a position, but author and inspirational speaker Sinek (2017) asserts, "When we choose to show up to serve the people around us, we become a leader. Regardless of our rank, title or position, we become a leader" (para. 5).

EMBRACING LEADERSHIP

While EAs do not hold a formal leadership position, they may be called upon to embrace a leadership role in order to advance the best interests of their student(s) or inclusive practices within the school. The complexity of leading within a hierarchy can be daunting. Developing some fundamental leadership skills and adopting some core leadership practices can increase competency and confidence and empower EAs in their advocacy for students.

Before one can lead others, it is imperative to truly know oneself. Accurate metacognition and clarity about one's own values, beliefs, and attitudes, as well as an understanding of one's strengths and weaknesses, increases an individual's ability to make good decisions and work in a consistent and authentic manner. Covey (2004) asserted that the inward journey of getting to know oneself is a precursor of finding and using one's voice to inspire change. He wrote extensively about the importance of engaging fully in one's work by developing mental energy into vision, physical energy into discipline, emotional energy into passion, and spiritual energy into consciousness or moral fortitude. Kouzes and Posner (2012) also emphasized that clarifying one's personal values is essential to affirming shared values in the workplace: "Values influence every aspect of your life: your moral judgements, your responses to others, your commitments to personal and organizational goals…. Values constitute your personal 'bottom line.' They serve as guides to action" (p. 49). Sharing their vision by talking comfortably and confidently about values like diversity, inclusion, and integration will strengthen EAs' ability to authentically model for others.

Kouzes and Posner (2012) identified modelling as the primary leadership practice. Their extensive research showed that the qualities needed to be seen in a credible model include being honest, forward thinking, competent, and inspiring. Modelling the way means offering the highest standard of support for students, consistently applying UDL principles, having impeccable communication skills, and demonstrating a consistent commitment to collaboration. To use a school metaphor, modelling the way is a bit like show and tell. Each and every day EAs have the opportunity to show others and tell others about how students can be fully included. Using every opportunity to talk about how to support students with complex needs and doing so with appropriate people-first language influences others over time. Telling stories about student success is an especially powerful way to model and inspire; if an EA has effectively supported a difficult child to be a meaningful part of the classroom, they should learn to tell that story well and tell it often.

By consistently sharing their vision for inclusion, EAs can inspire others to engage in continually improving the team's collective capacity to support all children in the school. The methods to accomplish this run parallel to the strength-based approach to supporting students that is part of EA practice. An attitude of affirming others and helping them see their gifts and their capacity to effectively include complex children increases engagement and confidence (Covey, 2004). An EA's passion can breathe life into a shared vision, whether they are charismatic or use quieter opportunities for persuasion. In either case, their capacity to envision possibilities for students and communicate these can enlist others. Kouzes and Posner (2012) emphasized that enabling others to take action toward a shared vision is accomplished by fostering collaboration, building trust, and facilitating relationships. Small successes strengthen others and generate competence. Education assistants can also engage others by piloting new ideas, seeking external resources for innovation, and taking calculated risks (p. 29).

Advocating for an individual student or for broader change can challenge the process that is in place to support students; however, this is often a critical part of an EA's role. Leadership skills are inherently a way of communicating and an EA's training, experience, and position alongside students provide them with a unique viewpoint. Honing communication skills and gaining the confidence to lead from their role within the hierarchy allows EAs to contribute to inclusive education for all students and paves the way for them to enjoy full and equitable citizenship in adulthood.

Voices from the Field

In the first weeks of working with Tish, Jane (her EA) realized the bright-eyed eight-year-old student with a diagnosis of autism spectrum disorder (ASD) would need adaptations to her classroom environment in order to be successful. Tish communicated with her feet: she would bolt from the class after 15 minutes, distracting nearby students. While limited in verbal expression, her sudden departures from class spoke volumes. Jane observed and documented the girl's behaviour and determined that Tish was bolting to avoid the noise and visual stimulation of the busy class. She believed that a change in seating to a quieter, less distracting corner of the class could improve Tish's school experience.

Jane chose a time that was convenient for the teacher to discuss her observations and her idea that they convert a large, unused cabinet into a quiet nook for Tish by adding a blanket door and a soft pillow. She also suggested that Tish's desk be right beside the quiet nook so that when Jane observed that her behaviour was escalating, she could give her a break and allow her time to self-regulate. The teacher was receptive to hearing Jane's ideas but was concerned that the nook and seating arrangement would isolate Tish from classmates and be perceived as a form of confinement. She agreed that something had to change so Jane provided her with a recent article that described self-regulation, which kept the dialogue open.

Jane had a good working relationship with the LST, Tish's case manager. She shared her observations with her at a weekly meeting and brought up the idea of the nook. The LST thought it was important to discuss the idea with the district behaviour specialist and to bring the teacher in on the conversation to hear concerns. A team meeting was called and while Jane waited for that day she continued with quiet determination to bring awareness to others about Tish's situation in ways that increased their connection to Tish and to Jane herself. When she solicited ideas from other EAs on strategies to help prevent a student from bolting, she was careful to keep her conversations with the classroom teacher and LST private. When the vice-principal asked Jane how her work with Tish was going, she provided a balanced update that included both her own observations and suggestions and the teacher's concerns. At the meeting, Jane shared her ideas with the team and listened to their concerns. A full discussion provided clarity regarding the difference between Jane's approach and seclusion and it was decided that the team would put Jane's plan into action.

It took a few days for Tish to make the transition to using the nook and new seating arrangement, but within two weeks her departures from class had decreased significantly and her ability to participate in classroom activities and interact with her peers had increased. Jane gave feedback to all the parties who had come together to support Tish and her classmates in a more positive classroom experience.

CRITICAL THINKING QUESTIONS

1. In the example provided, education assistant Jane advocates for her student, Tish. What type of advocacy does she demonstrate and what advocacy steps and ethical standards are in play? Based on this chapter, what more could Jane have done?

2. This chapter discusses many of the internal processes necessary to hone communication skills for effective advocacy. Based on this information,

what may be happening internally for Jane as she attempts to advocate for Tish?

3. The five most effective traits for leaders, as identified by Kouzes and Posner (2012), are as follows: model the way, inspire a shared vision, challenge the process, enable others to act, and encourage the heart. What leadership traits are demonstrated by Jane in the example provided? Explain.

REFERENCES

Adler, R. B., Rolls, J. A., & Proctor II, R. F. (2015). *Look: Looking out, looking in.* Toronto: Nelson Press.

"Advocacy." (n.d.). *Dictionary.com*. Retrieved from http://www.dictionary.com/browse/advocacy?s=t

British Columbia Ministry of Education and Training. (2006). *Special education.* Retrieved from https://www2.gov.bc.ca/gov/content/education-training/administration/legislation-policy/public-schools/special-education

British Columbia Teachers' Federation/CUPE British Columbia. (2009). *Roles and responsibilities of teachers and teacher assistants/education assistants.* Retrieved from https://bctf.ca/uploadedFiles/Public/Issues/InclusiveEd/RolesAndResponsibilitiesTeachersTAs.pdf

Canadian Association for Community Living. (2013a). *Assuring income security and equality for Canadians with intellectual disabilities and their families.* Retrieved from https://cacl.ca/wp-content/uploads/2018/05/CACL-Brief-Finance-Committee-Income-Equality-in-Canada-April-2013-2.pdf

Canadian Association for Community Living. (2013b). *Inclusion of Canadians with intellectual disabilities: A national report card 2013.* Retrieved from http://www.nlacl.ca/wp-content/uploads/2014/01/National-Report-Card-2013-ENG-Final.pdf

Canadian Association for Community Living. (2017). No excuses. Retrieved from https://inclusiveeducation.ca/take-action/no-excuses/

Covey, S. R. (2004). *The 8th habit: From effectiveness to greatness* [Kindle DX version]. New York: Free Press.

Covey, S. R. (2013, June 25). Leadership is a choice, not a position: Stephen R. Covey. *Business Standard*. Retrieved from http://www.business-standard.com/article/management/leadership-is-a-choice-not-a-position-stepen-r-covey-109020300076_1.html

Galinsky, A. (2017, February 17). How to speak up for yourself. *Ideas.Ted.com*. Retrieved from https://ideas.ted.com/how-to-speak-up-for-yourself/

Inclusion BC. (n.d.) Inclusive education. Retrieved from http://www.inclusionbc.org/our-priority-areas/inclusive-education

Inclusion BC. (2014). *Everyone belongs in our schools: A parent's handbook on inclusive education* (5th ed.). New Westminster, BC: Author. Retrieved from http://www.inclusionbc.org/parent-s-handbook-inclusive-education

Kippist, L., & Duarte, F. (2015). What does it mean having difficult conversations in the workplace? An exploratory literature review. *Employment Relations Record*, *15*(2), 61–74.

Kouzes, J. M., & Posner, B. Z. (2012). *The leadership challenge: How to make extraordinary things happen in organizations* (5th ed.). San Francisco: Jossey-Bass.

Lencioni, P. (2002). *The five dysfunctions of a team*. San Francisco: Jossey-Bass.

Levine, K., O'Hara, A., & Weber, Z. (2016). *Skills for human service practice*. Don Mills, ON: Oxford University Press.

Meeker, M. (2013). PowerPoint presentation on advocacy (module 1) for Diploma in Disability Studies, Vancouver Island University, Nanaimo, British Columbia.

Moore, S. (2016, April 4). *Transforming inclusive education* [Video file]. *YouTube*. Retrieved from https://www.youtube.com/watch?v=RYtUlU8MjlY

Penticton Advocacy Network. (1997). *The AdvoKit: A step-by-step guide to effective advocacy*. Penticton, BC: Author. Retrieved from https://ccsw2012.weebly.com/uploads/1/1/5/4/11542142/speakup.pdf

Representative for Children and Youth. (2011). *Champions for change: A guide to effective advocacy for youth and the adults who support them*. Victoria, BC: Author. Retrieved from https://www.rcybc.ca/sites/default/files/documents/pdf/rcy-champions-forchange.pdf

Ruiz, D. M. (1997). *The four agreements: A practical guide to personal freedom*. San Rafael, CA: Amber-Allen.

Schweitzer, A., & Wood, J. (2017). *Everyday encounters: An introduction to interpersonal communication*. Toronto: Nelson Education.

Sinek, S. (2017). Getting a better job [Blog post]. *Start with why*. Retrieved from http://blog.startwithwhy.com/refocus/2017/01/getting-a-better-job.html

Thompson, N. (2002). *People skills*. Hampshire, UK: Palgrave Macmillan.

The Education Assistant as a Professional

CHAPTER 3

What Makes an Outstanding Education Assistant? Best Practices in the Field

Victoria Johnston-Hatch

THREE KEY IDEAS

1. The fundamentals of effective practice include behavioural, social, and academic support.
2. Several key qualities of an education assistant contribute to the development of team collaboration and person-centred practice.
3. Awareness of barriers to best practice allows for an education assistant to develop a reflective approach to their role.

Inclusion BC defines an effective education assistant (EA) as a school employee who is "well-trained in several areas, including behaviour management and supporting students to develop social and communication skills" (2014, p. 13). The British Columbia Ministry of Education (2016, p. 10) defines EAs as follows:

- persons other than teachers [who] assist teachers in carrying out their responsibilities and duties under [the School Act] and the regulations

- persons employed under subsection (1) [who] work under the direction of a teacher and the general supervision of a teacher or school principal

The expectations of EAs within school settings have evolved significantly since the early 1990s (Groom & Rose, 2005). The above descriptions are generic definitions of only a portion of the daily work and tasks of an EA. In practice, EAs frequently support multiple students with complex needs throughout their day (Patterson, 2006). Both the required skill set and the expectations of EA work are increasing, as this position now plays a significant role in the education system (Burgess & Mayes, 2007). Wren (2017) listed the provision of academic, social, and behaviour supports as the main categories for the work of EAs. Behaviour support involves physical support; this is not as prevalent as the other categories and few of the EAs questioned for her study provide support in this area. There can also be a considerable discrepancy between how the EA role is defined and the work expected of EAs within each district, school, and classroom (Patterson, 2006).

WHAT IS EFFECTIVE PRACTICE?

Proximity

In their 1997 article "Helping or Hovering," Giangreco, Edelman, Luiselli, and Macfarland discussed how maintaining a high level of physical closeness between EAs and the students they are supporting was a documented practice. Does merely being close to students constitute effectiveness? While proximity to their focus students can be a useful behaviour tool, Giangreco et al. (1997) suggested that EAs should not rely solely on proximity. Instead, EAs need to be aware of how their presence can affect the students they are supporting, and layer it alongside other strategies and supports. Hemmingsson, Borell, and Gustavsson (2003) found that there were three levels of proximity for EAs: (1) sitting directly beside the students, (2) sitting one or two students away, or (3) sitting away from the group. With all three of these identified levels, they too found that the act of merely being close to a student was not enough to define effective practice. Causton-Theoharis (2014) discussed the importance of not sitting next to a student unless deemed necessary; however, in order not to miss a student's verbal or non-verbal communication cues, EAs must be close enough to engage. Knowing when to intervene and when to back off is a vital skill that EAs need to be effective. Students may require different levels of support at different times of day (Hemmingsson et al., 2003), so being able to read cues, step in and out as needed, and respond appropriately are vital skills EAs need to use continuously in their day-to-day work.

Hemmingsson et al. (2003) discussed the importance of allowing children to request support, while also standing back to let students move through the routine with as much independence as they need. Their research demonstrates that being available to students when they need assistance is still a primary skill for sufficient support; however, remaining close enough to assist when the student is willing to accept support, or even requires it, can be easier said than done!

Behaviour Support

Behaviour supports are becoming a critical factor in schools (Wren, 2017). Groom and Rose (2005) suggest that these supports are essential to the success of inclusion, and they illustrate how the role of the EA has become more complex and demanding. Implementing behaviour supports includes understanding how to implement behaviour plans (Walker & Snell, 2016). Patterson (2006) found that 90 percent of her study respondents indicated that the EA was responsible for attending to the behaviour of the student they were supporting. When the student engaged in challenging behaviour, the EA was expected to regulate their behaviour as quickly as possible. Patterson (2006) also notes that behaviour supports take top priority over all the other potential needs of the student.

Social Support

Hemmingsson et al. (2003) found that desire for social interaction was the primary motivation for students to allow EA support to occur. Saddler (2013) discussed how social and academic items are not only combined, but are also both very important to students in school. There is an expectation that EAs will facilitate social interactions and support their students in developing social skills. Causton-Theoharis (2014) has discussed the importance of friendships for students with disabilities and establishing social connections. Wren (2017) provided useful student perspectives on requiring support in social situations and indicated that students want assistance without feeling followed or intruded upon. Giangreco, Suter, and Doyle (2010) conducted a literature review into recent research on the work of paraprofessionals and found that, in fact, many student self-advocates saw their EAs as a possible barrier to social interactions. The EA is viewed by the student and their peers alike as more of a mother figure than an educator. Giangreco et al. (2010) also reported that students want to have more choices in terms of how they are supported and do not want to feel singled out for requiring adult supports. Helping students to indicate their choice is viewed not only as a beneficial behaviour support strategy but also as a critical item to assist with quality of life outcomes (Schalock, 2004). Within their work, EAs need to be able to involve their students in practical decision making to allow their voices to emerge.

Academic Support

Every year while out on practicum I have at least one student who is surprised, while working in high school Learning Support Services, when they need to assist students with high-level science and math. Working as an EA in high school can be daunting for those who do not feel confident in their academic skills; however, it is not always about knowing these subjects inside out, but rather about supporting students to complete their work and learning alongside their students. Causton-Theoharis (2014) noted the need for EAs to learn how to adapt the curriculum established by the teacher. They need to have strategies and ideas to provide differentiated instruction. Academic supports are one of the critical elements of EA practice.

ACTIVE SUPPORT: WHAT SKILLS DO OUTSTANDING EAs POSSESS?

Effective Collaboration

As discussed in the work of Saddler (2013) and Wren (2017), the roles of teacher and EA are often blurred, making it difficult for both students and EAs to know the boundaries of individual roles. Saddler (2013) mentioned that EAs are guided in practice by their individual school administrations, and this can mean that work and collaborative practices look very different in different schools. Patterson (2006) also discussed the necessity of collaboration and having everyone on the school team working together. During a 2018 practicum visit, a student recounted her initial visit to her classroom, and mentioned that she could not initially identify which adult was the teacher and which was the EA. Both adults were equally engaged in the class and supported all the students in the room. This is an excellent example of collaborative practice. The concept of the EA/teacher team is also noted in Wren (2017), as students within inclusive classrooms were also not always able to immediately identify the roles of the adults in their room.

Wren (2017) interviewed self-advocates and found that students did not always understand the supports their EA provided them in class; however, they understood that the EA was present to assist them in the classroom. The blurred lines mentioned in Wren (2017) and Saddler (2013) indicate that the collaborative method can make it difficult for students to understand the EA's role and the difference between the roles of teacher and EA. One question we need to ask is, should it matter? Ideally, students find support in the classroom from an adult whom they know and trust, who can assist in their work.

Groom and Rose (2005) mentioned the importance of students' perceptions of the EA in the success of their supports. It can be challenging to be firm and uphold expectations when students want to have their EA around. During an evaluation meeting, a teacher gave her EA practicum student a crucial piece of feedback: you are an educator, not simply a caregiver. This statement is in keeping with the best practices skills and needs of an EA. Fulfilling all these support responsibilities well is not just about being in the room, it is also about using multiple educational tools to teach students skills. Hemmingsson et al. (2003) have spoken about how EAs help teachers in many aspects of the work; in fact, "help teacher" is the term they use to define this role. This terminology supports the collaborative teams that successful teachers and EAs can create. It also speaks to this position's value in the classroom.

Glazzard (2011) discussed the importance of collaborative practice and meetings within the team of EAs. Individuals working in this position need time together to case conference and organize their work and supports. Effective practice does not happen by itself; EAs need to collaborate, and the whole EA team needs to use the individualized education plan (IEP) and support plan to guide their work.

Team Commitment

Parents often report that the EA's dedication and skills are crucial to their child's successful inclusion (Inclusion BC, 2014). Logan and Feiler (2006) discussed the importance of communication between parents and schools. They also noted that parents will occasionally not follow the school's IEP and supports. The main reason for this is that parents are worried about implementing supports incorrectly and derailing the plan. As a teacher, working with parents can be challenging, but building parents' confidence and skills so they can provide support at home is essential to students' success (Logan & Feiler, 2006). Patterson (2006) also indicated the need for parental involvement. All team members, including families, need support in order to be consistent with the process of supporting students.

Person-Centred Practice

As mentioned previously in this chapter, providing behaviour supports is an essential area of EA work (Groom & Rose, 2005). The functional behaviour assessment (FBA) process, which enables EAs to understand why a student is engaging in challenging behaviours, always begins with a personal profile that provides a comprehensive and robust overview of who students are (O'Neill, Albin, Storey, Horner, & Sprague, 2015). An FBA profile includes information on likes, dislikes, strengths, communication abilities, learning preferences, and any sensory and/or medical needs (O'Neill et al., 2015). This information is critical for an EA's work and effective practice. Even though it can be challenging when EAs are responsible for multiple students throughout the day, no two students are the same and the work of an EA needs to reflect this. Creating a connection with students provides an opportunity for the most effective support.

Creating Connection

While I was walking with an EA on a recent visit to a high school, a tall young man walked past us and said hello to the EA by name. She commented that he was not one of her students, but that she had created connections with students that extended past those for whom she was directly responsible. She circulated among a group of 30 students in the library during novel study, smiling and noticing the students that might need help but may not feel confident enough to ask. She noted a table to our right, indicating that these students likely needed help and might not ask or allow her to offer it. I asked her how she would assist in this situation, and she replied that being present to seize the opportunity when they did ask was vital. She also said that making time to create connections with students could open the door for times when they might need help. She had worked at this school for over eight years, and she mentioned that she enjoys her job. It was clear to me that she was both passionate and highly skilled. I left that school thinking about how lucky those kids were, and that she was definitely someone I would want working with my own children.

When I recently sat down with a school resource teacher, he made it very clear that he expects all his EAs, first and foremost, to connect and establish relationships with students. He recognizes that no supports will be useful until this has occurred. His expectations were valuable feedback for EA practicum students and essential for every EA to understand and implement daily. Establishing relationships as an EA creates trust with students and allows support to occur (Causton-Theoharis, 2014).

Stacey Wakabayashi, a provincial fetal alcohol spectrum disorder/ autism spectrum disorder outreach worker, mentions the importance of "connecting before you correct" (Wakabayashi, 2017). This relationship building is a vital starting point for the work of EAs. It is impossible to be effective without this connection occurring (Groom & Rose, 2005).

Taking and Displaying Initiative

Hemmingsson et al. (2003) have noted the importance of reading students' cues and adjusting accordingly. They spoke about the EA needing to take initiative to know when to use support strategies and provide intervention. These skills are difficult to teach. An EA must know how to read the room to determine where they are needed. They also need to know when to push a student and when to step back. Using initiative successfully is not only about using the right strategy, but also about using it when the student needs it.

PRE-SERVICE EAs' THOUGHTS ON ATTRIBUTES

When students begin their post-secondary education, they may view the role of an EA as easy to define. Individual values shape one's work as an EA (Glazzard, 2011). Being aware of the unique and varied experiences and values that an EA brings to their work can provide insight into one's own process. Barbara Cole's article on educational inclusion (2005) discussed the need for pre-service educators to not only focus on their work, but also to identify their guiding values. But what skills make an EA not only effective but outstanding? At the beginning of every course, I ask my pre-service EAs what skills they feel an effective EA possesses. They tend to mention patience, kindness, enjoying working with kids, and being knowledgeable. Their answers change as they move through the coursework and into practicum.

The list of skills and attributes possessed by outstanding EAs, as identified by pre-service EAs, includes the following:

- patience
- understanding
- taking a person-centred approach
- compassion
- initiative
- courage
- creativity

- honesty
- resourcefulness
- flexibility
- being caring
- creating meaningful connections
- being educated
- willingness to never stop learning
- being strategic
- resilience
- being hardworking

It is an extensive list! While thinking about your own practice, consider which items are important to you and how you might apply these in your practice. In considering this list, think about what skills you would work on developing and what skills are missing that you would add to your own practice.

BARRIERS TO EFFECTIVE EA WORK

There can be multiple barriers to effectively implementing IEP and support plans. Glazzard (2011) reported that the most significant obstacle to active practice is an attitude barrier. This includes the EA's attitude toward the student and their inclusion. Glazzard's example involves a preconceived notion about how a student will be based on the comments of others or on one's own previous experiences. Malette et al. (1992) also discussed the importance of overcoming attitudinal barriers. Of the three types of barriers they identified—attitude, knowledge, and accessibility/availability—attitude was the most difficult to remedy. Navigating change in this area is often challenging and frustrating. Allinder (1994) documented how feelings of useful work or progress can influence our success. Not only does one need to be aware of others' attitudes, but also of one's own.

Glazzard (2011) identified a lack of teamwork as another barrier to effective work. All team members need to work together to best support children and youth. Adding extra hands to the room can help with this, but achieving optimal support requires giving each other breaks and stepping in when needed. Wren (2017) also commented on the need for team collaboration in order to provide successful inclusion.

Finally, Glazzard (2011) noted other barriers that can also present challenges, including parental resistance, lack of resources, lack of training, and the standard curriculum. All these factors can make the EA's work more difficult.

When working as an EA, it is important to reflect on the following questions:

- Am I doing a good job?
- Where could I do better?
- Can I back up my position and choices with reliable data and research?
- Is the student I am supporting learning?
- Do I enjoy my work?

Too often we find ourselves going through the motions, and we forget that we are supporting our communities' most important resource: our children. Periodically returning to these questions helps EAs provide support to all students and work toward being outstanding in the field.

Voices from the Field

Ann's 14-year-old son, Josh, has 22q11.2 chromosome deletion syndrome. This syndrome often includes specific facial features, frequent infections, developmental delay, learning problems, and cleft palate. Josh struggles with academics due to these moderate to severe delays. He is extremely impulsive and has particular difficulty with his self-regulation skills. He is also small in stature and struggles with social cues, and these traits have affected his social skills and peer relationships. He has received EA support in school on a part-time basis. In his younger elementary school years, his EA would also assist his classmates to lessen any stigma he felt about requiring support. He is now in grade 9, participating in a modified high school diploma program with full integration in electives and chosen academic subjects. He receives support in his classes and has an IEP to provide academic, social, and behaviour supports. He is faced with wanting space and autonomy while also needing a high level of support to stay on task and be successful. He frequently comes home and indicates that he is not receiving support and his confidence and self-esteem are suffering. Ann is spending hours with him, trying to finish his work and send it back to school. Josh is frustrated and his behaviours are increasing both at school and at home. Ann feels that the best way for him to be more successful is to have more support and complete more school work at school; however, for that to occur, the EA needs first to connect and have a healthy relationship with Josh. This has not always happened, and her son is frequently not finishing his work in class and trying to avoid his EA at all costs. Ann has set up a meeting with the school to try to come up with ideas to assist Josh.

CRITICAL THINKING QUESTIONS

1. As an EA, how would one maintain support for Josh when he wants to avoid showing that he requires additional help?
2. What are some best practices strategies that might be of assistance when working with this specific age group?
3. Why is connecting with kids such an essential aspect of EA work? What could be done if an EA did not connect with the student to whom they were assigned?

REFERENCES

Allinder, R. M. (1994). The relationship between efficacy and the instructional practices of special education teachers and consultants. *Teacher Education and Special Education: The Journal of the Teacher Education Division of the Council for Exceptional Children, 17*(2), 86–95. doi:10.1177/088840649401700203

British Columbia Ministry of Education. (2016). *Special education services: A manual of policies, procedures and guidelines.* Victoria, BC: Ministry of Education.

Retrieved from https://www2.gov.bc.ca/assets/gov/education/administration/ kindergarten-to-grade-12/inclusive/special_ed_policy_manual.pdf

Burgess, H., & Mayes, A. S. (2007). Supporting the professional development of teaching assistants: Classroom teachers' perspectives on their mentoring role. *Curriculum Journal, 18*(3), 389–407. doi:10.1080/09585170701590056

Causton-Theoharis, J. (2014). *The paraprofessional's handbook for effective support in inclusive classrooms.* Baltimore: Brookes.

Cole, B. A. (2005). "Good faith and effort?": Perspectives on educational inclusion. *Disability and Society, 20*(3), 331–344. doi:10.1080/09687590500060794

Giangreco, M. F., Edelman, S. W., Luiselli, T. E., & Macfarland, S. Z. (1997). Helping or hovering? Effects of instructional assistant proximity on students with disabilities. *Exceptional Children, 64*(1), 7–18. doi:10.1177/001440299706400101

Giangreco, M. F., Suter, J. C., & Doyle, M. B. (2010). Paraprofessionals in inclusive schools: A review of recent research. *Journal of Educational and Psychological Consultation, 20*(1), 41–57.

Glazzard, J. (2011). Perceptions of the barriers to effective inclusion in one primary school: Voices of teachers and teaching assistants. *Support for Learning, 26*(2), 56–63. doi:10.1111/j.1467-9604.2011.01478x

Groom, B., & Rose, R. (2005). Supporting the inclusion of pupils with social, emotional and behavioural difficulties in the primary school: The role of teaching assistants. *Journal of Research in Special Educational Needs, 5*(1), 20–30. doi:10.1111/j.1471-3802.2005.00035x

Hemmingsson, H., Borell, L., & Gustavsson, A. (2003). Participation in school: School assistants creating opportunities and obstacles for pupils with disabilities. *OTJR: Occupation, Participation, and Health, 23*(3), 88–98. doi:10.1177/153944920302300302

Inclusion BC. (2014). *Everyone belongs in our schools: A parent's handbook on inclusive education.* Retrieved from http://www.inclusionbc.org/parent-s-handbook-inclusive-education/your-child-s-school-and-you-who-does-what/school-roles-and-r-4

Logan, E., & Feiler, A. (2006). Forging links between parents and schools: A new role for teaching assistants? *Support for Learning, 21*(3), 115–120. doi:10.1111/j.1467-9604.2006.00416x

Malette, P., Mirenda, P., Kandborg, T., Jones, P., Bunz, T., & Rogow, S. (1992). Application of a lifestyle development process for persons with severe intellectual disabilities: A case study report. *Journal of the Association for Persons with Severe Handicaps, 17*(3), 179–191. doi:10.1177/154079699201700306

O'Neill, R. E., Albin, R. W., Storey, K., Horner, R. H., & Sprague, J. R. (2015). *Functional assessment and program development for problem behavior: A practical handbook*. Stamford, CT: Cengage Learning.

Patterson, K. B. (2006). Roles and responsibilities of paraprofessionals: In their own words. *TEACHING Exceptional Children Plus, 2*(5). Retrieved from https://files.eric.ed.gov/fulltext/EJ967108.pdf

Saddler, H. (2013). Researching the influence of teaching assistants on the learning of pupils identified with special educational needs in mainstream primary schools: Exploring social inclusion. *Journal of Research in Special Educational Needs, 14*(3), 145–152. doi:10.1111/1471-3802.12019

Schalock, R. L. (2004). The concept of quality of life: What we know and do not know. *Journal of Intellectual Disability Research, 46*(3), 203–217. doi:10.1111/j.1365-2788.2003.00558.x

Wakabayashi, S. (2017, October 19). Introduction to FASD. Lecture presented at Kwantlen Polytechnic University, Surrey, British Columbia.

Walker, V. L., & Snell, M. E. (2016). Teaching paraprofessionals to implement function-based interventions. *Focus on Autism and Other Developmental Disabilities, 32*(2), 114–123. doi:10.1177/1088357616673561

Wren, A. (2017). Understanding the role of the teaching assistant: Comparing the views of pupils with SEN and TAs within mainstream primary schools. *Support for Learning, 32*(1), 4–19. doi:10.1111/1467-9604.12151

CHAPTER 4

The Education Assistant–Teacher Partnership in the Classroom: Maximizing Returns

Nan Stevens and Susan McKay

THREE KEY IDEAS

1. The relationship between the education assistant and the teacher is an important aspect of supporting students successfully within an inclusive classroom.
2. Teachers need a collaborative and communicative relationship with education assistants to serve students successfully.
3. Education assistants who have become teachers provide insight from their experiences, which may be beneficial in the field.

As a result of the mandated ideology of the full inclusion movement (FIM) in public and independent schools in Canada over the last two decades, the roles of the generalist teacher and the education assistant (EA) have changed significantly (Blatchford & Russell, 2012; Hutchinson, 2017). Additionally, the inclusive model has resulted in a dramatic rise in the number of EAs in schools, yet "there has been little systematic research looking into their effectiveness" (Symes & Humphrey, 2011, p. 57). Biggs, Gilson, and Carter (2016) suggest that more research is needed in the area of EA-teacher relationships: "Despite the prominence of teacher-paraprofessional partnerships, current research has not investigated ways to strengthen these relationships. Instead, most attention has been focused on what constitutes inappropriate and appropriate service delivery" (p. 257). Hill (2003) agrees that the frequency of EAs in inclusive classrooms has grown significantly and posits that EA support is the tool used to enable children with disabilities to be included. Hill notes that despite the increase in employment of EAs, there continues to be limited research on the topic and it "has been characterized as one of the least studied" topics in the field of education (p. 98). Similarly, Biggs et al. assert that "despite the number of teacher-paraprofessional partnerships, current research has not investigated ways to strengthen these relationships" (p. 257). The authors of this chapter, a teacher educator and an EA educator, believe that the relationship between the EA and the teacher may be the single most important aspect of serving students successfully within an inclusive classroom. This chapter will explore the relationship between the EA and the teacher by gathering feedback from three focus groups.

INSIGHTS UNCOVERED WITHIN THREE FOCUS GROUPS

Group #1: What Do EAs Need from Teachers to Be Able to Serve Students Successfully in the Generalist Classroom?

From interviews conducted with EAs, several insights emerged that are important for EAs to be successful in their work. These encompass the following areas: inclusive attitude; support from the teacher; skills, knowledge, and expertise; relationship; communication; and supervision.

Inclusive Attitude
A number of EAs expressed that teachers need to believe in inclusion and to "model it." Additionally, EAs want teachers to collaborate and co-operate more with them on instructional approaches to help optimize the educational potential of all students. Riggs (2004) notes that EAs "feel supported when the teacher acknowledges their work and

the children with whom they are working as important members of the classroom community" (p. 11). Within the inclusive classroom, EAs and teachers must work together to create and model a welcoming and inclusive environment.

Support from the Teacher

Education assistants want to remind teachers that they work with some of the most challenging students in the classroom and that this requires creativity, "thinking on the fly," patience, and accommodation. To carry out their work, EAs need the teachers' support and guidance, otherwise they may "burn out and feel isolated." They feel most valued when teachers trust their skill level and do not "micromanage" (Lori, EA, personal communication, May 14, 2018). For example, if there is an established behaviour plan in place, the teacher should try to trust the EA to follow through with it, rather than intervening or undermining the EA's efforts and skill level. According to Carnahan, Williamson, Clarke, and Sorensen (2009), EAs "value ongoing support and feedback about their efforts" (p. 42). Furthermore, Giangreco, Edelman, and Broer (2001) maintain that teacher recognition is important and may be demonstrated by "nonmonetary signs and symbols of appreciation" (p. 485), such as EAs being trusted with important responsibilities, being listened to, and supervising non-instructional tasks.

Skills, Knowledge, and Expertise

Education assistants have many skills to offer and want to be recognized and respected for their efforts and expertise. It helps when teachers are willing to listen to EAs' ideas and suggestions and not disregard their input. One EA commented that when working with children with exceptionalities, "there should be an unwritten rule where everyone demonstrates respect for one another and that neither professional knows everything!" (Lori, EA, personal communication, May 14, 2018).

Relationship

Developing familiarity and trust helps both professionals ensure a positive working relationship (Biggs et al., 2016). One EA suggested that if a teacher considers an EA to be subordinate in terms of their professional role, this may impair the effectiveness of the team (Lori, EA, personal communication, May 17, 2018). As Riggs (2004) posits, teachers and EAs benefit from taking time to get to know each other. Learning one another's name, family background, outside interests, skills, and strengths goes a long way. Blatchford, Russell, and Webster (2016) remind educators that if a teacher has concerns about giving up some control to an EA or feels threatened by an EA's skills and knowledge, the partnership may suffer.

Communication

Both teacher and EA are working to provide an optimal learning environment and it is important to recognize that each is doing their best to achieve this. A number of EAs interviewed noted that they are charged with a lot of responsibility with particular students. The EAs need the teacher to communicate strategies that work well with a student, as well as strategies that do not; in turn, EAs need to be listened to. Open communication is the key in the successful paraprofessional-professional relationship (Blatchford et al., 2016; Hill, 2003; Riggs, 2004). If the EA and teacher can communicate and function as a team, then the common goal of providing students with support can be reached (Kilanowski-Press, Foote, & Rinaldo, 2010).

Supervision

The EAs interviewed shared some common feedback about teacher supervision. Although teachers, at times, may not understand what an EA is doing for a particular student, it is essential that the teacher maintain an open mind. Teachers can learn a great deal from EAs, if they are flexible and willing to learn how to enhance a student's learning experience in a way that may not be "typical." In addition, as one EA pointed out, each teacher is unique in how they want their class managed, and it is important to know what they expect. EAs need direction, boundaries, and input from the teachers who supervise them. These sentiments echo the findings of Wadsworth and Knight (1996), who insist that for inclusion to succeed, team collaboration and communication must be essential aspects of the EA-teacher relationship. Similarly, Carnahan et al. (2009) posit that "effective supervision begins with effective communication" (p. 36).

Group #2: What Do Teachers Need from EAs to Be Able to Serve Students Successfully in the Generalist Classroom?

The following insights emerged from an analysis of correspondence from seven teachers regarding what teachers require from EAs:

- self-directed/know when to "jump in"
- collaboration and communication

Self-Direction and Knowing When to Jump In
Teachers need EAs in the classroom to be aware of what is going on around them and to take initiative in responding to students' needs. This theme resonated for every teacher who responded to the inquiry. Teachers need EAs to look around the class and see who needs support. Students' needs change daily, and within each subject and/or project. According to classroom teachers, the EAs who are most effective are those who do what needs to be done, without needing continuous reminders and guidance. Teachers need EAs who are confident in making decisions in the moment, and who act professionally and independently. As teachers' responsibilities have grown, they claim they are too busy to supervise an additional person in the classroom (Villa, Thousand, Nevin, & Liston, 2005). It is interesting to note that teachers expressed a need for EAs to be self-directed, yet, as discussed in the previous section, EAs voiced a need for more explicit direction and supervision from the teachers with whom they work.

Collaboration and Communication
Creating a culture of respect, collaboration, and ongoing communication is essential to successfully serve all students within a classroom (Calder-Stegemann & Aucoin, 2018). Similar to Calder-Stegemann and Aucoin, the classroom teachers interviewed expressed a need for EAs to be part of a communicative team. The teachers maintain that EA

feedback is absolutely welcome and necessary. One teacher noted that the EAs who focus on relationship building are successful; students respond better when they have a relationship with an adult that is personal. Hill (2003) studied the activities and interactions of EAs and teachers and found that the EAs "indeed had an important role in influencing inclusive practices" (p. 100). Moshe (2017) found that specific expertise for student support rested with a small number of staff (EAs). Additionally, Symes and Humphrey (2011) and Taylor and Edwards (2016) concur that more training in specific instructional methods or educational pedagogy for EAs would help to develop capacity in the classroom.

While team collaboration between teachers and EAs is desirable, Villa et al. (2005) caution that in a classroom of multiple instructional agents, "an 'only as much as necessary' support principal needs to be observed. For example, if a paraprofessional is in the classroom, this person becomes a co-teacher and a support to the class rather than a 'velcroed' personal assistant to one lone student" (p. 42). Biggs et al.'s (2016) study focusing on the paraprofessional-professional relationship found that "teachers are the leaders of classrooms.… They have considerable potential to cultivate or hinder strong cooperative relationships with paraprofessionals through their mindset, proficiency, and leadership" (p. 270). These scholars suggest that it is the responsibility of teachers to cultivate good communication and effective teamwork.

Group #3: For EAs Who Are Enrolled in a Teacher Education Program, What Aspects of Your Journey Will Help to Inform the EA-Teacher Partnership?

Seven teacher candidates in the bachelor of education program at Thompson Rivers University in Kamloops, British Columbia, who once worked as EAs in schools, commented on their unique journeys and provided feedback that may help paraprofessionals and professionals increase the efficacy of their work.

All individuals expressed that working as an EA made them more empathetic to students with diverse needs and felt that their experiences will make them more effective and responsive teachers. They discussed how learning strategies for identified students are also helpful to other students in the classroom. Additionally, the teacher candidates identified that the main difference between the role of an EA and the role of a teacher lies within the expectations for each. EAs are expected to help students on a one-to-one or small group basis, while teachers are expected to design lessons that reach *all* learners in the class. One of the challenges the teacher candidates noticed during their practicum experiences was the need to shift from focusing on single students who may need support to seeing their role as caring for the entire class.

After reviewing the feedback from the three focus groups, a number of common themes were uncovered that may be compared to findings from the literature.

DISCUSSION

The literature from the 1990s maintained that the role of paraprofessionals in classrooms was disciplinary in nature, as EAs helped teachers by working with students with behaviour challenges (Bowers, 1997; Homer, Diemer, & Brazeau, 1992). More recently, research has focused on EA efficacy and the blurred boundaries between teacher and EA roles (Alborz, Pearson, Farrell, & Howes, 2009; Blatchford et al., 2016; Clarke & Visser, 2016; Cockroft & Atkinson, 2015).

Upon review of information from research and focus groups, evidence supports two themes as having the most significance for the EA and teacher groups: (1) the changing roles of the EA and the generalist teacher in the inclusive classroom, and (2) blurred boundaries require defined roles and responsibilities. These themes are discussed next; the discussion includes an exploration of how these themes relate to a co-teaching model.

The Changing Roles of the EA and the Generalist Teacher in the Inclusive Classroom

First, a brief review of the "push in" and "pull out" models of support will assist in the discussion. In a survey of current practices,

Kilanowski-Press et al. (2010) found that the push in model, where the special education teacher enters the classroom to provide instruction and support to children, is still the most widely used. In this model, "the 'push in' teacher will bring materials into the classroom and work cooperatively with the classroom teacher" (Webster, 2018, para. 5) and EA(s) assigned to the class. Swartz (2003) cites the following as benefits of the push in model: increased collaboration between specialists and classroom teachers, alignment of teaching strategies, and reduced stigma for students typically pulled from the classroom.

The pull out model of providing special education services can be defined as any program that removes students from the general classroom to special classrooms to receive instructional support (Swartz, 2003). It is a standard practice that "students continue to be pulled out of the classroom for various services such as counseling, speech therapy, occupational therapy, [and] physical therapy" (Barton, 2016, p. 2). According to Fernandez and Hines (2016), students work in a separate area for individualized or small group instruction with the purpose of targeting instruction to the students' learning needs.

The full inclusion mandate has resulted in a greater adherence to the push in model and, as a result, there has been a dramatic rise in the number of EAs in classrooms (Symes & Humphrey, 2011; Vincett, Cremin, & Thomas, 2005). Kilanowski-Press et al. (2010) share a caution from their findings that is relevant to the increase in EA numbers:

> One-to-one student support, plausibly the least inclusive form of instruction … emerged as the most prevalent type of support provided in inclusive classrooms.… The role of such instructional formats must be carefully monitored to ensure compatibility with best practice. (p. 53)

Although, the traditional push in model of support has demonstrated success with inclusive education, educators are exploring alternatives. Educators (and parents) wish to place students with diverse learning needs into the least restrictive environments (Calder-Stegemann & Aucoin, 2018; Rozalski, Stewart, & Miller, 2010); however, the overuse of paraprofessionals to replace teachers' instruction is not ideal. Giangreco and Broer (2005) are "concerned that the longer the pressure of inclusion continues to be shifted onto the backs of paraprofessionals, the more this delays attention to the root problems in general and special education" (p. 24). The evidence may suggest that paraprofessionals are situated in classrooms to meet the needs of "full inclusion," yet this may be compromising the least restrictive approach.

Co-Teaching Model

The co-teaching model, blending both generalist and special education teachers, is gaining attention (Villa et al., 2005). As inclusion shifts in pedagogy, special education services need to evolve away from either a pull out or push in delivery model to foster a co-teaching model (Friend, Cook, Hurley-Chamberlain, & Shamberger, 2010). Peery (2017) defines *co-teaching* as a team that "works in the general education classroom for the majority of the time; students with special needs are not pulled out to receive services in another location" (para. 4). As educators are leaning in to a co-teaching modality, Moore (2016) asserts that "professionals and experts can work together within the general classroom with a collaborative teaching model in order to bridge the gap between special education and 'teaching to the diversity of all'" (p. 5).

Friend et al. (2010) further explain that co-teaching is "the sharing of instruction by a general education teacher and a special education teacher, or another specialist in a general class that includes students with disabilities, and is a relatively recent application" to special education pedagogy (p. 9). Co-teaching may resemble the push in model of providing student support but, according to Beninghof (2012), co-teaching differs "because both educators are simultaneously engaged in the instructional process" (p. 8). Woodward and Talbert-Johnson (2009) claim that students benefit from co-teaching as they feel they can get help when they need it with two teachers present. One concern that has arisen out of the co-teaching model is the "overlap" or "blurred boundaries" of teacher and EA roles and responsibilities, which can be problematic.

BLURRED BOUNDARIES REQUIRE DEFINED ROLES AND RESPONSIBILITIES

Co-teaching is gaining ground as an innovative way to meet students' needs in an inclusive classroom. There are now multiple instructional agents in the classroom and working as a collaborative team is the key (Villa et al., 2005). Friend et al. (2010) assert that "co-teaching is becoming more and more of a necessity as a response to the increasing difficulty of a single professional keeping up with all the knowledge and the skills necessary to meet the instructional needs of the diverse student population attending public schools" (p. 11). In response to difficulties experienced by generalist teachers, Villa et al. (2005) suggest that "educators and other support personnel have redefined their roles to that of collaborative team members who jointly plan, instruct and solve the daily problems of teaching in today's diverse classrooms" (p. 42). Due to the expanded role of the EA, Moshe (2017) wonders if "inclusion assistant" would be a more apt title for an individual who supports both the teacher and the student.

The data gathered from interviews and email conversations revealed that EAs wish to have their role clearly defined. They wish to know what is expected of them. At the same time, teachers want EAs to be self-starters and initiators (to "jump in") so that they are not burdened with the responsibility of directing another person in the classroom. Teachers and EAs need to find that "dance" or balance with one another so that they can perform their jobs optimally, independently yet together.

Biggs et al.'s (2016) findings include the following: teachers should have an attitude of openness and professionalism when working with paraprofessionals, and should lead by "fostering paraprofessional strengths, and making efforts to show paraprofessionals they are valued and appreciated" (p. 270). Fisher and Pleasants (2012) support these findings, suggesting that besides supporting students directly, paraprofessionals can have a significant impact on classrooms by being a direct support to teachers. Salter, Swanwick, and Pearson (2017) found that the onus for creating a classroom culture of collaboration is on the teacher: "Within a classroom, an environment dedicated to interaction and to the transfer of information from one individual to a number of others[,] … the attitude and the expectations of the teacher will shape the nature of the interaction" (p. 47). Even with the onus placed on teachers to create a culture of collaboration, both EAs and teachers may consider Peery's (2017) list of the seven factors of best practice that contribute to high quality EA-teacher partnerships:

- respect each other
- clearly define roles and responsibilities
- be flexible
- plan together
- don't take yourself too seriously
- communicate
- seek administrative support

Both the EA and the teacher can benefit from defined roles and responsibilities, while at the same time delivering quality instruction as a high-functioning team.

The full inclusion movement has resulted in multiple educators providing instruction in a general classroom. To reach the needs of all students in a class where diversity is the norm, an increased number of paraprofessionals is required. In addition to the increased number of EAs in the room, the roles of both teacher and EA have expanded considerably. The classroom culture has resulted in a more dynamic and responsive educational setting, yet there are issues to resolve—specifically, how EAs and teachers can best work together.

Practicing EAs and teachers provided insight and feedback about their needs in their respective roles. Additionally, a unique population of respondents (EAs studying to be teachers) shared aspects of their journey while enrolled in a pre-service teacher education program. EAs identified their need for teachers to have an inclusive attitude, be supportive and respectful of their work, and communicate clear expectations. Teachers expressed their need for EAs to show initiative, be self-starters, demonstrate flexibility, and share strategies when they are effective.

The teacher candidate group shared their knowledge regarding specialized instructional methods that work with designated and undesignated pupils, the expectations of the EA and teacher roles, and the need to shift their focus from supporting individuals to working with the whole class. All three groups expressed the need for clear and consistent communication, and teamwork and trust as essential aspects of a positive and effective relationship. When these aspects co-exist, the EA-teacher partnership will be able to maximize returns for both eduators and students.

Voices from the Field

EAs' Voices

The EA is "the lubricant that makes the wheel turn more smoothly!" —Deb, personal communication, May 2, 2018

"Mutual respect and rapport in an honest, open relationship are essential for student success." —Lori, personal communication, May 14, 2018

"It is absolutely crucial to have an open dialogue and positive communication with the teacher." —Taylor, personal communication, May 14, 2018

"I need information about classroom routines, rules, instructions for working with students, etc., and I need the teacher to clarify this so that I can do my work effectively." —Deb, personal communication, May 12, 2018

Teachers' Voices

"An ideal EA is a self-starter. They are able to look around the room and support students who need it, without being asked. Having an awareness of the learning needs within the class and intuitively seeking ways to support all students requiring assistance while encouraging not being helpless as a learner assists the teacher a great deal." —Beth, grade 6/7 teacher, personal communication, May 15, 2018

"I need them (EAs) to be adaptable and flexible because my class is always changing. I also appreciate it when EAs see a need and just jump in without needing direction." —Justin, grade 5/6 teacher, personal communication, May 7, 2018

"I think of EAs as equal and never feel like they are stepping on my toes if they jump right in. I need an EA who can deal with behaviour and academics." —Kim, grade 5 teacher, personal communication, May 10, 2018

"An effective EA is invaluable to a classroom teacher." —Beth, grade 6/7 teacher, personal communication, May 7, 2018

"I need an EA with a sense of humour and a willingness to communicate with me. We are a team!" —Kim, grade 5 teacher, personal communication, May 10, 2018

"I currently have an amazing EA. We will often 'tag' in and out of stressful moments. I trust her and we support each other. Although she is not part of the decision making so to speak, she stays current on all information regarding the child and she will offer her thoughts. I feel that this has a direct impact on the positive climate in my classroom. Daily operations run smoothly and when a problem arises we are able to respond quickly. Together we built a safe, productive space for learning." —Andrea, grade 6/7 teacher, personal communication, May 15, 2018

The Voices of EAs Becoming Teachers

"With 10 years of focus being on a select few students with exceptionalities, I am challenged to give my attention and resources to all the students." —Tanya, teacher candidate, personal communication, May 21, 2018

"My experiences as an EA provided me valuable skills with special needs, including learning, emotional, and physical challenges, on a one-to-one basis and in small groups that I will build upon as I transition to an entire classroom's scale." —Magalie, teacher candidate, personal communication, May 21, 2018

CRITICAL THINKING QUESTIONS

1. How do teacher education and education assistant programs work together to cultivate the kinds of best practices uncovered in this chapter?
2. How is the inclusive education model of co-teaching changing the landscape of EAs and teachers working together?
3. What are some of the systemic barriers that prevent all students from being well served in an inclusive classroom?

REFERENCES

Alborz, A., Pearson, D., Farrell, P., & Howes, A. (2009). *The impact of adult support on pupils and mainstream schools.* London: DCSF.

Barton, K. (2016). Pull-out or push in? Impact on students with special needs social, emotional, and academic success. *Education Masters*, paper 334.

Beninghof, A. M. (2012). *Co-teaching that works: Structures and strategies for maximizing student learning.* San Francisco, CA: Jossey-Bass.

Biggs, E. E., Gilson, C. B., & Carter, E. W. (2016). Accomplishing more together: Influences to the quality of professional relationships between special educators and paraprofessionals. *Research and Practice for Persons with Severe Disabilities, 41*(4), 256–272. doi:10.117715407696916665604

Blatchford, P., & Russell, A. (2012). *Reassessing the impact of teaching assistants: How research challenges practice and policy.* New York: Routledge.

Blatchford, P., Russell, A., & Webster, R. (2016). *Maximizing the impact of teaching assistants: Guidance for school leaders and teachers* (2nd ed.). London: Routledge.

Bowers, T. (1997). Supporting special needs in the mainstream classroom: Children's perceptions of the adult role. *Child: Care, health and development, 23*(3), 217–232.

Calder-Stegemann, K., & Aucoin, A. (Eds.). (2018). *Inclusive education: Stories of success and hope in a Canadian context.* Toronto: Pearson Canada.

Carnahan, C. R., Williamson, P., Clarke, L., & Sorensen, R. (2009). A systematic approach for supporting paraeducators in educational settings: A guide for teachers. *Teaching Exceptional Children, 41*(5), 34–43.

Clarke, E., & Visser, J. (2016). Teaching assistants managing behaviour: Who knows how they do it? A review of literature. *Support for Learning, 31*(4), 266–280. doi:10.111/1457-9604.12137

Cockroft, C., & Atkinson, C. (2015). Using the wider pedagogical role model to establish learning support assistants' views about facilitators and barriers to effective practice. *Support for Learning, 30*(2), 88–104.

Fernandez, N., & Hynes, J. (2016). The efficacy of pullout programs in elementary schools: Making it work. *Journal of Multidisciplinary Graduate Research, 2*(3), 32–47.

Fisher, M., & Pleasants, S. L. (2012). Roles, responsibilities, and concerns of paraeducators: Findings from a state-wide survey. *Remedial and Special Education, 33*(5), 287–297. doi:10.1177/0741932510397762

Friend, M., Cook, L., Hurley-Chamberlain, D., & Shamberger, C. (2010). Co-teaching: An illustration of the complexity of collaboration in special education. *Journal of Educational and Psychological Consultation, 20*(1), 9–27. doi:10.1080/10474410090 3535380

Giangreco, M. F., & Broer, S. M. (2005). Questionable utilization of paraprofessionals in inclusive schools: Are we addressing symptoms or causes? *Focus on Autism and Other Developmental Disabilities, 20*(1), 10–26.

Giangreco, M. F., Edelman, S. W., & Broer, S. M. (2001). Respect, appreciation, and acknowledgement of paraprofessionals who support students with disabilities. *Exceptional Children, 67*(4), 485–498. doi:10.1177/001440290106700404

Hill, C. (2003). The role of instructional assistants in regular classrooms: Are they influencing inclusive practices? *Alberta Journal of Educational Research, 49*(1), 98–100.

Homer, R. H., Diemer, S. M., & Brazeau, K. C. (1992). Educational support for students with severe problem behaviour in Oregon: A descriptive analysis from the 1987–1988 school year. *Research and Practice with Severe Disabilities, 17*(3), 154–169. doi:10.1177154079699201700304

Hutchinson, N. (2017). *Inclusion of exceptional learners in Canadian schools: A practical handbook for teachers* (5th ed.). Toronto: Pearson.

Kilanowski-Press, L., Foote, C. J., & Rinaldo, V. J. (2010). Inclusion classrooms and teachers: A survey of current practices. *International Journal of Special Education, 25*(3), 43–56.

Moore, S. (2016). *One without the other: Stories of unity through diversity and inclusion.* Winnipeg: Portage and Main Press.

Moshe, A. (2017). Inclusion assistants in general education settings: A model for in-service training. *Universal Journal of Educational Research, 5*(2), 209–216. doi:10.13189/ujer.2017.050206

Peery, A. (2017, February 5). Co-teaching: How to make it work. *Cult of pedagogy.* Retrieved from https://www.cultofpedagogy.com/co-teaching-push-in/

Riggs, C. G. (2004). Top 10 list to teachers: What paraeducators want you to know. *Teaching Exceptional Children, 36*(5), 8–12.

Rozalski, M., Stewart. A., & Miller, J. (2010). How to determine the least restrictive environment for students with disabilities? *Exceptionality: A Special Education Journal, 18*(3), 151–163. doi:10.1080/093628352010.491991

Salter, J. M., Swanwick, R. A., & Pearson, S. (2017). Collaborative working practices in inclusive mainstream deaf education settings: Teaching assistant perspectives. *Deafness and Education International, 19*(1), 40–49. doi:10.1080/14643154.2017.1301693

Swartz, S. L. (2003). Working together: A collaborative model for the delivery of special services in general classrooms. Retrieved from http://www.stanswartz.com/collaboration.html

Symes, W., & Humphrey, N. (2011). The deployment, training and teacher relationships supporting pupils with autism spectrum disorders (ASD) in mainstream secondary school. *British Journal of Special Education, 38*(2), 54–64. doi:10.111/j.1467-8578.2011.00499.x

Taylor, J., & Edwards, M. (2016, July 12). 5 ways to improve relationships with educational assistants and paraprofessionals [Blog post]. Retrieved from https://www.crisisprevention.com/Blog/July-2016/working-relationships

Villa, R. A., Thousand, J. S., Nevin, A., & Liston, A. (2005). Successful inclusive practices in middle and secondary schools. *American Secondary Education, 33*(3), 33–50. Ashland, OH: Ashland University.

Vincett, K., Cremin, H., & Thomas, G. (2005). *Teachers and assistants working together: A handbook.* New York: Open University Press.

Wadsworth, D. E., & Knight, D. (1996). Professionals: The bridge to successful full inclusion. *Intervention in School and Clinic, 31*(3), 166–171. doi:10.1177/105345129603100306

Webster, J. (2018, January 17). Inclusion: What is inclusion? *Thought Co.* Retrieved from https://www.thoughtco.com/what-is-inclusion-3111011

Woodward, M. M., & Talbert-Johnson, C. (2009). Reading intervention models: Challenges of classroom support and separated instruction. *Reading Teacher, 63*(3), 190–200. doi:10.1598/rt.63.3.2

SECTION II

MENTAL HEALTH AND WELLNESS

Mental health and wellness has been illuminated over the last decade as a critical element of support within the school system. Health Canada studies suggest that as many as 14 to 25 percent of children and youth experience significant mental health issues (School-Based Mental Health and Substance Abuse Consortium, 2013). Mental health problems can often be detected before the age of 24, and half of these difficulties show up before the age of 14 (Kessler, Berglund, Demler, Jin, & Walters, 2005). Difficulties with mental health contribute to challenges in achievement and relationships at school (School-Based Mental Health and Substance Abuse Consortium, 2013). Students struggle on a daily basis, leading to social and academic isolation.

Considering the high prevalence of mental health issues and low levels of community service use, it is important to consider alternative sites and methods for promoting students' social emotional well-being. Education assistants in the classroom are in a position to engage with students directly and are often the team members that can bring forward anecdotal information that can lead to more formal supports. In addition, classrooms need to embrace a trauma sensitive approach as all students benefit from a more empathetic and mindful environment. In this section, chapters 5 and 6 focus on behaviour and communicative intent. Chapter 5 invites the reader to explore communication and assumptions to avoid reactionary responses. Chapter 6 provides an introductory overview of developing relationships within the context of a trauma sensitive approach. Chapters 7, 8, and 9 explore the importance of social emotional learning connecting to the work of an education assistant in the classroom to continuously support opportunities for social inclusion. It is our hope that those using this book will ensure the critical analysis of this topic and place trauma and mental health issues in a broader socio-political context. This big picture perspective enables us to develop a stronger ecological framework when supporting students within a larger system context.

REFERENCES

Kessler, R. C., Berglund, P., Demler, O., Jin, R., & Walters, E. E. (2005). Lifetime prevalence and age-of-onset distributions of DSM-IV disorders in the National Comorbidity Survey Replication. *Archives of General Psychiatry, 62*(6), 593–602.

School-Based Mental Health and Substance Abuse Consortium (2013). *School-based mental health in Canada: A final report.* Ottawa: Mental Health Commission of Canada. Retrieved from https://www.mentalhealthcommission.ca/sites/default/files/ChildYouth_School_Based_Mental_Health_Canada_Final_Report_ENG_0.pdf

Behaviour

CHAPTER 5

Understanding and Honouring Communicative Intent: Shifting from Judgment to Curiosity with Kindness and Intention

Jane Green, Michelle Pozin, and Lisa Gates

THREE KEY IDEAS

1. Communication comes in multiple forms to support practice and inform perceptions of behaviour.
2. Behaviours always serve a function and provide a means of communication for the education assistant to interpret and respond with positive supports.
3. A practical approach for interpreting behaviour is by answering the question "What are you trying to say?"

Understanding and honouring communicative intent: shifting from judgment to curiosity with kindness and intention. What do these words mean? And, more relevantly, how do we actually do this?

From a practical perspective, the education assistant (EA) is in a unique position to facilitate or interpret the communicative intent of students they support. The EA is the student's coach, facilitating and making easier the flow of information and interaction between the learner and their classroom community.

All behaviour communicates verbally and non-verbally. There is a message inherent in every behaviour. This includes the times when our silence speaks volumes. Some of these messages/behaviours have been present over long periods of time; some may be the result of trauma. The EA role is similar to that of a private investigator, respectfully exploring possible interpretations of sometimes puzzling behaviour. The EA serves as a compassionate detective—one with big eyes and ears, and an open and curious mind and heart.

In this chapter, the reader is asked to consider their own experiences of communication going awry, of being misunderstood. The learning from this chapter is quite simple; however, supporting students effectively is by no means "easy" and requires practice and openness. This chapter provides the tools and ideas to support the reader to feel and be more effective as an EA, and to experience an increase in compassion and understanding. The information shared in this chapter may help reduce the stress, confusion, and challenges encountered by EAs, both professionally and perhaps in other areas of their lives as well. The reader may indeed experience "aha" moments, both personally and professionally, as a result.

THE NATURE OF COMMUNICATION AND PERCEPTIONS

Communication comes in many forms (Wood, 2015). Verbal communication encompasses the words spoken and heard in conversation. Non-verbal messages also communicate. The eye roll, the eyebrow lift, the smile, that look of stress or disgust or delight—all are forms of behavioural communication. Think about a conversation between two people who know each other fairly well. They can tell from the expressions on each other's faces, which is technically a behaviour, enough information to help them think about what the other person would be communicating if there was a speech/thought bubble (like in a cartoon) above their head.

The study of non-verbal messages, including very subtle cues called micro expressions, has become a science of late (Ekman, 2018; Haggard & Isaacs, 1966). In the television series *Lie to Me*, the main character is a psychologist who is able to decipher and clearly understand what the expressions on a person's face are communicating. Whether we think of these micro expressions as "behaviours" is another matter. For EAs, all the subtle micro expressions displayed by students send a clear message, if one knows what to look for and how to effectively discern the message being sent (Fernández-Dols & Russell, 2017). Barthel (2013) illustrates the functions of non-verbal communication:

> Sometimes children with sensory processing challenges become excited when they are actually connected to themselves! The excitement or increased arousal that we observe may be about feeling present and in their body. This is an increase in emotional arousal resulting from experience rather than an arousal created by too much sensory feedback. Discerning this situation requires an especially fine magnifying glass. Children who seek to repeat and repeat and repeat an activity often are emotionally charged by the successful processing of the experience. "I like this feeling."

"Holistic" communication considers both verbal and non-verbal expressions. In addition, there is the perception of what is being communicated or the filter through which this information is received. Too often, filters are distorted and lenses are inaccurate, like a carnival mirror that shows someone as taller or shorter, wider or thinner—much different than the reality of their true stature.

Context

Context is everything. What do we mean by the word *context*? Here, context refers to the specific time, place, situation, people, and any other variable that has an impact on an individual. When we understand context as an important factor that influences behaviour, we understand why certain behaviours happen only at school, only in the morning or at bedtime, or only on the Tuesday morning after a long weekend in a particular homeroom situation with a particular request made by a particular teacher. People say, "Oh my, this never happens when we're at home—only at the grocery store!" or "I only see him behaving like this after he's had too much sugar or not enough sleep." That's context.

Sometimes people's circumstances change, for example, through a move to a new community, a changing home situation, a different medication, or a new teacher. These changes can impact individuals in different ways. Altering just part of one's context can have a major impact on an individual. Perhaps an unexpected visitor affected bathroom availability in one's home. Perhaps there was a boil water advisory in one's town, or an environmental change such as a power failure. All these have an impact on behaviour.

Resilience to navigate changing context—our capacity for "bouncing back"—is different for each individual and can result in behavioural responses that can be interpreted by others as "maladaptive." Individuals usually do the best they can at the time to cope with changing circumstances; however, for many individuals with "different" brain wiring, these common changes or "bumps in the road" may be perceived as enormous and cataclysmic.

In the classroom, there are typical patterns in the schedule and structure of the day, creating comforting routines; however, when there is a substitute teacher or EA, or a special assembly, or perhaps an event like a track meet or field trip that alters this structure, it's difficult to anticipate how students who struggle without these routines will react. Students who have difficulty with executive functioning—organization, transitions, and planning—may find themselves significantly disadvantaged and without the capacity to transition skilfully or to self-regulate their emotional state in what would normally have been a smooth day. With this may come frustration, confusion, or anger; emotions expressed or communicated through behaviour. Sometimes behaviour may be very subtle or small, for example, a slightly raised or elevated voice volume or tone, while at other times it can look like a full-blown tantrum involving physical or verbal aggression or a "meltdown."

For individuals who do not have natural or developed coping strategies to navigate changes in context, an EA needs to supplement or augment this skill set. Education assistants are most helpful if they can predict, through observation and perhaps data analysis, what might be distressing or disturbing to an individual they are supporting and then offer information and insight about the anticipated change in advance, so there is time for the individual to prepare for the disruption. The EA may also be able to make adaptations to the instructions for a particular activity. For example, if a student is going on a field trip, it is important to prepare them in advance for the change in routine. A few days ahead, inform the student that they will be riding the bus at a different time and that it will go not to their home but to a different location.

The effective EA will be able to offer insight into changes and predict ways in which these changes may impact learners who receive their support. Education assistants set up and structure interactions to offer reassurance, information, and practical tools that guide the learner to make more effective and appropriate decisions about their behaviour. This approach is empowering and non-judgmental. Some context shifts are not easily predictable and require the EA to be able to "think on their feet," demonstrating quick responses to changing circumstances.

BEHAVIOUR

All behaviour is communication and the task and role of the EA is to decipher the message conveyed by the behaviour. The EA may not know or accurately understand the message that a particular behaviour is attempting to communicate; however, they can develop a hypothesis based on kindness, curiosity, and contextual understanding.

Consider a child who is tearing up a picture they have drawn. What function or purpose might that child have had in mind, consciously or unconsciously, when they were tearing the paper? Perhaps some aspect of the drawing was too large or too small or was done in the "wrong" colour. Perhaps they misspelled a word on a diagram. Perhaps the drawing was of a dog but it looked more like a cat.

In relation to this example, it is also useful to consider "setting events" or "slow triggers"—what might have happened earlier in the day or at some other point in recent or even distant history for that student that may be influencing their current behaviour. For example, has there been a lack of predictability in their routine? Perhaps they ran out of their favourite cereal for breakfast and had to have an alternative that they did not want. Perhaps their favourite shirt was in the wash. Perhaps they had their hair cut and do not like the way it looks. Perhaps their parent was out of town and called in the morning rather than being there in person—or had forgotten to call. Any of these factors could be enough to "unsteady" a person. The job of the EA is to offer support to regain steadiness. Tearing the paper is a message; perhaps it means "I'm upset." The task of the EA is to observe, listen, and decipher. Setting events *do not* cause behaviours, but they can increase the likelihood that an individual will engage in challenging behaviour.

In addition, it is important to also consider and understand that some behaviours may result from traumatic origins in a child's life. These may be considered coping mechanisms and, whether effective or ineffective in accurately communicating a message, they are a likely response to post-traumatic stress disorder (PTSD). Barthel (2013) has done some revolutionary work in the area of PTSD, trauma-informed practice, and sensory difficulties, including therapeutic work, with former professional hockey player Theo Fleury. Their book, *Conversations with a Rattlesnake* (2014), offers more about this approach.

Functions of Behaviour

The function of behaviour is the reason people behave in a certain way. People engage in millions of different behaviours each day, but the reasons for displaying these different behaviours often fall into four main categories. The four main functions that maintain behaviours are as follows:

1. Escape/avoidance: The individual behaves in order to get out of doing something they do not want to do.
2. Attention seeking: The individual behaves to get focused attention from parents, teachers, siblings, peers, or other people around them.
3. Seeking access to materials: The individual behaves in order to get a preferred item or participate in an enjoyable activity.
4. Sensory stimulation: The individual behaves in a specific way because it feels good to them.

David Pitonyak (2018), whose consulting work lends kindness and compassion to the total framework of understanding communicative intention, helps us to see behaviours differently:

> Imagine is the name I give my consulting practice which is dedicated to supporting people who experience disabilities and exhibit, what some have called, "difficult behaviors." In my view, what's most needed when a person engages in difficult behaviors is *imagination*. The story-line that is floating around about the person is a *major* part of the problem. What's needed is a new story.
>
> My practice is based upon a simple idea: *difficult behaviors result from unmet needs*. In a sense, difficult behaviors are messages which can tell us important things about a person and the quality of his or her life. People with difficult behaviors are often missing: meaningful and enduring relationships; a sense of safety and well-being; joy in ordinary and everyday places; power and choice; a sense of value and self-worth; relevant skills and knowledge; supporters who are themselves supported. (emphasis in original)

Once an EA has identified what function or functions are producing a student's challenging behaviour, they can start to implement an intervention that will help decrease the inappropriate behaviour and increase more appropriate behaviours (North Shore Pediatric Therapy, 2012).

From this perspective, one can look at the function of a particular behaviour, use this information, and act as a detective: What needs might be expressing themselves through a learner's behaviours in class or on the playground? How is this particular behaviour supporting the learner to get their needs met? How can EAs support learners to express these needs with greater clarity, and increase their success in getting these needs met? How can EAs effectively and gently shift their understanding of another's behaviour as communication and support others in the environment to do the same?

The following situations provide examples: (1) If Jeremy has a tantrum, he does not have to go to gym class—or math class. He can avoid a situation he does not enjoy and, as a bonus, he receives attention from his EA. (2) If Joanna sits quietly during the reading circle, she will receive a bookmark and perhaps be able to choose the next story. (3) Chris is struggling to pay attention as he feels agitated, so he is spinning his plastic dinosaur by the tail, which is soothing and helps him to focus.

In the first example, we see that the EA and the support team may need to consider an alternate way to support Jeremy to make a skilful transition and offer him positive supports so that he has his need for attention met in ways that are respectful and affirming. The role of the EA may be to teach him an appropriate (more positive) way to communicate his needs to get them met, for example, a new way to communicate that he needs help or a break.

In the second example, Joanna is motivated to sit quietly because she wants a bookmark and to have a voice in the choice of the next story. This works because the bookmark and the choice option are reinforcers. If she did not want a bookmark or to express her choice, the situation might require a different form of reinforcement or an exploration of why it is difficult for Joanna to sit still (e.g., is it the type of activity? Does she need to sit on a cushion? Does she need more frequent breaks? Does she have self-regulation strategies?).

In the third example, Chris playing with his dinosaur is fine, as long as the others in the situation accept that he has a need for this particular tool, and as long as the dinosaur is available.

These examples clearly demonstrate that understanding the function of a particular behaviour helps one to answer the question of what is the feeling that is not verbalized: "I don't want to go to gym class! And you can't make me!" "I really want a bookmark." "I need to get calm and spinning my dinosaur helps."

Social Skilfulness and Communicative Intent

As learners develop social skill competence, their verbal and non-verbal communication becomes clearer; however, learners can sometimes be misunderstood in seriously undermining ways. A person may struggle with basic social interactions such as greeting skills and have their overly warm welcome be misunderstood. Sadly, these misinterpretations can sometimes set up people for abuse.

In *Ethics of Touch*, Dave Hingsburger offers examples of common misunderstandings based on context and learning (Hingsburger, Weinstock, & Harber, 2003). One example is the story of an individual who is hoping to buy something in a shop, and what happens when his touch is misunderstood by the store clerk. When he tries to get her attention, as he is trying to tell her something important, he reaches out to touch her; this is a skill he has learned. This touch is misinterpreted and launches police and security actions.

The Flash Curriculum, exploring social skilfulness and sexuality education, supports learners with diverse abilities who may struggle with verbal or non-verbal communication. This resource supports learners to develop congruence with their communication and social skills so that they are empowered to effectively express themselves and meet their needs (Stangle, 1986/2011). The units are carefully designed with clear examples to illustrate learning about essential communication skill sets.

Practical Approaches for Interpreting Behaviour: "What Are You Trying to Tell Me?"

From "To" to "For" to "With" to "From"

Historically, support services have been provided "to" learners or individuals with differences in many contexts. Think of institutional settings, where, within the medical model, a patient was seen as someone who required "fixing." Services then moved to the "for" stage, as in "this will be good *for* you"; an example of this is the normalization movement in the 1960s and the well-meaning social approach to ensure that people had a "normal" rhythm of the day and year. This movement launched community-based supports and a shift to more typical daily activities and environments like group homes and day services. From this stage, services moved toward the "with" stage, which featured person- or student-centred support, and working *with* individuals to ensure participation in planning. Support services are currently at the "from" stage. We are listening and learning more *from* the voice of the individual receiving services and are being guided by their wisdom about themselves, regardless of how that is expressed. If EAs trust that the learners they are supporting have their own strategies, and truly believe in them, they can honour student voices and invite them to develop and implement their own effective self-regulation and support strategies.

Walk a Mile in My Shoes

Empathetic detective work is important, and we often ask people to think about what it is like to walk in another person's experience before we judge. Education assistants can, metaphorically, place themselves in the "shoes" of the person they are supporting. They can understand the setting events for students, possible triggers, and other factors that might impact their experience. The EA may also be aware or gain knowledge of the learner's overall skill set (e.g., ability to communicate, cognitive functioning, social skills, learning challenges), which can help them to support their learner.

As the EA moves into a kinder, more intentional response, they can show the learner that they recognize them as a person and see their situation. The EA can reflect back what they are seeing or hearing and what they think it means, and then become supportive as the learner chooses their best coping mechanism and response. Rather than controlling or trying to control the learner, the EA can instead "be" with them in their situation while they sort things out and move to a clearer, more appropriate way of moving forward. The EA does not have to take power away by imposing punishments or consequences; they can instead support a balanced relationship and show students that they trust them to return to a more settled state "in a good way."

HALT: Hungry, Angry, Late, Lonely, or Tired

The acronym HALT (hungry, angry, late, lonely, or tired) is interpreted in multiple ways in many different contexts (Ragau, Hitchcock, Craft, & Christensen, 2018). Simple and clear, it provides an excellent and easily remembered approach to understanding factors that are likely to influence behaviour. These would be considered "antecedents," or things that happen just before a behaviour occurs. Is it possible that the learner's behaviour is a result of their experiencing one of these five states? While the learner experiences the emotion, the EA sees the behaviour that reflects that emotion.

Hunger: Is the learner experiencing a blood sugar challenge? Would a healthy snack be a good idea?

Anger: Is the learner dealing with something stressful and is that stress making them feel angry? Would it be helpful for the learner to have a chance to express those feelings in a healthy way?

Late: Is the learner feeling pushed to keep to a schedule that is unrealistic for them? Are they behind in an assignment? Do they need more time in a transition? Would an extension offer some comfort?

Lonely: Does the learner have any unpaid friends? Are they feeling alone? Is it time for some fun social time, or to play a game and include another learner?

Tired: Has the learner had enough sleep? Have they had enough breaks? Would a body break or a nap be a good idea?

So many circumstances impact emotions and the way individuals express them: transitions between homes, feeling sleepy or ill, a disagreement with family members or peers, missing a bus, running late, feeling hungry, or some other less clear reason.

In addition to noticing these behaviours in students, EAs can ask themselves if they are experiencing these feelings, and whether the learner may be picking up on their behaviour. The EA-student relationship works in two directions, and the individual receiving support may be as sensitive to the EA's tone or demeanour as the EA is to theirs. Think of a clerk in a store who is having a hard time and finding it difficult to smile. If their feet are tired or sore, or they are worried, or hungry, or lonely, it can be difficult to behave in a cheerful way. The effective EA will be mindful of their own needs, take note of the HALT elements in their own situation, and address them.

Seek First to Understand, Then to Be Understood

In his book *The 7 Habits of Highly Effective People* (1989), Stephen Covey identifies the fifth habit as follows: "Seek first to understand, then to be understood" (p. 247). In the context of an EA-learner relationship, this habit moves the EA directly into a role of extremely active listening. Before a learner is ready to listen to anything the EA has to say, they need to be understood, and, as noted, they may be communicating with behaviour rather than words. The EA needs to focus on shifting away from assumptions, and instead be open to the learner and what they are trying to express. Alan Alda, who developed the Alda Method of communication, speaks to the critical importance of deep listening and explores the science behind why we connect, why we don't, and why listening is the best strategy (Keohane, 2017). As Alda notes, it is obvious that paying attention to the person you are communicating with is important, but it is not that easy to do! This approach is inherent in the work of the effective EA. This work requires being fully present to the unique reality of the student and then responding in real time. And it works. Simply slowing down enough to be present is a very demanding task, but is highly effective.

All behaviour communicates. It is up to the EA to carefully listen and respond with curiosity, kindness, and respect.

Voices from the Field

Special education teacher Michelle Pozin and EA Lisa Gates share their curiosities and perspectives in response to the following case study.

Case Study

Melinda is an active 11-year-old in grade 6. She is a strong learner in all areas; however, it is reported that she seems to be enveloped in her own fantasy world. Melinda has a teenage sister who is involved in drug use and no longer attending school, which is a constant stress and worry. Her parents are together; however, her father works out of town and her mother's job requires shift work. It is often a struggle to get Melinda to school. She is not readily accepted by her peers and does little to reach out to them; she tends to isolate herself from them during group activities and breaks. Melinda was recently diagnosed with an anxiety disorder.

When the classroom teacher verbally indicates there is a transition (change of activity), Melinda argues with her and refuses to change activities. This usually results in Melinda having to sit out in the hallway or in the school office until she calms down, which can take up to 30 minutes. When she arrives back in the classroom, unless the class is engaged in a highly preferred activity, she will often refuse to participate. The teacher will often let her sit in the class and do something else (for example, draw, which is her favourite activity) as long as she does not disrupt the rest of the class.

Start with Curiosity

EA-in-Training Perspective

- Based on what you have just read, what do you know or think you know about Melinda?
- What are your perceptions of the classroom teacher?
- Try to put your opinions and judgments aside; just look at the facts.

Explore Vantage Points and Perspectives: Be a Detective

Special Education Teacher Perspective

- Ask, "Is this typical behaviour for Melinda? How long has the behaviour been happening? Is this a safety concern? Is this disruptive to the learning environment? Have we been in contact with the family?"
- Look at the school file for assessments that may have been done previously and/or previous report card comments. What is Melinda's profile (cognitive ability, learning strengths and challenges, medical conditions, etc.)? What types of strategies have been implemented? What was successful?
- Set up an individual school support meeting with current and past teachers and any other school support staff to identify strengths/interests, challenges, behaviour(s) of concern. This will help to determine how long Melinda has been displaying the behaviours and if she is doing so in all settings. How do these behaviours impact learning for Melinda and others? What social or emotional impact do they have?

Continued

EA Perspective

- What strategies have been used in Melinda's case? What has worked? What hasn't?
- How could we use what we know about Melinda's specific strengths and other assessments that may have been done as identified in the education plan? What are useful insights?

Strengths: Melinda is highly verbal, likes to draw, does better with written than verbal directives, likes to help, is a strong academic student, loves animals, wants friends

Challenges: anxiety, self-regulation

Problem behaviour: refusal to do activities (saying "No, I won't" followed by no response)

Other Questions to Ask as an EA

- How am I reacting? Are my reactions creating a reaction in Melinda?
- How can I be most reassuring to her? How can all our interactions be relationship building?
- What are her favourite TV shows, foods, and friends? These questions are aimed at getting to know Melinda better and establishing a rapport.
- It is established that she likes to draw. What subjects does she like to draw? Does she have a wide or narrow repertoire of subjects? Are there other clues here?
- Is anything in particular happening before the teacher asks the students to change activities—is Melinda deeply involved in the current work? Does she need time to complete what she is doing?
- What are Melinda's body language and facial expression when she is comfortable as opposed to when she becomes upset?
- Is there time and space in the schedule (perhaps when Melinda is outside the classroom) to help her explore her emotional range—to recognize and name what her feelings are when she is calm and when she is anxious?

Discern Your Skilful Response as an EA

- How can I be fully present to what Melinda needs and serve as interpreter of her behaviour with kindness and compassion?
- What respectful response is called for that meets Melinda's needs? How can I respectfully go forward as a team player?
- Celebrate gaining a clearer understanding of Melinda's voice!

CRITICAL THINKING QUESTIONS

1. Think of a time when your predictable rhythm was thrown off by an external change in your context. What happened? How did you react? What was helpful in your environment to assist you with managing the change in your circumstance? What message would you like to have heard at that time?
2. Have you ever been completely surprised when you learned more about someone's context (had that "aha" moment)? Has someone responded differently to you after they respectfully listened to what was going on "behind the scenes"? How did that feel?
3. How might you mindfully put this approach in place in your own life? Practice makes perfect—who could you be listening to and watching more closely, honing your detective skills to better prepare you for your work as an EA?

REFERENCES

Barthel, K. (2013, March 3). Becoming a detective. *Kim Barthel*. Retrieved from http://kimbarthel.ca/becoming-a-detective/

Covey, S. R. (1989). *The 7 habits of highly effective people: Restoring the character ethic*. New York: Simon and Schuster.

Ekman, P. (2018, July 23). What are micro expressions? *Paul Ekman Group*. Retrieved from www.paulekman.com/micro-expressions/

Fernández-Dols, J.-M., & Russell, J. A. (2017). *The science of facial expression*. New York: Oxford University Press.

Fleury, T., & Barthel, K. (2014). *Conversations with a rattlesnake*. N.p.: Jaguar.

Haggard, E. A., & Isaacs, K. S. (1966). Micro-momentary facial expressions as indicators of ego mechanisms in psychotherapy. In E. A. Haggard (Ed.), *Methods of research in psychotherapy* (pp. 154–165). New York: Appleton-Century-Crofts.

Hingsburger, D., Weinstock, J., Harber, M., Young Adult Institute and Workshop, & National Institute for People with Disabilities. (2003). *Ethics of touch: An interactive discussion with David Hingsburger.* Newmarket, ON: Diverse City Press.

Keohane, J. (2017, June). Famed actor Alan Alda on the secrets to better communication. *Entrepreneur.* Retrieved from https://www.entrepreneur.com/article/294433

North Shore Pediatric Therapy. (2012, August 12). What are functional assessments and the four main functions of behavior? Retrieved from https://nspt4kids.com/therapy/what-are-functional-assessments-and-the-four-main-functions-of-behavior/

Pitonyak, D. (2018, July 18). Finding new stories for people with disabilities. *David Pitonyak: Imagine.* Retrieved from www.dimagine.com/

Ragau, S., Hitchcock, R., Craft, J., & Christensen, M. (2018). Using the HALT model in an exploratory quality improvement initiative to reduce medication errors. *British Journal of Nursing, 27*(22), 1330–1335.

Stangle, J. (2011). FLASH lesson plans for special education. *King County.* Retrieved from https://www.kingcounty.gov/depts/health/locations/family-planning/education/FLASH/special-education.aspx (Originally published in 1986)

Wood, J. T. (2015). *Interpersonal communication: Everyday encounters.* Boston: Nelson Education.

CHAPTER 6

Trauma Sensitivity in the Classroom: Developing Trusting Relationships

Mary Harber and Asha Rao

THREE KEY IDEAS

1. In order to create a safe learning environment, trauma-informed and sensitive practice is critical for education assistants.
2. It is the role of an education assistant to contribute to and maintain a trauma-informed/sensitive school climate.
3. Trauma-informed practice is inclusive and beneficial for all students.

TRAUMA IN THE CLASSROOM

In school settings, education assistants (EAs) witness students who seem to be out of "control" in terms of their emotions, who break down under the slightest pressure or are withdrawn or aggressive for what seems to be no apparent reason. There may be many reasons for this behaviour, but one may be that these students are impacted by trauma or chronic stress. As a part of the educational team, it is important to understand trauma in the classroom and trauma-informed practice (TIP).

DEFINING TRAUMA

The understanding of trauma has evolved from the early identification of post-traumatic stress disorder (PTSD) to a broader application within the mainstream population (Wilson, Pence, & Conradi, 2013). Trauma can be described as simple, complex, developmental, and intergenerational, all of which focus on the impact versus the nature of the trauma (Poole & Greaves, 2012). A trauma response is individualized and influenced by factors such as genetics, previous life experiences, and support in the aftermath of an event. A supportive professional response to trauma positively influences the longer term effects when delivered in a trauma-sensitive manner (Wilson et al., 2013).

Trauma can be defined as "an exceptional experience in which powerful and dangerous events overwhelm a person's capacity to cope" (Rice & Groves, 2005, p. 3). Although we may intuitively consider the emotional impact of trauma, the physiological impact, which contributes to emotional and behavioural reactivity, is important. When there is a threat, real or perceived, the body responds with the fight, flight, or freeze response, activated by the amygdala in the brain: the body's alarm system. This system detects sensory cues through sights, sounds, body sensations, and smells, which are like files in a filing system. These files are reviewed during an event and cue the brain to respond to danger quickly and without thinking—in other words, to react (Haskell, 2012).

Now let's think about students in the classroom. There are students who experience environments in which they are constantly under the threat of danger, either directly or indirectly. These children and youth live in a state of hyper arousal—always ready for fight, flight, or freeze, which exhausts the nervous system. Eventually, the system is less able to differentiate between cues that are truly a threat and those that are not. As a result, individuals may interpret all events as threatening and respond to harmless situations in a defensive and emotionally charged manner (Haskell, 2012). Students impacted by trauma distrust their own feelings, and everything and everyone becomes a potential threat.

Many children and youth have been impacted by adverse childhood experiences (ACEs). The Centers for Disease Control and Prevention and Kaiser Permanente in California conducted a large sample study (Felitti et al., 1998) in which 40 percent of respondents reported two or more ACEs and 12.5 percent experienced four or more. Because ACEs cluster, many studies now look at the cumulative effects of ACEs rather than the effects of each individual occurrence (Felitti et al., 1998). In the study, ACEs included familial substance use, divorce or separation, witnessing family violence, incarceration of a parent, mental illness, and physical, sexual, or emotional abuse and/or neglect.

In a Canadian research study, 30 percent of those aged 15 and over reported physical and/or sexual abuse at the hands of an adult before the age of 15 (Statistics Canada, 2014). This type of epidemiological research has shown that many children and youth experience exposure to one or more traumatic events in their lifetime (Fairbank, 2008).

Impact

The experience of abuse, neglect, or instability from people and in environments that traditionally represent a safe place physically and emotionally is confusing for children. They can feel alone and ignored, may hide their anxieties and fears, and often distrust their own feelings or relationships in the environment. This directly affects their ability to learn, as being in a state of chronic stress results in cognitive and attention difficulties and an inability to regulate emotions and impulses (Haskell, 2012). Trauma changes the way students make sense of their world, their relationships with others, and where they belong. Trust is undermined and, to feel safe, they develop rules and ideas about relationships, built on mistrust, fear, and betrayal. They overthink situations with their peers and feel out of place with family and friends. They miss that essential feeling of belonging (Australian Childhood Foundation, 2010). The world itself is experienced as potentially dangerous for trauma-impacted children and youth; therefore, it is critical that we not only understand this, but also create a safe learning environment through TIP.

TRAUMA-INFORMED PRACTICE

Trauma-informed practice recognizes the potential impact of ACEs and that students may experience triggers in the school environment. Triggers occur when the stress response fails to differentiate between real and imagined danger, so everything causes anxiety and fear. As a result, a student will do whatever is necessary to decrease the perceived threat. These behaviours often manifest as attention deficits, learning disabilities, or behavioural conduct issues (Downey, 2007).

An understanding of TIP is important in the context of a classroom. We understand that children experience trauma and vulnerability, but fail to see how the impact of trauma may show up in various environments. We talk about the importance of reporting abuse and neglect, but fail to talk about what happens next: what happens when a child comes to the classroom after they have been moved from their home into foster care, or a child has witnessed violence in the home and comes to school in the morning after a night of anxiety and fear? Although a student may identify an experience as part of their home life, this impacts the ability to learn, integrate knowledge, and function in terms of social learning and connection at school. Trauma-informed practice is an overarching approach that is both preventative and healing in nature. It acknowledges and addresses the relationship between triggers and perceived dangers in direct practice. It moves from the question, "what is wrong with you?" to "what happened to you?" (Richardson, 2018). When educators are aware of and understand TIP, they are fully inclusive in their classrooms, schools, and communities.

INCLUSION

The Salamanca Statement on special needs education (UNESCO, 1994) recognized the need for access to education in the regular classroom for all students and, in particular, made an international call to countries to address students with diverse learning needs. Inclusive practice in education invites students with a variety of strengths and needs to be a part of the general education classroom.

Educational reforms like the Salamanca Statement are shifting practices provincially, nationally, and internationally. As such, ministries of education are restructuring curricula to teach to all learners. The BC Ministry of Education (2015) asserted that "personalized learning is at the heart of the new curriculum." This shift in practice in public education coincides with Moore's (2016) statement: "Teaching to diversity and inclusion is where we value the characteristics that are diverse, and not try and homogenize them" (p. 9). In other words, there are no restrictions on who can be in classrooms. It is more a question of how all students can be part of an education system that is engaging and appropriate for each student's learning needs, and that builds on individual strengths and interests. Inclusive education is about providing opportunities in a variety of ways for all students to have access and contribute to content in the classroom with their peers. Moore (2016) contended that there is more than one way to be inclusive and that practice will vary between individuals. Building on the knowledge that inclusion is a right of the individual, we work together as a team to create inclusion that is meaningful and personalized for each student.

Classrooms and schools are becoming more flexible, and as choices in learning and shared ownership of students' successes increase, so will opportunities for them to succeed both in school and community. A classroom is like a woven tapestry in which all students belong to part of the whole (Causton-Theoharis, 2009). When students are part of a group, they have numerous opportunities to be supported academically, socially, and emotionally and feel successful amongst their peers. Students need opportunities throughout the day to show their strengths and to have the support to grow. When educators understand TIP, they can better support all students and further inclusion in schools and society.

ROLE OF THE EA

When a child has experienced any form of trauma, relationships and trust have eroded. Their beliefs about relationships are often skewed; therefore, it is difficult for them to know who to trust, when to trust, and whether people have their best interests at heart. This lack of trust is compounded by the fact that a trauma response can impair a student's ability to self-regulate their emotions, behaviour, and attention, making it difficult to form and maintain relationships (Cole, Eisner, Gregory, & Ristuccia, 2013).

The cornerstone of TIP in the school setting is understanding the need for connection and using empathy to build trusting relationships. When a child's development has been impacted by trauma, subsequent dependable relationships support healing and growth along with learning in social, emotional, and academic areas (Masten, 2014; Matto, Strolin-Goltzman, & Ballan, 2014). Resilience is created when the vulnerable child is engaged in caring relationships and structures that support internal competence and growth, when a child feels safe enough to form a sense of self and personal power (Treptow, 2017). Positive school-based connections with teachers, friends, and mentors are implicated in many studies on resilience; they are what Ann Masten (2014) refers to as "ordinary magic."

When EAs create a trusting relationship through understanding, empathy, and support, children and youth thrive. The "ordinary magic" of building resilience helps to protect a person against the effects of trauma and chronic stress (Stipp & Miller, 2018). In addition, the brain develops new neural pathways that enable individuals to improve their adaptive thinking, self-regulation, academic learning skills, and problem solving. Relationships are not simply an act of kindness and understanding, rather they are the very pathways to healing, growth, and learning (Masten, 2014; Matto et al., 2014).

An EA who understands TIP has the power to support students in the classroom and the responsibility to reduce the impact of trauma and chronic stress:

> The greatest hope for traumatized, abused and neglected children is to receive a good education in schools where they are seen and known, where they learn to regulate themselves, and where they can develop a sense of agency. At their best, schools can function as islands of safety in a chaotic world[;] ... [they can] be the place where children are taught self-leadership and an internal locus of control. (Van der Kolk, 2014, p. 3)

KEY STRATEGIES FOR EAs

For EAs to successfully support students, they need to have a varied skill set. Being calm, aware, present, predictable, and compassionate are key attributes to building safe, strong relationships with students (Health Federation of Philadelphia, 2010). With these attributes in mind, there are many strategies that EAs can use to support students. Three foundational strategies that EAs may use to develop a TIP are as follows: (1) supporting self-regulation, (2) being structured and consistent, and (3) providing strength-based opportunities for success in social, emotional, and academic contexts.

Self-Regulation

Students who have experienced trauma often have difficulties with self-regulation and modulation, thus, one of the key areas that EAs can work on is developing strategies and skills to help students to self-monitor and regulate. Validating students' feelings and providing comfort and ways for them to self-manage emotions is key for their personal, social, and academic development. It is important for EAs to understand that trauma manifests in different ways: some children who have experienced trauma may act out aggressively, while others may be withdrawn. Thus, self-regulation strategies can be different for different students. The ability to regulate is a key predictor of academic success and, arguably, success as a whole being (Massachusetts Advocates for Children, 2005).

When we are teaching students to regulate their nervous systems and the toxic stress in their bodies, we need to be aware that this may be a challenge for them on multiple levels, including learning that they are in control of their emotions and recognizing what they may be feeling at any given time (Shanker, 2018). Students need strategies that they can use for their own self-care and soothing. Providing opportunities throughout the day for students to learn and try new self-regulation skills teaches them to have control (Echo Parenting & Education, 2017).

The following are suggested techniques that can be used by EAs working with students in implementing trauma-informed self-regulation practices:

1. Mindfulness exercises and breathing techniques
2. Body exercises such as yoga or circuits
3. Walking or movement breaks
4. Muscle relaxation techniques
5. Creative opportunities such as drawing and painting
6. Grounding exercises
7. Use of sensory rooms

Structure and Consistency

The experience of trauma is chaotic and unpredictable; in contrast, routine, consistency, and structure provide a safe environment that enables students to engage in learning rather than being distracted by fight, flight, or freeze mode (Alberta Education, 2018). Their brains can relax and develop in the areas that they need to be working. In the classroom, EAs can help by being predictable, calm, and sensitive in their relationship with students. According to TIP, all school staff should maintain settings in which they, as well as their students, are calm, relaxed, and focused in a learning environment that encourages shared control or power with strategies (Echo Parenting & Education, 2017).

The following are actions EAs can display when working with students to develop structure and consistency:

- use a calm and respectful tone
- warn about transitions
- model behaviours and routines
- be consistent in choices and expectations
- be open and honest in discussions
- acknowledge good decisions and choices—positive reinforcement (Downey, 2007)

Strength-Based Opportunities for Success

Educators empower students to make positive choices and work to their highest potential. To do so, "we must discover what students are asking for, help them make sense of that need and teach them to express it in a productive way" (Souers & Hall, 2016, p. 77).

In TIP, EAs help students build competency across multiple domains: academic, social, and emotional. By drawing on their strengths and giving them a voice in daily activities (Zacarin, Alvariz-Ortiz, & Haynes, 2017), they can empower students who did not have choice in their trauma experience.

It is vital to provide students with choices throughout the day, which can help them build a sense of self, trust, and identity as learners (Massachusetts Advocates for Children, 2005). The Child Safety Commissioner (Downey, 2007) suggested that children may find the social aspects of relationships difficult given that the trauma they experienced may have occurred in a relationship. Children who have experienced trauma may not have created secure attachments to adults in their lives and, thus, may struggle with being in a class and connecting with peers. They may struggle with being present, and reading body language and facial expressions (Downey, 2007). These students may need both social and emotional support to learn the skills required to develop healthy relationships.

EAs can provide social and emotional support to students in the following ways:

1. Model open discussions and emotions
2. Communicate clearly and honestly
3. Provide and support creative and group play
4. Provide opportunities to work with partners and small groups
5. Teach to strengths
6. Create safe spaces
7. Be caring, nurturing, and compassionate
8. Use "I" statements

9. Play games around emotions and feelings
10. Overall, promote post-traumatic growth skills, such as problem solving and support seeking, to give students a sense of place, belonging, and identity (Echo Parenting and Education, 2017)

BEING PART OF A TEAM

All students benefit from a team of professionals working together to support their learning, sense of safety, and belonging. Education assistants work alongside multiple educators such as teachers, inclusive education teachers, counsellors, and therapists. Inclusive practice invites educators to spend less time in isolation and more time being involved in a collaborative model of support. To contribute to the team, EAs must understand their roles and responsibilities, be effective communicators, and identify when it is time to set boundaries and make referrals (British Columbia Teachers' Federation/CUPE British Columbia, 2009). If each member of the team remembers that everyone is there to support student growth and school success on multiple levels they can work collaboratively toward these goals.

Roles and Responsibilities

It is important for EAs to fully understand their role, job description, and the policies of the school district. Since each school district may specifically define the responsibilities of EAs differently, it is important to understand both individual and shared roles. Souers and Hall (2016, p. 76) suggest that when thinking about supporting a student, educators should ask themselves the following questions:

- What is my role?
- Who am I working for?
- What will drive my behaviors?

Communication

Making time to communicate with the team is an important skill for EAs to develop. It is critical to find ways and times to meet. This could include meeting before or after school or during a walk-and-talk time, building meetings into the school schedule, or asking an administrator to cover a class during a meeting time. It is essential to share with the team what is going on with a student and to review any plans and strategies for support on an ongoing basis. Communication always has challenges, but when the team members know they are working for student success, they will ensure that their communication is effective. The following are suggestions for how to facilitate strong communication:

- send a daily communication email to the team or teacher
- ask questions about what is required to support and implement plans
- initiate conversations with the team about different strategies
- share knowledge about TIP strategies with the team

BOUNDARIES AND REFERRALS

While an EA may work closely with students to support their success, it is important to know when to set a professional boundary with students and families. They need to be aware of their professional ethics and know when it is critical to refer students and families to someone else on the team, such as a counsellor, administrator, or mental health support worker. In situations in which they are unsure, EAs who understand these boundaries consider ethical dilemmas and reach out for support to bring clarity to who is responsible for taking action. The following section describes indicators that boundaries need to be set.

SELF-CARE

Care for the caregiver is an element of TIP. We discuss self-care in the context of helping relationships, but what about self-care when supporting students who are triggered by what we do in the classroom? When students are triggered, an EA can feel frustrated, inadequate, and hopeless, and can sometimes experience vicarious or secondary trauma.

Secondary trauma happens when an EA takes in the trauma stories of those they support and this triggers feelings of sadness, betrayal, or fear and causes them to feel unsettled. If this feeling is ignored, the EA may experience difficulty in terms of their own physical or emotional wellness. How often do educators hear difficult family stories and feel shocked and think, how can a family do that? After a while, stories can start to break down their own confidence in keeping children safe and they may start to feel angry and hopeless. In addition, educators may have had their own experiences of trauma that can be triggered in the classroom. Issues that they have not dealt with in their past come into their consciousness and impact their ability to be supportive. Self-care in any helping profession is not a luxury but a necessity, and EAs must learn to be as compassionate toward themselves as they are to others.

A trauma-informed organization increases safety for all, and care for the caregivers creates a community of hope and health (Bowie, 2014). The essence of self-care is as follows:

- finding balance in our lives in terms of external and internal needs
- being able to set limits and boundaries
- being aware of what we are feeling (attuned to ourselves)
- connection with our supports, our community, and/or mentors and in meaningful relationships (Bowie, 2014)

Education assistants also have a responsibility to tune in to their own feelings before they are able to tune in to the students they are supporting. Blaustein and Kinniburgh (2010) developed a model for trauma-informed schools that supports the idea that well-regulated, attuned, and mindful adults create environments where children feel safe to learn. Self-care is critical for the development of a balanced relationship, which is the most important support for individuals who have experienced trauma.

Voices from the Field

Monique Moore, District Inclusion Teacher and Clinical Counsellor

The role of the EA may include supporting students who have experienced trauma, which requires a skill set in demonstrating compassion, empathy, and presence. School personnel do not necessarily need to know the cause of the trauma, but simply that it is a presenting factor for the student and may be impacting their success at school. The actual trauma incident, whether known or unknown, also never needs to be discussed with the student by school personnel, as this is the role of the mental health support personnel in place for the student. Just as the trauma is an individual experience, the demonstrated behaviour is also unique to the individual. Since these students can be highly reactive, they often require numerous movement and break options throughout their day to support self-regulation. In contrast, other individuals may withdraw and communicate so little that they may profile as having selective mutism. Regardless of the presenting behaviours, the following strategies are best practice in supporting these students:

- connect and build relationship
- use consistency in your approach

Case Study

Alex, an 11-year-old Indigenous grade 6 student, did not speak during his first year at middle school. He attended school regularly. He would nod in response to questions and after almost four months of building relationships, he would occasionally offer a shy smile to a joke. Physically, he had significant scarring on his body and some minor scars on his face. Learning difficulties were present due to missing a year of school, but he also had a diagnosed learning disability in reading and writing. The school team was aware of Alex's history through school transition meetings and communication from the family. This young man had been hit by a car and missed his

Continued

entire grade 4 year due to surgeries and trauma. His family lived in poverty and there were six children that lived in the home. Violence was witnessed intermittently in the home. Generational trauma was a factor as the mother shared that she had attended residential school.

In this case study, how might an EA use TIP to support Alex?

CRITICAL THINKING QUESTIONS

1. What does it mean to have a practice that is trauma-informed/sensitive?
2. What might an EA do if they believe that a student has experienced trauma but they are not sure how to respond?
3. How might an EA understand the impact of trauma for individuals with a developmental disability?

REFERENCES

Alberta Education. (2018). *What is trauma informed practice?* [Video file]. Retrieved from https://www.alberta.ca/trauma-informed-practice.aspx?utm_source=redirector

Australian Childhood Foundation (2010). *Making space for learning: Trauma informed practice in schools*. Ringwood, Australia: Author. Retrieved from https://www .theactgroup.com.au/documents/ makingspaceforlearning-traumainschools.pdf

Blaustein, M. E., & Kinniburgh, K. M. (2010). *Treating traumatic stress in children and adolescents: How to foster resilience through attachment, self-regulation, and competency.* New York: Guilford Press.

Bowie, V. (2014). Trauma informed self-care: Building resilient staff and teams. In I. Needham, M. Kingma, K. McKenna, O. Frank, C. Tuttas, S. Kingma, & N. Oud (Eds.), *Proceedings of the Fourth International Conference on Violence in the Health Sector: "Towards safety, security and wellbeing for all"* (pp. 215–216). Retrieved from http://www.oudconsultancy.nl/Resources/Proceedings%20 4th%20Workplace %20Violence.pdf

British Columbia Ministry of Education. (2015). BC's new curriculum. Retrieved from https://curriculum.gov.bc.ca/curriculum-updates

British Columbia Teachers' Federation/CUPE British Columbia. (2009). *Roles and responsibilities of teachers and teacher assistants/education assistants.* Retrieved from https://bctf.ca/uploadedFiles/Public/Issues/InclusiveEd/RolesAndResponsibilities TeachersTAs.pdf

Causton-Theoharis, J. (2009). *The paraprofessional's handbook for effective support in inclusive classrooms.* Baltimore: Brookes

Cole, S. F., Eisner, A., Gregory, M., & Ristuccia, J. (2013). Helping traumatized children learn II: Creating and advocating for trauma-sensitive schools. Boston: Massachusetts Advocates for Children, Trauma and Learning Policy Initiative.

Downey, L. (2007). *Calmer classrooms: A guide to working with traumatised children.* Melbourne, Australia: Child Safety Commissioner. Retrieved from http:// education.qld.gov.au/schools/healthy/pdfs/calmer-classrooms-guide.pdf

Echo Parenting and Education. (2017). *What do I do? Trauma informed support for children.* Retrieved from https://www.echotraining.org/trauma-informed-support-for-children/

Fairbank, K. (2008). The epidemiology of trauma and trauma related disorders in children and youth. *PTSD Research Quarterly, 19,* 1–7.

Felitti, V., Anda, R., Nordenberg, R., Williamson, D., Spitz, A., Edwards, V., … Marks, J. (1998). Relationship of childhood abuse and household dysfunction to many of the leading causes of death in adults: The adverse childhood experiences (ACE) study. *American Journal of Preventive Medicine, 14*(4), 245–258.

Haskell, L. (2012). A developmental understanding of complex trauma. In N. Poole & L. Greaves (Eds.), *Becoming trauma informed* (pp. 9–27). Toronto: Centre for Addiction and Mental Health.

Health Federation of Philadelphia. (2010). *CAPPD: Practical interventions to help children affected by trauma.* Philadelphia: Author. Retrieved from http://www.multiplying connections.org/become-trauma-informed/cappd-interventions-guide

Massachusetts Advocates for Children. (2005). *Helping traumatized children learn: Supportive school environments for children traumatized by family violence.* Boston: Author. Retrieved from http://www.washtenawisd.org/sites/ default/files/WISD/HandleWithCare/PDF/HelpingTraumatizedChildren-Learn.pdf

Masten, A. S. (2014). *Ordinary magic: Resilience in development.* New York: Guilford Press.

Matto, H. C., Strolin-Goltzman, J., & Ballan, M. S. (2014). *Neuroscience for social work: Current research and practice.* New York: Springer.

Moore, S. (2016). *One without the other: Stories of unity through diversity and inclusion.* Winnipeg: Portage and Main Press.

Poole, N., & Greaves, L. (Eds.). (2012). *Becoming trauma informed.* Toronto: Centre for Addiction and Mental Health.

Rice, K., & Groves, B. (2005). *Hope and healing: A caregiver's guide to helping young children affected by trauma.* Washington, DC: Zero to Three Press.

Richardson, S. (2018). Awareness of trauma informed care. *Social Work Today.* Retrieved from http://www.socialworktoday.com/archive/exc_012014.shtml

Shanker, S. (2018). Calm, alert and learning: Classroom strategies for self-regulation. *Mehrit Centre.* Retrieved from https://self-reg.ca/cal-guide/

Souers, K., & Hall, P. (2016). *Fostering resilient learners: Strategies for creating a trauma-sensitive classroom.* Alexandria, VA: ASCD.

Statistics Canada. (2014). *General social survey: Victimization.* Retrieved from https://www.statcan.gc.ca/eng/survey/household/4504

Stipp, K., & Miller, K. (2018). Self-care as a trauma-informed practice. *Social Work Today.* Retrieved from http://www.socialworktoday.com/archive/exc_1117.shtml

Treptow, R. L. (2017). Book review: *Ordinary magic* by Ann S. Masten. *Infant Mental Health Journal, 38*(2), 318–320.

UNESCO. (1994). *The Salamanca Statement and framework for action on special needs education.* Salamanca, Spain: UNESCO and the Ministry of Education and Science, Spain. Retrieved from http://www.unesco.org/education/pdf/SALAMA_E.PDF

Van der Kolk, B. (2014). *The body keeps the score: Brain, mind, and body in the healing of trauma.* New York: Viking.

Wilson, C., Pence, D., & Conradi, L. (2013). Trauma-informed care. *Encyclopedia of Social Work.* Retrieved from http://socialwork.oxfordre.com/search?siteToSearch=oresw&q=wilson+pence+conradi&searchBtn=Search&isQuickSearch=true

Zacarin, D., Alvariz-Ortiz, A., & Haynes, J. (2017). *Teaching to strengths: Supporting students living with trauma, violence, and chronic stress.* Alexandria, VA: ASCD.

Social Emotional Learning

CHAPTER 7

Social Emotional Learning and the Work of Education Assistants

Nancy Norman, Janine Fajenski, and Jessica Mantel

THREE KEY IDEAS

1. The theoretical framework of social emotional learning can be used as a foundation for fostering the social emotional development of students in the classroom.
2. Education assistants use specific strategies to support the development of social emotional competence for students with diverse learning needs.
3. Social emotional learning can be used to promote the self-care, emotional resilience, and well-being of education assistants.

In today's inclusive schools in Canada, it is common for students with diverse learning needs to receive additional support from an education assistant (EA). This support often includes EAs facilitating and directly teaching social emotional competence to their students. This chapter presents the theoretical framework of social emotional learning (SEL) as a foundation for understanding social emotional development of children with exceptionalities and connects how SEL is supported in the work of EAs. It concludes by highlighting strategies for EAs to consider when supporting their own social emotional competence and well-being.

SOCIAL EMOTIONAL LEARNING

Social emotional learning refers to the development of skills related to recognizing and managing emotions, developing care and concern for others, establishing positive relationships, making responsible decisions, and handling challenging situations constructively and ethically (Collaborative for Academic, Social, and Emotional Learning, 2018; Zins, Bloodworth, Weissberg, & Walberg, 2004). The Collaborative for Academic, Social, and Emotional Learning (CASEL; 2018) has put forward a theoretical framework for SEL that outlines five widely agreed-upon interrelated dimensions (also referred to as core competencies or essential skills), including cognitive, affective, and behavioural domains.

> Self-awareness: The ability to accurately recognize one's emotions, thoughts, and values, and understand their influence on behaviour. This includes accurately assessing one's strengths and limitations and possessing a well-grounded sense of confidence, self-efficacy, and optimism.
>
> Self-management: The ability to regulate one's emotions, thoughts, and behaviours effectively in different situations. This includes managing stress, controlling impulses, motivating oneself, and setting and working toward achieving personal and academic goals. It also includes one's ability to delay gratification and have the self-discipline and organizational skills necessary to achieve success.
>
> Social awareness: The ability to take the perspective of and empathize with others from diverse backgrounds and cultures, to understand social and ethical norms for behaviour, and to recognize family, school, and community resources and supports.
>
> Relationship skills: The ability to establish and maintain healthy and rewarding relationships with diverse individuals and groups. This includes communicating clearly, listening actively, co-operating, resisting inappropriate social pressure, negotiating conflict constructively, and seeking and offering help when needed.

Responsible decision making: The ability to make constructive and respectful choices about personal behaviour and social interactions based on consideration of ethical standards, safety concerns, social norms, the realistic evaluation of consequences of various actions, and the well-being of self and others.

WHY IS SEL IMPORTANT?

Social emotional competence is necessary for success in school and life. It is well established that the development of SEL skills in children and youth significantly improves their attitudes about themselves and others, positively affects social interactions, increases positive attitudes toward school and classroom participation and engagement, improves efforts to achieve academic success and problem-solving and planning skills, and decreases emotional distress and conduct disorders (see, for example, Zins et al., 2004; Zins, Elias, & Greenberg, 2003). The development of these skills may also have positive effects on academic performance (see, for example, Zins & Elias, 2006). In addition, children and youth with well-developed SEL skills tend to have a higher sense of self-efficacy, better sense of community, more involvement in positive behaviours (such as sports or engagement in their community), higher interpersonal engagement and motivation, and increased prosocial behaviours, as compared to students without this competence (Durlak, Weissberg, Dymnicki, Taylor, & Schellinger, 2011). In fact, SEL skills have been shown to provide benefit to physical health, mental health, and a sense of wellness (Elias et al., 1997; Zins et al., 2004), having far-reaching and long-lasting effects on overall development.

The five domains of SEL are central to emotional health and well-being for all children and youth; however, they are particularly important for students who have diverse or complex learning needs. Norman and Jamieson (2015) point out that students who have difficulty acquiring and maintaining SEL skills across the five domains—most commonly, self-awareness (identifying emotion) and self-management (self-regulation and impulse control), as well as social awareness (perspective taking and empathy)—often need additional supports within the school environment. Given that EAs work closely (often one-to-one) with students, they are uniquely positioned in their role to support the development of SEL skills in their students.

HOW CAN EAs SUPPORT THE DEVELOPMENT OF SEL?

Education assistants can support the development of social emotional competence across the five SEL core competencies by using the following suggested strategies.

Self-Awareness

Facilitating growth and development of self-awareness is central to effective EA support. Experienced EAs use a variety of strategies to support their students' ability to recognize emotional responses, identify and name emotion, accurately assess self-perceptions, recognize individual strengths, and build self-confidence and self-efficacy. Effective strategies used by EAs include the following:

- Encourage acceptance of the full range of emotions. Remind students that no feelings/emotions are wrong; it is what we do with those feelings/emotions that it is important to manage.
- Check-in with students about their feelings throughout the school day (morning, after recess/lunch, and/or end of day); for example, asking, "How are you feeling/how do you know?"
- Create a break card for students who are non-verbal or cannot verbalize/articulate their need for a break.
- Develop a safe, quiet place for students to take a break that includes objects, books, and visual cues to help calm the mind and body.
- Include strategies for de-escalation/returning to a calm emotional state as part of the student's emotional management plan.
- Give students examples that illustrate strategies for self-regulation.
- Directly teach emotion literacy and include appropriate strategies for self-regulation.

- Use teachable moments when opportunities arise in class where the student has/has not identified appropriate emotions. Include reflection and discussion: What happened? What worked? What didn't work? Why was/wasn't it appropriate?
- Practice strategies and responses that students can use in a variety of circumstances or situations.

Self-Management

In addition to self-awareness, EAs facilitate growth and development in students' self-management skills. Specifically, EAs support students' self-regulation of emotion and thoughts with emphasis on developing skills connected to impulse control, stress management, self-discipline, self-motivation, goal setting, and organization. Effective strategies used by EAs include the following:

- Provide a "go-to" list of strategies/activities students can use in their quiet spot.
- Allow students to choose one goal to focus on, such as "when I feel angry I will ___." Then, create a picture reminder for their desk; this can include a checkmark chart, where they decide how many times/hour/days they will do the strategy in order to feel they have accomplished the goal. Together, decide what the "reward" for accomplishing the goal will be. Begin by helping them know when to check their chart and then slowly allow the student to take this over.
- Develop an individualized social story for difficult situations students are struggling with, and include multiple endings using a variety of self-management strategies; this can be done in consultation with the integration/resource teacher.
- Encourage motivation by keeping a checklist of items/tasks students need to complete and/or organize daily. This will help students remember to complete these tasks. For example, a checklist for starting the day: hang up backpack and jacket, put planner in the bin, sit at the carpet. Verbal instructions can be accompanied (or replaced) by picture symbols.

Social Awareness

Many students who receive support from an EA have difficulty connecting socially with others, which has a significant impact on their ability to make and maintain friendships with peers. Education assistants support their students' social awareness by providing opportunities for students to gain skills in perspective-taking, empathy, appreciating diversity, and respecting others. Effective strategies used by EAs include the following:

- Create clear step-by-step pictures/words of how to work with a peer partner.
- Give support for peer work, games, and unstructured times, such as recess and lunch. Step in only when witnessing major issues arising (preferably before emotional escalation). Recognize and discuss how each person is feeling and why they are feeling that way. Over time, slowly give more space as students develop skills when working and playing with others.
- When problems occur between students, allow time for each student's voice to be heard: "I feel _____ because _____." It will be very challenging the first few times, as the other student will want to interject with their perspective. Have each student repeat why the other student is upset: "You feel _____ because _____." The role of an EA is to mediate the discussion help the students share their perspectives.
- Teach students that self-management is necessary in order to be able to connect socially with others. This is particularly important when disagreements between peers occur. In these situations, students might need a quiet space to calm down. Once calm, students are able to rejoin discussions and work through problems.
- Create social stories of common interpersonal disagreements. Have students identify helpful strategies and then choose one strategy to use if disagreements happen during that day. Be sure to have the student identify a backup solution, in case the first solution is unsuccessful or inappropriate.

Relationship Skills

The development of students' relationship skills is an essential part of the work of EAs, as it is common for students who have additional learning needs (including challenging behaviour) to struggle with interpersonal communication, which affects social engagement, building relationships, and effective teamwork. Effective strategies used by EAs include the following:

- Practice appropriate ways to gain the attention of other students. This includes how to ask permission to join another student to play, how to invite others to play, and how to ask to share toys or games.
- Include co-operative games with a focus on collaboration rather than winning.
- Practice turn-taking between peers.
- Directly teach students how to recognize and interpret facial expressions and body language. Discuss the connection between feeling and facial expression and body language ("What might that person be feeling and what should/shouldn't you do in response?")
- Role play strategies for conflict resolution (e.g., listening/working with peers, ethical issues, what to do if one witnesses bullying) by using ideas about both what to do and what not to do in situations. Teach relationship skills through the use of social stories; include multiple endings and provide choice so students have the opportunity to problem solve.

Responsible Decision Making

The ability to make good decisions is critically important for success in life. Not only do EAs promote and facilitate the development of good interpersonal skills, demonstrating how to collaborate with peers and communicate effectively, but they also provide opportunities for students to learn how to make good decisions autonomously. Ethical decision making includes the ability to identify problems, analyze situations, solve problems, evaluate outcomes, reflect on experiences, and take responsibility. Effective strategies used by EAs include the following:

- Provide choice in a variety of contexts, learning environments, and opportunities for students to practice decision making in a safe environment.
- Read the book *Have You Filled a Bucket Today?* by McCloud, Lundgren, and Messing (2006). Discuss each day ways the student's own bucket has been filled, ways other people's buckets have been filled, and what they would do if they saw someone's bucket was running low.
- Read books that explore moments where characters display great emotion. Discuss how that character feels and what strategies they could use to deal with their emotions.
- Create clear pictures/symbols with words displaying cause and effect: "When I find a quiet space and breathe deep, then ___ happens," or "If I use my words, then ___ happens." This teaches positive behaviour rather than punishing unwanted behaviour, using the principles of positive behaviour support (PBS).
- Role play so students can practice making wise choices in the moment. Where possible, include a peer to role play together.
- Positively reinforce any time you see students making responsible decisions—celebrate the successes. Have a conversation about why it worked, and ask, "How did it feel to make this decision?"
- Teach responsible decision making through the use of social stories; include multiple endings and provide choice so students have the opportunity to problem solve.
- Create open-ended scenarios related to decision making, problem solving, and analyzing situations. Discuss potential positive decisions students can make and what the outcome of these decisions may be. Discuss what the negative decision in the same situation would look like and the potential consequences of that decision.

SELF-CARE FOR EAs (AND OTHER SCHOOL-BASED PROFESSIONALS)

The work of an EA can be stressful as it often requires moment-to-moment decision making and flexibility, as well as patience and understanding while working with students with diverse needs and challenging behaviours (Causton-Theoharis, 2009). As a result, it is common for EAs to experience signs of physical exhaustion (e.g., yawning midday, lack of energy) and emotional exhaustion (e.g., forgetfulness, insomnia, anxiety, depression) (see, for example, Garwood, Van Loan, & Werts, 2018; Shyman, 2010). If left untreated and unsupported, ongoing (chronic) stress may lead to EAs experiencing burnout (cynicism, detachment, feeling ineffective), which has a great impact on quality of life and well-being (Ghere & York-Barr, 2007; Tillery, Werts, Roark, & Harris, 2003). With the impact of chronic stress in mind, it is important for EAs to develop their own social emotional competence across the five domains of SEL. An important consideration for stress management is the inclusion of regular self-care strategies in their lifestyles through mindfulness practices (Jennings, 2016). One evidence-based SEL intervention specifically designed to help teachers and other school-based personnel develop social emotional competence and well-being is the Cultivating Awareness and Resilience in Education (CARE) program, which includes three components: emotion skills instruction, mindfulness and stress reduction practices, and caring and listening strategies (Jennings, 2015). Each of the three components promotes social emotional competence by reducing neurological stress responses (flight, fright, freeze) (Jennings, 2016). Strategies highlighted in the CARE program include the following:

- Emotion skills instruction includes experiential activities (self-reflection and interpersonal role plays) with a focus on the recognition of emotional states and an exploration of participants' own behavioural and emotional patterns. The emphasis of the CARE program is to encourage self-awareness and self-understanding with the goal of regulation of emotion.

- Mindfulness and stress reduction practices include deep breathing, focused attention, mindful awareness, body awareness, and emotional awareness. Yoga is an effective way to include mindfulness practices in regular wellness routines. Mindful minutes, or short mindfulness practices throughout the day, are also an easy way to gain benefit. Gratitude practices such as reflecting on things one is grateful for, keeping a personal journal, and expressing gratitude to others by showing appreciation and kindness also increase mindfulness. The goal of mindfulness and stress reduction practices is to facilitate self-management, social awareness, and relationship skills.
- Caring and listening strategies include mindful listening and generating feelings of care for self and others. When practiced over time, caring and listening strategies increase positive emotions and reduce emotional reactions. Further, caring and listening encourage interpersonal sensitivity to the experiences of others, which supports social awareness and relationship skills through conflict resolution (Jennings, 2016).

The five domains of the SEL framework (self-awareness, self-management, social awareness, relationship skills, and responsible decision making) are central to success in school and in life. Within the school environment, SEL instruction and support is often provided through structured class- or school-wide interventions (using, for example, formalized SEL programs such as MindUp, Roots of Empathy, and Zones of Regulation). Increasingly, this is also being taught through learning outcomes (such as self-reflection and self-regulated learning) included in provincial K–12 curricula. Within the work of EAs, SEL competencies are increasingly included in individualized education plans and in direct instruction of individualized interventions and supports. In addition, with the widespread implementation of SEL initiatives in schools, EAs are also involved in supporting class-wide SEL interventions with all students.

Voices from the Field

Andrea, a grade 2 student, joined the grade 2/3 blended class halfway through the school year. Andrea was a perfectionist who was never satisfied with her written output, thus, she would constantly restart her assignments as she felt her work was not "good enough." In fact, she rarely began her work and would try anything to avoid written tasks, exhibiting many signs of anxiety: obsessively worrying about what was coming next, worrying about keeping her desk neat and tidy, obsessing over whether or not she was forgetting/missing something, and extreme fatigue (occasionally falling asleep in class), as well as constant stomach aches and headaches.

In addition to her incapacitating anxiety, Andrea had high-functioning autism, and had significant trouble in her social interactions with peers. Andrea would often misinterpret social cues and catastrophize situations with peers, believing that her friends did not want to play with her. In these situations, Andrea would either get upset and cry, have a tantrum and de-friend her peers, or tattle on the other students—each reaction added to her anxious state of being.

As an EA, I recognized that Andrea needed to develop skills in SEL in order to understand her own feelings and their effects on her body. When she began crying or exhibiting escalating emotions (heavy breathing and dazing out), she would shut down and was not able to self-manage. Fortunately, I was trained to use two SEL intervention programs: Zones of Regulation (Kuypers, 2011) and the CALM Curriculum.

This training emphasizes direct teaching of self-regulation skills (e.g., managing stress and worries), as well as self-awareness skills (e.g., recognizing and naming feelings and emotional triggers). The classroom teacher welcomed the CALM program into the class, and we began by identifying emotions and verbally explaining what that emotion feels like in our own bodies. Throughout the lessons, I gave examples of how my body feels when I'm worried, anxious, or stressed. Each student described an event or activity that made them feel worried, anxious, or stressed, and how their body reacted.

Continued

As the students began to understand their emotions and emotional responses, we incorporated the Zones of Regulation SEL intervention into the class's daily vocabulary. Zones of Regulation uses colour names to indicate emotional states (blue: low (sad, tired, sick, bored); green: calm alertness (happy, focused, content, ready to learn); yellow: heightened alertness (stress, frustration, anxiety, excitement, silliness); red: extremely heightened alertness/intense emotion (anger, rage, explosive behaviour, devastation/terror). As we worked through the SEL interventions with Andrea, we began to see great improvement in her coping skills. After a week, she was able to identify to her teacher when she was feeling worried or anxious about her work. After two weeks, she was beginning to use strategies to help her get back into the green zone. And after a month, she was completing her work on a regular basis, with minimal one-on-one support, and having much more positive social interactions with peers.

To further support the development of Andrea's social awareness and relationship skills, I created individualized social stories that were specifically tailored to her social emotional needs and emphasized different ways that she could respond to social situations. Each day, we would read the story and discuss how to use the various strategies embedded within the story, and then she would choose one of the strategies to practice during recess and lunch that day. Not long after we began the use of social stories, I could see Andrea's social skills improving and she was able to converse with her friends more effectively. The combination of predictability and repetition of strategies in these social stories was a very effective tool for Andrea's social success and self-management of emotion and impulse control.

CRITICAL THINKING QUESTIONS

1. How are the domains of SEL connected to each other? How are the domains of SEL related and interconnected to each other?
2. Why are EAs uniquely situated to teach SEL skills to their students?
3. What are the key facilitators to effective SEL instruction? What are some barriers to effective SEL instruction?

REFERENCES

Causton-Theoharis, J. (2009). *The paraprofessional's handbook for effective support in inclusive classrooms*. Baltimore: Brookes.

Collaborative for Academic, Social, and Emotional Learning. (2018). Social and emotional learning core competencies. Retrieved from http://www.casel.org/social-and-emotional-learning/core-competencies/

Durlak, J. A., Weissberg, R. P., Dymnicki, A. B., Taylor, R. D., & Schellinger, K. B. (2011). The impact of enhancing students' social and emotional learning: A meta-analysis of school-based universal interventions. *Child Development, 82*(1), 405–432. doi:10.1111/j.1467-8624.2010.01564.x

Elias, M. J., Zins, J. E., Weissberg, R. P., Frey, K. S., Greenberg, M. T., Haynes, N. M., & Shriver, T. P. (1997). *Promoting social and emotional learning: Guidelines for educators*. Alexandria, VA: ASCD.

Fraser Valley Child Development Centre. (n.d.). Connect with CALM. Retrieved from https://www.connectwithcalm.ca

Garwood, J. D., Van Loan, C. L., & Werts, M. G. (2018). Mindset of paraprofessionals serving students with emotional and behavioral disorders. *Intervention in School and Clinic, 53*, 206–211. doi:10.1177/1053451217712958

Ghere, G., & York-Barr, J. (2007). Paraprofessional turnover and retention in inclusive programs: Hidden costs and promising practices. *Remedial and Special Education, 28*, 21–32. doi:10.1177/07419325070280010301

Jennings, P. A. (2015). *Mindfulness for teachers: Simple skills for peace and productivity in the classroom*. New York: Norton Series on the Social Neuroscience of Education.

Jennings, P. A. (2016). CARE for teachers: A mindfulness-based approach to promoting teachers' well-being and improving performance. In K. Schonert-Reichl & R. Roeser (Eds.), *The handbook of mindfulness in education: Emerging theory, research, and programs* (pp. 133–148). New York: Springer-Verlag. doi:10.1007/978-1-4939-3506-2_9

Kuypers, L. (2011). *The zones of regulation: A curriculum designed to foster self-regulation and emotional control*. San Jose, CA: Think Social Publishing.

McCloud, C., Lundgren, M., & Messing, D. (2006). *Have you filled a bucket today?: A guide to daily happiness for kids*. Northville, MI: Ferne Press.

Norman, N., & Jamieson, J. R. (2015). Social and emotional learning and the work of itinerant teachers of the deaf and hard of hearing. *American Annals of the Deaf, 160*(3), 273–288. doi:10.1353/aad.2015.0024

Shyman, E. (2010). Identifying predictors of emotional exhaustion among special education paraeducators: A preliminary investigation. *Psychology in the Schools, 47*(8), 828–841. doi:10.1002/pits.20507

Tillery, C. Y., Werts, M. G., Roark, R., & Harris, S. (2003). Perceptions of paraeducators on job retention. *Teacher Education and Special Education, 26*(2), 118–127.

Zins, J. E., Bloodworth, M. R., Weissberg, R. P., & Walberg, H. J. (2004). The scientific base linking social and emotional learning to school success. In J. Zins (Ed.), *Building academic success on social and emotional learning: What does the research say* (pp. 3–22). New York: Teachers College Press.

Zins, J. E., & Elias, M. J. (2006). Social and emotional learning. In G. G. Bear & K. M. Minke (Eds.), *Children's needs III* (pp. 1–13). Bethesda, MD: NASP.

Zins, J., Elias, M. J., & Greenberg, M. (2003). Facilitating success in school and in life through social and emotional learning. *Perspectives in Education, 21*(4), 55–67.

CHAPTER 8

The Role of the Education Assistant in Developing Play, Recreation, and Social Skills

Joan Astren

THREE KEY IDEAS

1. Inclusion benefits everyone.
2. Educators' attitudes impact the depth and scope of the social abilities of students with diverse needs.
3. Opportunities for play result in positive development.

Play: one word with monumental implications. Opportunity to play is a fundamental element of children's overall growth and development. The nature and location of the play, the child's ability, and the support available determine which resources and skills are needed to help a student with diverse abilities participate. To be able to play generally requires the use of numerous developmental abilities, such as gross and fine motor skills, the ability to observe others, and to problem solve, wait, and practice using appropriate social skills. Through play, the child may discover the sheer emotional joy of being with another peer. To experience a sense of belonging and acceptance from one's peers can be a motivating factor for students with diverse needs. As play activities can broaden students' knowledge of self and their world, it is important that education assistants (EAs) recognize the importance of play and commit to ensuring that all students are offered the opportunity to participate in play. Children make meaning of their world through active engagement of materials and with peers. Through play, children construct knowledge, make hypotheses, and develop their social abilities. Play offers opportunities to take risks and build a sense of positive self (Gonzalez-Mena, 2014). Students with diverse needs often require the support of an EA to make modifications with materials and the environment in order to facilitate successful inclusion. The nature and degree of the student's need shapes the resources required. For example, a student with a visual impairment wishing to participate in play or recreational activities requires different adaptions to their environment than a student with high-functioning autism (Trawick-Smith, 2014, p. 279).

Fiore (2012, p. 107) noted that if a goal of education is to help students develop skills, abilities, and competencies, then play needs to be an important part of their development; therefore, educational settings need to acknowledge and provide venues for play and recreational activities, which can enhance future student success. Education assistants are on the front line of practice and know that most individuals have the basic need to belong; when students with diverse needs experience a sense of belonging and have positive relationships with their peers and adults within the school setting, they report "feelings of acceptance" (Rose & Shevlin, 2017, p. 76). When they have the opportunity to take risks and navigate through an experience or interaction while supported by an EA, they build competence and autonomy and feel empowered, all of which can lead to being resilient. As noted by Brooks (1994, p. 546), "resilient children appear to have a high level of self-esteem, a realistic sense of personal control and a feeling of hope."

Inclusion invites growth and awareness for all individuals involved. In spite of this awareness and knowledge, why is it that there are fragmented and limited opportunities for some students with diverse needs to participate with their peers in play and recreational activities?

GAPS AND BARRIERS

From a societal perspective, including students with diverse needs can amplify awareness, tolerance, compassion, and acceptance for all students. As noted by Dyson (2014), an inclusive school is one where everyone is accepted and supported by their peers and other individuals in the school. As a broad concept this makes sense and seems right, yet it is not always carried out in educational settings. Different factors can hinder inclusion, such as the physical layout of the school, teacher availability, commitment of the classroom teacher, ability of the EA, and the availability of appropriate resources. These can all influence the degree of social inclusion. One foundational element that can either support or detract from inclusion is an individual's belief about whether inclusion is seen as a benefit or a hindrance. These beliefs impact overall attitudes and the effort people make to support inclusion in practice.

Social activities in which all students can participate can help those students with diverse needs learn and develop social skills, such as how to enter into a conversation or activity, how to maintain an interaction, and how to end a conversation/activity in a positive manner. In a cross-national study of teachers in Canada and China, Dyson (2014) examined the depth and scope of social inclusion in the elementary school system and found that "social inclusion most often took place in the classroom and under teachers' supervision" (p. 110). With this in mind, EAs can create peer-to-peer interactions in the classroom environment.

Education assistants must consider the strengths and needs of the individual student and how to address these in any activity. For example, if the student is proficient in math, the EA could support them to participate in a card game that requires mathematical calculations. Their peers could model appropriate social skills, such as learning reciprocity, while the student uses their math skills.

Attitudinal Barriers

There are two constructs of inclusion: the philosophy that denotes beliefs about the rights of others and the actual implementation in the education system. As noted by Glazzard (2011), it is difficult to separate one's beliefs from one's actions, as the commitment of one's beliefs determines the authenticity of inclusion. For example, if an EA consistently strives to include all students, this demonstrates a strong belief; therefore, EAs need to be willing to examine their beliefs and values about inclusion and be honest in their self-reflection. When there is an understanding that inclusion is as diverse and distinct as each student, one can begin to formulate approaches and strategies that are respectful of individual student needs.

Glazzard (2011) states that in order for practitioners to embrace inclusion fully, they need to be open to making changes to their teaching style and overall pedagogical approach. For example, if an EA reduces the complexity of their instruction with a student using a "first do this and then you can do this" framework, the student is clear about the sequence of tasks. This clear and concise language lends itself to greater student success. In contrast, if the EA uses too many words when giving instruction the student may become overwhelmed, resulting in negative behaviour as a result of frustration. This example illustrates how an EA can shape their approach to fit the ability of the student.

Changing approaches requires a paradigm shift in order to separate the behaviour from the student. This reinforces the view of the student as capable rather than unwilling or difficult. The student is trying to communicate needs and wants and it is the educator's job to identify these in order to provide responsive support. This mindset is central to the development of inclusive educational environments. If an EA practices from a competency-based model, they see opportunities for students to participate and take risks, whether it be in play, during structured or unstructured activities, outdoors or indoors. Inclusion is greatly influenced by the educational team and often begins with the EA. When belief and practice are congruent, true inclusion results.

Physical Barriers

Attitudes are not the only barriers to inclusion. As noted by Eynat, Schreur, and Engel-Yeger (2010), structural or physical barriers such as the absence of a ramp or elevators for wheelchairs, automatic doors, large signage, and railings for location definition restrict and impede an individual's ability to be included. There may be uneven ground or large pebbles in the schoolyard that can hinder the manoeuvrability of a wheelchair. When a student is using climbing equipment or other structures, once they have made it to one level there may be barriers to accessing other features or activities. The EA is called upon to be creative and develop games or activities that will be engaging for the student. A study conducted by Pivik (2010) found that students with diverse needs reported that the highest number of barriers were simply doorways that opened up into hallways, classrooms, the library, and recreational facilities (p. 514). It is often the everyday structures that can create a lack of accessibility.

Lack of Resources

Lack of resources has also been cited as a possible barrier to inclusion, especially in physical activities. In one study, Carbonneau, Roult, Duquette, and Belley-Ranger (2017) found that adaptive and specialized material was often absent in schools because of a lack of knowledge about where to purchase the material. In addition, there may be an absence or shortage of school funding for purchasing specialized equipment.

Absence of Expertise

Limited opportunity for inclusive play may also be attributed to a lack of interest on the part of the EA or the classroom teacher. The EA may also lack knowledge and skill in terms of how to organize and orchestrate an inclusive activity. Education assistants can ask, what is this student good at and how best can I bring their ability into this activity? This facilitates creative thinking and allows for successful inclusion. Lindsay, Proulx, Thomson, and Scott (2013) found that unpredictable student behaviour, in addition to an absence of training on how to best respond to the student's outburst, could be a possible factor hindering inclusion. Activities that are out of the usual classroom routine, such as field trips or speakers coming into the classroom, can cause upset for students who are very routine-bound. An EA can help the student prepare for these types of activities by using pictures of change and giving them a choice about how they wish to participate. There may also be a lack of time or opportunity and available expertise to teach EAs about specific technology-based communication devices. Many children use iPads with communication applications as their means of communicating. Speech therapists usually know how to use these applications and many are very willing to explain and demonstrate programs to educators.

There are numerous factors (identified here) that limit or prevent inclusion; however, there are numerous strategies EAs can use to facilitate successful inclusion that require few resources and simply require the willingness to think of alternative ways to offer opportunities for learning and play.

ADAPTATIONS AND ACCOMMODATIONS

According to Horn, Palmer, Butera, and Lieber (2016), a teacher who acts with intentionality supports a valuable and meaningful learning experience and provides equal opportunities for students with diverse needs. This approach supports students to process new information, acquire new skills, and build social competence. As noted by Evans and Adirim (2007), there are very few conditions that prevent students with diverse needs from participating in sedentary recreational activities; even with limited mobility and ability there is always something they can do, so it is important never to discount their ability to participate.

One overarching question an EA needs to ask is, "What adaptations or accommodations do I need to use to ensure positive engagement for this student?" Or, alternatively, "How does this student learn best and what adjustments do I need to make to facilitate meaningful participation?" There may be the same overall objective for this student as there is for the rest of the class, but variation in how the student attains the objective. Creating ways for them to be included while on the playground can help with inclusion; though this requires some thought, it can have positive outcomes and is worth the effort. It may be comfortable, but not optimal, to have the student remain beside the EA when outside. Instead, an EA can facilitate peer interaction by arranging in advance for other students to play together on the playground (Beninghof, 1997).

An EA can set up a prearranged peer buddy who can play or be with the student with diverse needs during an activity. A student with diverse needs may require visual, sensory, or auditory adaptations or adjustments in terms of planning or navigating the physical environment. The following sections address general considerations for adaptations for students with diverse needs in specific areas of engagement.

Sport Adaptations

There are numerous ways to maximize involvement for students with diverse needs playing a ball sport. For example, the distance to transport the ball can be shortened, or a larger ball that is easier to grasp and hold can be used, or a squeeze ball or a ball with nubs on the outside that provides sensory input. To assist students with a visual impairment, a larger, brightly coloured ball can be used in conjunction with a large visual that marks the spot they need to take it to. Making available a quiet place where students can retreat and compose themselves when they are overwhelmed will help them to retain their dignity, knowing they can resume the activity when ready. It is generally agreed that having a perimeter fence or clearly marked boundary is necessary for all students.

According to Proud (2014), offering students with diverse needs "orientation opportunities" allows them time to think about where and how they might engage outside. This promotes the use of executive function skills such as planning and implementing a plan. It also facilitates independence and builds competence, which can mitigate negative behaviour. From a broader perspective, this is what educators want for any student—to build competence and positive social ability.

Haugen (1997, p. 3) suggests that students with diverse needs should be given the opportunity to take on a leadership role and should not always remain on the peripheral of activities. Pairing a peer with a student with diverse needs can build understanding and social inclusion.

For example, educators can organize a sport in which the student with diverse needs is the manager of the equipment and others on the team engage with the student to use the equipment.

As noted by L. Maslen (personal communication, June 17, 2018), willingness to consider alternative ways to help a student participate in sport can support inclusion:

> When I look at students being included on teams, in clubs, in sports, in physical education classes, on the playground, full inclusion looks different for everybody. My approach is to ask, are they happy, do they want to be there, and are they doing what they can be doing? That opens the doorway so a student that is interested in a particular sport can be included even if they are not on the field, on the rink or on the deck. As an example, last year I had a student who was interested in hockey and joining the hockey team. I talked with the hockey coach and he was fully supportive of this student's goal. We had everything set up but we soon discovered this student did not have the physical stamina or skill set to participate at the level the team was working. The coach and I agreed this student needed to participate so we re-examined his goal to be on the team. We explored different jobs that occur on the team that aren't necessarily on the ice, for example, scorekeeping, equipment manager, or statistician. The coach created a brand-new job of opening and closing the penalty door and when we approached the student, he loved the idea! He worked at home games and he got to be part of the team. He had a hockey jersey with his name on the back, attended school functions that are hockey oriented, and was part of the team photo in the yearbook. When he walked down the hallway, the hockey kids high-fived him, recognized him, saying, "Hey, how's it going." They recognize that he is a teammate and that is full inclusion!

Environmental Adaptations

Using visual schedules is an effective method of supporting students who learn best visually. Placing the visual schedule of the day in full view at the front of the class can benefit all students. The schedule can illustrate both expectations and sequence of activities. For example, it may include a drawing of students standing in one line waiting for outside time or a turn. This is an example of positive behaviour support, setting students up for success, because they are aware of the expected behaviour prior to the activity. It also assists with comprehension, leads to independence, and promotes a positive sense of self and identity. Another example is the use of a visual that illustrates the number of players for a game and when to participate in the game. Students may refer to these illustrations, enhancing their resourcefulness and competence. The drawings do not need to be elaborate—they can depict stick people, easy and uncomplicated. To support understanding, the visual should be easily visible at eye level and not surrounded by distracting materials. Various items can be attached to the schedule with Velcro, which allows students to remove the pictures of the tasks they have completed, aiding in focus and transitions to the next activity (Haugen, 1997).

An EA can also use simplified and animated gestures to help convey expectations or reinforce behaviour. A welcoming wave along with a visual direction is a simple and effective tool. Education assistants can also create visual reminders or visual sequences of activities that are small enough to fit in a student's pocket; this is an effective and dignified tool.

Student Adaptations

When explaining concepts or transmitting information, EAs can use multiple methods simultaneously. When providing an explanation or direction, EAs should use wording that is easy to follow, pause, allow for processing time, and use gestures to accompany the verbal explanation. Concrete examples or objects can be used to illustrate expectations. Educators may need to repeat their directions/explanations and allow extra time for students to process instructions. This is important, as the EA may think the student is being non-compliant when, in fact, they are processing information. Tasks should be broken down into manageable steps. For example, if the class is outside and the student wishes to join a peer who is already playing a game, the EA may say, first, think of what you will say; second, approach and get their attention; third, ask; and fourth, wait for an answer. To build flexibility in thought and social ability, the EA may also offer the following insight: "They might say yes and they might say no." This lays out the process and defines it in navigable steps, setting up the student to accept that the invitation may be declined. Decluttering language improves understanding and can support student success. It is crucial for an EA to know the comprehension level of a student so their support matches student need.

An awareness and understanding of temporal expectations can assist in student task completion and transition to the next activity. Temporal aids can include a timer or buzzer, or a verbal or gestural warning. These can help students begin to process an end time and emotionally and cognitively prepare for a shift in activity.

Some students are very sensitive to noise level and type of noise, and this can be quite problematic. To cope with this, students can be given noise-cancelling headphones or the amount of time spent in the environment can be adjusted. Some students may be hypersensitive to certain types of noise; for example, the hum of fluorescent lights can be very bothersome. In this case, dimming the lights and providing alternate lighting is helpful. Pivik (2010) made a valid point when he suggested that flashing lights could be used to indicate period changes or fire drills instead of bells or alarms (pp. 514–515). Some schools have placed slit tennis balls on the bottom of chair legs to lessen the noise as the chairs are moved across the floor. Some students may be tactile defensive, which means that an individual is reactive to or avoids touching certain textures. If, for example, a student does not like the feel of clay or a similar medium, it can be placed in a plastic bag and the student can "touch" it through the bag, allowing for participation. If a student seeks motion and movement within the classroom, an EA can provide a break for the individual student or the whole class can engage in a sensory break. For example, students can do wall push-ups or can place the palms of their hands together and push. These actions address the need for sensory stimulation and can calm the body.

CONCLUSION

There are many ways to facilitate inclusive social opportunities using play and recreational activities. As Proud (2014) so aptly stated, play is the venue that unites us; it strengthens our sense of community by including everyone. Play "enhances understanding, tolerance, empathy and cooperation" (2014, p. 63).

It is important that EAs practice from the belief that students with diverse needs have the same right as any other child to participate and have their dreams realized. This can enhance students' competence and positive sense of self, leading to positive outcomes. This truly exemplifies the EA's role: facilitating and promoting inclusion!

Voices from the Field

Linda Maslen, Inclusion Support Educator, Cowichan Secondary School, Duncan, British Columbia

What Would an Ideal EA Look like in Terms of Skills and Knowledge?

The ideal EA comes with an open mind and with the skills necessary to be able to connect with students on an authentic level. They must be team players and open to working with their fellow EAs, teachers, administration, and the students' families. They also need to have knowledge of relevant subject matter so they can support students in the classroom. Connecting with students is by far the most important attribute to have and EAs who are willing and able to do that are able to help their students more.

What Are Some Barriers That Would Prevent an EA from Connecting with a Student?

I think EAs do the best that they can; however, if I had to suggest one barrier to their being able to connect with a student, I might suggest fear.

Continued

I think that some EAs are scared of potential physical or verbal student outbursts, especially if they feel that they are not fully supported. Also, some EAs may be afraid of being judged by peers and other adults in the school or looking like they are incompetent and unable to manage the behaviour of a student. Like all of us, I think they fear being perceived as inadequate.

How Do You Encourage EAs to Be Willing to Have an Open Mind and Take Risks in Their Practice?

The EA needs to know that their work is valuable, that the work they do is necessary, and that they are part of the team. My aim is to help them keep an open mind and challenge their own personal beliefs and, sometimes, I help them shift those beliefs to help them see that what they are doing is valuable.

In Your Role as Inclusion Support Educator How Have You Facilitated Teamwork?

I try to always include EAs and everything I say and do is designed to let the EAs know how valuable they are. I ask and value their opinions, I offer additional training, I have them do observations in the classroom, and I corroborate their observation with the teachers. They participate in individualized education plan meetings, as they are with the student the most and sometimes have the most insight. I also try to ensure that parents know how valuable they are so it's inclusive for everybody.

CRITICAL THINKING QUESTIONS

1. What measures do we need to take to offer optimum participation for all students?
2. In what ways can participation enhance student success?
3. What is the importance of an EA's attitude in educational settings?

REFERENCES

Beninghof, A. M. (1997). *Ideas for inclusion: The classroom teacher's guide to integrating students with severe disabilities.* Longmont, CO: Sopris West.

Brooks, R. B. (1994). Children at risk: Fostering resilience and hope. *American Orthopsychiatric Association, 64*(4), 545–553.

Carbonneau, H., Roult, R., Duquette, M., & Belley-Ranger, E. (2017). The determining factors in school contexts which lead to active lifestyles among young people with disabilities. *International Journal of Applied Sports Sciences, 29*(2), 13–30. doi: 10.24985/ijass.2017.29.1.13

Dyson, L. (2014). Teachers' perspectives and experiences of the contexts of social inclusion within elementary school classrooms in Canada and China. *Journal of International Association of Special Education, 15*(2), 108–117.

Evans, S., & Adirim, T. (2007). Exercise, sports and recreation. In M. Batshaw, L. Pellegrino, & N. Roizen (Eds.), *Children with Disabilities* (6th ed.; pp. 581–589). Baltimore: Brookes Publishing.

Eynat, G., Schreur, N., & Engel-Yeger, B. (2010). Inclusion of children with disabilities: Teachers' attitudes and requirements for environmental accommodations. *International Journal of Special Education, 25*(2), 89–99.

Fiore, L. B. (2012). *Assessment of young children: A collaborative approach.* New York: Routledge.

Glazzard, J. (2011). Perceptions of the barriers to effective inclusion in one primary school: Voices of teachers and teaching assistants. *British Journal of Learning Support, 26*(2), 56–63.

Gonzalez-Mena, J. (2014). *Foundations of early childhood education: Teaching children in a diverse society.* New York: McGraw Hill.

Haugen, K. (1997, March/April). Using your senses to adapt environments: Checklist for an accessible environment. *Child Care Exchange.* Retrieved from https://www.childcareexchange.com/article/using-your-senses-to-adapt-environments-checklist-for-an-accessible-environment/5011450/

Horn, E., Palmer, S., Butera, G., & Lieber, J. (2016). *Six steps to inclusive preschool curriculum.* Baltimore: Brookes Publishing.

Lindsay, S., Proulx, M., Thomson, N., & Scott, H. (2013). Educators' challenges of including children with autism spectrum disorder in mainstream classrooms. *International Journal of Disability, Development and Education,* *60*(4), 347–362.

Pivik, J. (2010). The perspective of children and youth: How different stakeholders identify architectural barriers for inclusion in schools. *Journal of Environmental Psychology, 30*(4), 510–517.

Proud, I. (2014, July/August). Every playground, every child: Inclusive playground design. *Child Care Exchange.*

Rose, R., & Shevlin, M. (2017). A sense of belonging: Children's views of acceptance in "inclusive" mainstream schools. *International Journal of Whole Schooling,* Special Issue (January), 65–80.

Trawick-Smith, J. (2014). *Early childhood development: A multicultural perspective.* Hoboken, NJ: Pearson.

CHAPTER 9

Finding Connection: Developing Social Competence

Mary Harber

THREE KEY IDEAS

1. Education assistants have a unique opportunity to support the development of social competence within the school community.
2. Social competence and social capital are important in developing connections and learning about relationships, which support quality of life for students with disabilities.
3. Creative drama can be used as a strategy to teach and support social competence.

SOCIAL SKILLS VERSUS SOCIAL COMPETENCE

The term *social skills* often brings to mind concrete behaviours used to connect with others. Greeting skills, eye contact, body language, and use of personal space are identified as social skills. If this were all that was needed to make connections, then it would be easy to do so, as people would simply learn and memorize a set of behaviours and act on them. Unfortunately, navigating the subtle cues of the social world can be difficult and is far more complex than a set of behavioural skills. Social behavioural skills are one of the many components that make up social competence. Bierman and Welsh (2000) identify the following elements of social competence: the ability to understand and use appropriate interpersonal communication skills; the ability to understand give and take in terms of regulating behaviour, responding to what the other person is saying or doing; and the ability to read social situations and environments.

Marcia Winner (2002), who developed the framework of social thinking skills, defines *social competence* as the ability to adapt to a changing environment while thinking about the context, the people involved, and the thoughts, beliefs, and needs of the individual or group. Social competence also includes the personal history of knowledge and experience of each individual, which influences communication choices; therefore, social competence is more than just a "skill set." Social competence is an umbrella term highlighting both internal and external factors that influence the development of social connection. For example, think about when two individuals first meet. How they respond depends on the setting (e.g., at a pub versus a professional meeting), how they greet each other (e.g., making eye contact or not, formal or informal, smiling or bored looking), and their tone of voice and rate of speech. As a result of evaluating these cues one may respond differently. Does one person sense that the other is tired or bored? If so, they may make a joke to lighten the mood or perhaps decide that this is inappropriate. If they have tried to make a joke in the past (history) and it fell flat when meeting a new person, they may choose not to do this. This brief example illustrates that there are many decisions that occur in the moment of simply meeting a new person while initiating or responding to communication. Social skills used in the moment come together to create a social interaction; this goes far beyond shaking someone's hand and making eye contact. These micro-level skills are highly important and the more an individual is able to integrate skills with specific reactions, the more likely the interaction will be satisfactory for both participants (Spence, 2003).

Social competence is the ability to behave in a satisfactory manner in public or during interpersonal situations. To be socially competent, one must be able to adapt to listeners' needs, tune in to others' perspectives, build upon past interactions, and have empathetic skills. Social competence is usually associated with other characteristics such as social skills, interpersonal communication, and social ability.

KEY ELEMENTS OF SOCIAL COMPETENCE

When defining social competence, it is critical to break this broad concept down into several elements or key areas. As noted by Han and Kemple (2006), the following five key areas are important.

1. Adoption of Social Values

When students begin to realize that they are part of a larger group and that their own personal needs are not always paramount, they are beginning to adopt social values. Social values relate to caring, social justice, honesty, flexibility, and sexuality, to name a few, and are created by cultural and community norms. As an education assistant (EA) it is important to consider what values are being promoted in the school community and the classroom while considering your role in supporting student participation. The adoption of social values highlights the importance of being considerate of others' needs and understanding that co-operative interaction benefits the group, not just the individual.

2. Developing a Sense of Personal Identity

When people feel good about themselves and have a sense of personal power, belonging, self-worth, competence, and purpose, relationships are enriched and interactions are more likely to be positive and connected (Walsh, 1994). A well-developed personal identity reinforces confidence and success, which leads to greater connection. This also helps break the cycle of low self-esteem and reduces feelings of rejection and exclusion.

3. Learning Interpersonal Skills

This element is most commonly referenced when discussing social skills and relates to actual "skill" development. Students learn to read others' feelings and articulate their own needs and feelings. This creates a balanced relationship in which individuals can meet the demands of various social situations and can adjust their behaviour accordingly. Not only do students need to acquire these skills, but they also need decision-making abilities in order to know when and where to use their skills and how to choose from among them (McCay & Keyes, 2001).

4. Regulating Personal Behaviour in Line with Social Expectations

This element refers to balancing personal and relationship expectations with social values. What happens when a student does not get what they want or need? How do they react? EAs are very aware of the need for emotional regulation and that a reaction impacts behaviour and peer interaction. Regulation includes monitoring reactions, understanding how to cope with frustration and overexcitement, and being able to evaluate and monitor the impact that these reactions have on others.

5. Planning and Decision Making

This is the ability to act in a meaningful and purposeful way and to understand that each person has the power to make choices and, as a result of our choices, there are consequences. In addition, it is important for students to understand how others may react to choices or decisions and how this impacts relationships.

Developing Cultural Competence

Culture plays a role in how individuals interact with each other. Cultural competence encourages us to consider how others want to be treated, for example, in relation to touch, tone of voice, topics of discussion, eye contact, or physical proximity. Cultural competence is not only about knowledge of other cultures but also how we respect and interact comfortably with people of different ethnic backgrounds (Kostelnik, Whiren, Soderman, Stein, & Gregory, 2002).

When considering the above five elements of social competence, we begin to realize that learning skills related to social interaction may seem simple but that this is actually a complex area of learning. The term *social skill* fails to fully represent the complexity of social competence.

Although difficult to achieve, it is understood that social competence is a strong predictor of success in many areas of life and that a lack of ability has negative outcomes, especially for those with disabilities. Frostad and Pijl (2007) state that social skills are essential for academic development and social inclusion and participation, and contribute to a more successful transition to adult life and work. As such it is necessary to consider these short- and long-term impacts as key elements in inclusion programs (Vlachou, Stavroussi, & Didaskalou, 2016).

WHY IS SOCIAL COMPETENCE IMPORTANT FOR ADOLESCENTS WITH DISABILITIES?

While supporting adolescents, it can be challenging for EAs not to evaluate a lack of skill as defiance or adolescent rebellion. Instead, through empathy and compassion, EAs can demonstrate an understanding that challenges related to social competency can get in the way of positive academic peer collaboration and relationships with both peers and teachers. This becomes more of an issue in the context of middle and high school as social demands increase dramatically and support often diminishes (Sutherland, Lewis-Palmer, Stichter, & Morgan, 2008). Lee, Yoo, and Bak (2003) state that students without disabilities tend to act as helpers, caregivers, and tutors to students with diverse needs, rather than becoming their friends; this is highlighted by a lack of social interaction. Research by Peterson and McConnell (1993, as cited in Terpstra & Tamura, 2008), identified that students with disabilities demonstrate lower rates of social interaction including, but not limited to, social initiation, response, and use of appropriate social skills than their typical peers. Social skill difficulties are associated with many critical outcomes such as peer rejection, social isolation, poor academic achievement, and aggressive behaviour (Frostad & Pijl, 2007). When students with disabilities are included in the classroom they are visible to other students, they feel a sense of belonging, and other students want to interact with them (Chamberlain, Kasari, & Rotheram-Fuller, 2007).

Assumptions to Avoid in Practice

To avoid stereotypes around social learning, it is important to recognize assumptions that EAs may have about the ability of a student. Winner (2002) highlights three major assumptions that get in the way of successful socially based teaching and support.

The first is the assumption that the EA thinks they know what a person understands and how they interpret and respond to social information. This is often based on anecdotal information rather than building a relationship with the student and getting to know them; therefore, it is important to observe them in social situations prior to establishing a plan.

The second assumption is that if a student demonstrates an understanding of the concepts, EAs expect them to "perform" successfully in a social interaction. Often this is not possible, because the student has not been supported in developing foundational knowledge in the areas of problem solving, social attention, and interpreting social cues.

The final assumption is the belief that social skills are "intuitive" because the EA knows how to respond in the moment to information. In turn, they may believe that they naturally know how to teach these skills to others who may have a weak learning system. As a result, EAs may simply teach based on what they know as social "behaviours." It is important for EAs to research elements of social skill training and develop a sound framework for practice. Social competence begins with learning how to attend to and interpret the social world and using that information to problem solve and make decisions about the social response (Winner, 2002).

Since social competency is critical and influential, it is curious that there is often a lack of emphasis on social goals or learning social emotional concepts in the individualized education plan. This seems somewhat short-sighted as evidence clearly supports the premise that social goals are linked to academic goals (Winner, 2002), and are critical for building social capital in the school and broader community. Social capital is an important concept for framing the purpose of developing social skill and competency.

SOCIAL CAPITAL AND RELATIONSHIPS

When students feel successful at developing and maintaining social connections, they are building social capital. Social capital refers to the network of people with whom individuals have a trusting relationship and who provide support and connection necessary for a sense of belonging. Social capital refers to relationships and social ties with both organizations and individuals. These social ties support a person's choices, create opportunities, increase options, and can lead to an enriched quality of life (Gotto, Calkins, Jackson, Walker, & Beckmann, 2010). To support people with disabilities to be more connected with community it is important to consider the power and potency of relationships.

Studies on social capital over the past 40 years show clearly that health, happiness, and longevity are all enhanced by our social capital, the relationships in our lives. As Condeluci (2000) notes, "it is quite simple—the more relationships in your life, the healthier you are, the happier you are … and the longer you live" (p. 3).

The literature identifies two types of social capital: bonding and bridging (Putnam, 2000). Bonding social capital refers to the connections between individuals who share similar values, interests, and characteristics. Bridging social capital refers to when people from different groups come together and develop associations and links in order to support each other (Putnam, 2000). It is important for EAs to understand both when determining how to support social competency for students, and to keep in mind the necessity of supporting the development of both types of social capital in the classroom and in the broader school community. Education assistants work within school goals to establish transferable social competency skills to support citizenship and community participation.

BECOMING A BRIDGE

An EA can sometimes fall into a practice of working too closely with a particular student and, as a result, fail to support a broader context for practicing social skills. Although an EA may be teaching skills directly on an individual basis, this may be inadvertently preventing the student from practicing with others. The responsibility of the EA is to ensure that there are multiple opportunities for student engagement and to act as a bridge to other students, social groups, and learning groups in the classroom and school.

There are many strategies and programs that address social skill development, but very few respond to the broader issue of social competency and incorporate the understanding of social context. An EA has a very specific role in supporting students' social development, especially in middle and high schools, which can be both challenging and rewarding. In typical secondary school environments, social interaction between students with disabilities and general education peers is limited and for some students non-existent. Although social skill development is important for all ages, it is intensified during middle and high school.

INTERVENTION

An EA is positioned to promote social interaction among students and to play a key role in facilitating and supporting peer interaction through both support-based intervention and skill-based intervention (Carter & Hughes, 2005). While teaching these skills, it is important to reinforce appropriate interactions rather than focus on the reduction of inappropriate or negative behaviours (Vlachou et al., 2016).

Support-based interventions occur in both natural ways, through unplanned opportunities for teaching, and purposeful manipulation of the environment to encourage peer connection. Skill-based interventions are an intentional teaching of a set of skills and competencies identified as part of an overall strategy. Under the umbrella of these two types of interventions, strategies may be organized as environmental arrangements, peer strategies, natural strategies, and more direct and purposeful intervention (Han & Kemple, 2006).

SUPPORT-BASED INTERVENTIONS

Environmental Arrangements

EAs working with teachers in a classroom can influence the elements needed to facilitate social interaction. Students with disabilities often demonstrate lower rates of social interaction, which includes the ability to initiate connection, respond with social awareness, and use skills that foster connection (Peterson & McConnell, 1993). There are many ways to utilize the environment to encourage peer interaction. Strategies include, but are not limited to, the following:

- arranging the physical environment in a classroom to include those with and without disabilities in group arrangements
- ensuring that there are private/quiet spaces in the classroom
- providing well-planned schedules and routines, which assist in individual self-regulation (Han & Kemple, 2006)

Peer Strategies

Intentional peer support strategies also create a socially supportive environment. EAs may use collateral skill instruction, for example, teaching students with support needs a game that they could play with others on the computer (Carter & Hughes, 2005). In addition, with training and support within the school system, peers can be used as mentors, social buddies, and instructional helpers. Peers use modelling, shaping, and reinforcement to support students, which is associated with longer social interaction. In addition, Shukla, Kennedy, and Cushing (1999) identify that when students interact with peers there is a greater variety of social interaction in comparison to interactions with adult support.

Natural Strategies

Natural strategies link to those natural opportunities that arise in the environment whereby the EA must be observant and quick thinking.

This refers to seeing opportunities for spontaneous coaching such as the following:

- in the moment conflict resolution, e.g., how might you solve this problem? what do you need to say to _____?
- promoting self-regulation needs, e.g., do you need a break or what do you need right now?
- seeing moments for facilitating connection and coaching through reinforcement, e.g., that was a nice thing to do with _____.
- gentle correction, e.g., what might be another way to ask that question? (Han & Kemple, 2006)

PURPOSEFUL INTERVENTION AND SUPPORT

Social Skill Instruction

Social skill instruction is a deliberate and intentional effort to teach needed skills based on assessment. This intervention includes the use of a specific curriculum or set of strategies or a combination of these to support student learning and integration of knowledge, experience, and skill (Strawhun, O'Connor, Norris, & Peterson, 2014). Effective social skills instruction encourages reflection and self-awareness linked to social emotional learning while practicing both as individuals and in groups. Although direct instruction is effective there are some cautions surrounding the need to ensure that skills can be generalized to different situations (Strawhun et al., 2014). In their review of the literature, Carter and Hughes (2005) identified four basic types of direct instruction: self-management and social interaction instruction, group skill instruction, social interaction skill instruction using a communication book, and social skill instruction alone.

The EA, with support of the teacher, must understand the student's social goals, which should be incorporated into the individualized education plan along with academic goals. Skills can be taught but opportunity to practice these skills must be created to build competence in reciprocal social interaction and in maintaining friendships.

Although there are many programs and models, how one will teach these skills is an important consideration.

DRAMA AND SOCIAL SKILLS

Considering the interactive and kinetic elements of drama, it is no wonder that this is considered one of the more effective strategies for supporting the development of social skills. This method includes mind-body language, relations history, and culture in a comprehensive context (Costa, Faccio, Belloni, & Iudici, 2013), which reflects the key elements of social competence discussed earlier. Individuals are able to recreate real or imagined scenes to increase the range of possibilities in terms of choice making. Students are able to practice reading social situations, reacting in different ways, and making mistakes without consequence.

Freeman, Sullivan, and Fulton (2003) note that although creative drama can be used for a variety of purposes (note that this is not audience-based), it is always based on improvisation, which begins with a story or scene that participants develop. Leaders guide participants to think about situations and offer gentle feedback on what could be different. Using improvisation allows participants to feel empowered and create what is "real" for them. This process facilitates co-operation skills. Participants develop situations, dialogue, and spontaneous actions and reactions. Specific feedback and the ability for a re-do in a safe space when an individual makes a social "mistake" increases confidence in the development of social skills. Creative drama provides the experience and development of social response, initiation, emotional regulation, and the understanding of the reciprocal nature of communication (Freeman, Sullivan, & Fulton, 2003).

Creative drama also has the ability to impact self-concept and increase confidence for future social situations. We often assume that social skills are "intuitive," but they are not for everyone. For those with disabilities, having a safe place in which to practice these skills and develop competency increases the likelihood of engagement.

Creative drama not only lends itself to ensuring that students see the interplay between action and consequence, which can be discussed, replayed, and understood, but it is also kinetic and fun. Learning by doing involves energy, participation, laughter, support, and connection (Bailey, 1997). Creative drama activities create a place in which different choices can be explored without real-life consequences, where students receive help trying things out without fear of rejection. As a drama therapist so aptly states,

> the quandary lies not in knowing what social skills young people need but in how best to teach them. I believe drama is the best vehicle for social skills development because drama involves students in concrete, hands on practice of behavior[;] ... the abstract becomes bodily concrete. (Bailey, 1997, p. 3)

It is important for EAs to understand the area of skill development for a student that needs support. For example, if an EA wants to teach in a group setting how to initiate a conversation and how to ask someone to do an activity (for example, go to a movie), the sequence for planning may look like the following:

- in preparation for the activity the EA should break down the task by thinking about the steps of inviting a person to do an activity and list them
- ask group participants to brainstorm activities they like to do with friends
- have the students create a scene to practice using an activity from the list
- have two students act out the scene; the other students can say "freeze" (only after a few minutes) and take the place of either person in order to create different outcomes
- once the person who is being asked to do an activity in the scene accepts the invitation, the scene moves on to next steps of planning (where, when, how are they going to get there, etc.)
- if the responder says "no" to the invitation, the group might explore how the inviter feels and how they might respond

This is just one basic outline of an idea that could be used, but there are many possibilities when using creative drama and activities to support "in situation" learning.

If the EA is not working with a group, this method could be practiced with an individual; however, the caution is that the more work is done solely with the individual, the less opportunity they have to practice and connect with peers and others. Peer interaction is critical to the development of social competency.

There has been promising research into the efficacy of creative drama in developing social competency, as these activities are interactive and focus on relationships, emotions, communication, co-operation, and reading verbal and non-verbal cues (Spolin, 1986). Results of a recent study by Guli, Semrud-Clikemen, Lerner, and Britton (2013) note that using drama resulted in an improvement in positive interaction with peers, a decrease in solitary play, and the generalization of skills.

Creative drama is a positive method for supporting students in learning and practicing skills related to social competence. Drama allows the learner to exist in the "as-if" world. The EA and teacher create a context that enables participants to build skills and practice roles that are developmentally appropriate (Andersen, 2010). Current literature suggests that the structure and content of creative drama methods are suited for use in a school setting and provide a fun and engaging way to build social competence and friendships (Guli et al., 2013).

As discussed in this chapter, social competence and skills are described in many ways. Unfortunately, a commonly accepted definition of social skills is lacking in the literature, which results in ongoing difficulty with regards to teaching, evaluating, or integrating research into models of practice. With a lack of consistency, practitioners in the field find it difficult to understand and implement support strategies (Vlachou et al., 2016).

Regardless, it is critical that social competence is supported and that EAs take initiative and incorporate this support into daily practice. Social competence directly impacts inclusion and, while students with disabilities are physically present in the classroom, students who struggle to interact with their peers are not fully included (Waltz, 1999). As Judith Snow says, "the only disability is having no relationships," and recognizing that relationships and social networks are a determinant of both physical and mental health is paramount to the quality of life of every individual (Lord & Hutchison, 2011, p. 184).

Voices from the Field

Erica May-Wood is a professional actor and artist educator who has delivered arts programming to participants aged 6 months to 60 years. She has facilitated workshops in schools, agencies, theatres, and conservatories with toddlers, children, teens, at-risk youth, and youth and adults living with mental and physical health challenges and lived experience of homelessness.

In 2012, I worked on a project at a specialized (high school) learning community for students with unique needs. The project, involving five classes of students living with developmental and physical disabilities, created music, poetry, art, and scenes for a collaborative video representing various scenarios of bullying, exclusion, and discrimination that were part of their worlds. With a simple "rewind" technique they re-enacted different approaches to the conflict or issue, and through a collectively created choral poem, explored what we can all do to create more inclusive connections in our communities.

Communication, co-operation, and choice were not only the main themes of their project, but also the key elements of the collective creation process; negotiating skills were not only applied in the re-enactment, but also in the incorporation of all their ideas and deciding who would play what role. Some students were particularly challenged, through drama, in areas such as making eye contact or being in closer proximity to other students. Students also interacted outside their school peer groups, building bridges and creating more accepting relationships in place of former challenges. All students found their way into participating, with some thriving and excelling beyond all expectations. Education assistants were an integral part of the process and, through the project, learned more about their students' skills and hidden talents.

CRITICAL THINKING QUESTIONS

1.   If an EA does not have a "specific" time allotted for creative drama activities, how might they incorporate this into their practice on a daily basis?
2.   What are some strategies that an EA can use in the moment when supporting the learning of social skills and social competencies?
3.   What is the difference between social skill and social competency and why is this important?

REFERENCES

Andersen, C. (2010). Learning in "as-if" worlds: Cognition in drama in education. *Theory into Practice, 43*(4), 281–286. doi:10.1207/s15430421tip4304_6

Bailey, S. (1997). Drama: A powerful tool for social skill development. *Disability Solutions, 2*(1), 1, 3–5.

Bierman, K., & Welsh, A. (2000). Assessing social dysfunction: The contributions of laboratory and performance-based measures. *Journal of Clinical Child Psychology, 29*(4), 526–539.

Carter, E., & Hughes, C. (2005). Increasing social interaction among adolescents with intellectual disabilities and their general education peers: Effective interventions. *Research and Practice for Persons with Severe Disabilities, 30*(4), 179–193.

Chamberlain, B., Kasari, C., & Rotheram-Fuller, E. (2007). Involvement or isolation? The social networks of children with autism in regular classrooms. *Journal of Autism and Developmental Disorders, 37*(2), 230–242. doi:10.1007/s10803-006-0164-4

Condeluci, A. (2000). Social capital: The real route to community inclusion. *Langley Association for Community Living*. Retrieved from https://www.langleyacl.com/documents/Route_to_Community_Inclusion.pdf

Costa, N., Faccio, E., Belloni, E., & Iudici, A. (2013). Drama experience in educational interventions. *Social and Behavioral Sciences, 116*, 4977–4982.

Freeman, G., Sullivan, K., & Fulton, R. (2003). Effects of creative drama on self-concept, social skills, and problem behavior. *Journal of Educational Research, 96*(3), 131–138. doi: 10.1080/00220670309598801

Frostad, P., & Pijl, S. (2007). Does being friendly help in making friends? The relation between the social position and social skills of pupils with special needs in mainstream education. *European Journal of Special Needs Education, 22*(1), 15–30.

Gotto, G., Calkins, C., Jackson, L., Walker, H., & Beckman, C. (2010). *Accessing social capital: Implications for persons with disabilities.* N.p.: National Gateway to Self Determination, US Department of Health and Human Services. doi:10.1080/08856250601082224

Guli, L., Semrud-Clikemen, M., Lerner, M., & Britton, N. (2013). Social competence intervention program (SCIP): A pilot study of a creative drama program for youth with social difficulties. *The Arts in Psychotherapy, 40*(1), 37–44.

Han, H. S., & Kemple, K. M. (2006). Components of social competence and strategies of support: Considering what to teach and how. *Early Childhood Education Journal, 34*(3), 241–246. doi:10.1007/s10643-006-0139-2

Kostelnik, M. J., Whiren, A. P., Soderman, A. K., Stein, L. C., & Gregory, K. (2002). *Guiding children's social development: Theory to practice* (4th ed.). New York: Delmar.

Lee, S., Yoo, S., & Bak, S. (2003). Characteristics of friendships between children with and without mild disabilities. *Education and Training in Developmental Disabilities, 38*(2), 157–166.

Lord, J., & Hutchison, P. (2011). *Pathways to inclusion: Building a new story with people and communities.* Concord, ON: Captus Press.

McCay, L., & Keyes, D. (2001). Developing social competence in the inclusive primary classroom. *Childhood Education, 78*(2), 70–78. doi:10.1080/00094056.2002.10522707

Peterson, C. A., & McConnell, S. R. (1993). Factors affecting the impact of social interaction skills intervention in early childhood special education. *Topics in Early Childhood Special Education, 13*(1), 38–56.

Putnam, R. D. (2000). *Bowling alone: The collapse and revival of American community.* New York: Simon & Schuster.

Shukla, S., Kennedy, C. H., & Cushing, L. S. (1999). Intermediate school students with severe disabilities: Supporting their social participation in general education classrooms. *Journal of Positive Behavior Interventions, 1*(3), 130–140.

Spence, S. (2003). Social skills training with children and young people: Theory, evidence and practice. *Child and Adolescent Mental Health, 8*(2), 84–96. doi:10.1111/1475-3588.00051

Spolin, V. (1986). *Theater games for the classroom: A teacher's handbook.* Evanston, IL: Northwestern University Press.

Strawhun, J., O'Connor, A., Norris, L., & Peterson, R. L. (2014, September). *Social skills instruction.* Strategy brief. Lincoln, NE: Student Engagement Project, University of Nebraska-Lincoln and the Nebraska Department of Education.

Sutherland, K., Lewis-Palmer, T., Stichter, J., & Morgan, P. (2008). Examining the influence of teacher behavior and classroom context on the behavioral and academic outcomes for students with emotional or behavioral disorders. *Journal of Special Education*, *41*(4), 223–233.

Terpstra, J., & Tamura, R. (2008). Effective social interaction strategies for inclusive settings. *Early Childhood Education Journal*, *35*(5), 405–411. doi:10.1007/s10643-007-0225-0

Vlachou, A., Stavroussi, P., & Didaskalou, E. (2016). Special teachers' educational responses in supporting students with special educational needs (SEN) in the domain of social skills development. *International Journal of Disability, Development and Education*, *63*(1), 79–97. doi:10.1080/1034912X.2015.1111305

Walsh, J. (1994). Moral development: Making the connection between choices, responsibility and self-esteem. ERIC Document 369555.

Waltz, M. (1999). Pervasive developmental disorders: Finding a diagnosis and getting help. O'Reilly & Associates.

Winner, M. (2002). Assessment of social skills for students with Asperger syndrome and high-functioning autism. *Assessment for Effective Intervention*, *27*(1–2), 73–80. doi:10.1177/073724770202700110

SECTION III

CULTURAL DIVERSITY

This section provides the reader with the opportunity to explore issues related to the intersection of culture and disability, and the importance of recognizing and responding to inclusive practice in this context. With this in mind, the authors reflect on not only *what* we teach, but also *how* we teach and culturally sound practice. It is important to be aware of the messages about diverse cultures that can be subtly reinforced within the school setting through policy and practice as these directly translate into the wider community and relational context.

Chapter 10 identifies for education assistants the importance of practicing from a culturally safe framework. It is one thing to note that one is "sensitive" to the ways of other cultures and individuals, but another to create a culturally safe space. With an Indigenous lens, the author explores the necessity of cultural safety for colonized Indigenous populations. Chapters 11 and 12 explore the intersection more generally of cultural diversity in the classroom and how students are supported in the context of disability. In the presence of a disability, families of diverse cultural backgrounds living at the intersection of race, culture, language, and disability often encounter systems and structures that are unable to help them navigate services. This results in a lack of culturally responsive and appropriate services and/or interventions (Blanchett, Klingner, & Harry, 2009).

REFERENCE

Blanchett, W. J., Klingner, J. K., & Harry, B. (2009). The intersection of race, culture, language, and disability: Implications for urban education. *Urban Education*, 44(4), 389–409.

Indigenous

CHAPTER 10

Cultural Safety: A Foundation for Working with Indigenous Students

Joanne Mitchell

THREE KEY IDEAS

1. Cultural safety explores the relationship between Indigenous Peoples and settlers and seeks to build an understanding of the differences between dominant and Indigenous cultures.
2. Understanding Indigenous perspectives can help reconcile relationships and build cultural competence.
3. Education assistants can support Indigenous students in the classroom by understanding practice in the context of cultural safety.

This chapter uses the concept of cultural safety to provide a foundation for education assistants (EAs) to support students with Indigenous ancestry. Cultural safety, a concept developed by the late Maori nursing scholar Dr. Irihapeti Ramsden, is an educational framework for the analysis of power relationships between professionals and those they serve (Ramsden, 2002). Since it is important for all Canadians to understand Indigenous perspectives to reconcile our relationships and build a more just society, culturally safe EAs can influence a broad group of students that includes those from both Indigenous and settler cultures. The term *settler* refers to any Canadian who does not have Indigenous ancestry. It is a term used by a growing number of researchers and academics and is preferred over terms that begin with "non," as in non-Indigenous. Cultural safety is a concept that looks at the relationship between Indigenous Peoples and settlers and seeks to build an understanding of how it came to be that Indigenous Canadians are overrepresented in virtually all negative social statistics.

As Canadian citizens, we have been called to action by the Truth and Reconciliation Commission (TRC) of Canada to examine the strategic implementation and devastating consequences of the Canadian residential school system, and to work toward reconciliation of the relationship between Indigenous Canadians, the Government of Canada, and settler Canadians. When a government's policies and actions harm its own people, truth commissions are enacted to reveal the crimes (truth) and offer formal apologies and reparations (reconciliation). Dozens of truth commissions have taken place around the world, from South Africa, Chile, and Sierra Leone, to the United States, Rwanda, Peru, and Nepal, and, of course, Germany, where the Nuremberg trials were held following World War II. They are a national response with an international audience.

> Too many Canadians know little or nothing about the deep historical roots of these conflicts [between Indigenous Peoples and the government]. This lack of historical knowledge has serious consequences for First Nations, Inuit, and Métis peoples, and for Canada as a whole. In government circles, it makes for poor public policy decisions. In the public realm, it reinforces racist attitudes and fuels civic distrust between Aboriginal peoples and other Canadians. Too many Canadians still do not know the history of Aboriginal peoples' contributions to Canada or understand that by virtue of the historical and modern Treaties negotiated by our government, we are all Treaty people. History plays an important role in reconciliation; to build for a future, Canadians must look to, and learn from, the past. (TRC, 2015, p. 14)

A cultural safety framework addresses the TRC Calls to Action by guiding individuals toward a deeper understanding of themselves as individuals and as Canadians. It was originally developed for those working in nursing, and can be used by EAs in a similar way: "The dream of Cultural Safety was about helping the people in nursing education, teachers and students, to become aware of their societal conditioning and how it has affected them and their practice" (Ramsden, 2002, p. 2). Cultural safety is about more than understanding that there are differences in dominant and Indigenous cultures, and it is not about learning the cultural expressions of Indigenous Peoples; it is about understanding how dominant society's historical and contemporary practices have impacted Indigenous people and cultures. A cultural safety framework allows EAs to analyze their own knowledge base regarding Indigenous issues (what do I know and where did I learn it?), challenge that knowledge base (why and how did this happen?), and consider how it relates to their work in classrooms (how will this help the students in my charge?). They can evaluate themselves individually with regards to their own knowledge base and then choose to address any gaps in their knowledge, as there is a continuum for all Canadians with regards to their understanding of the history, cultures, and worldviews of Indigenous Peoples. When EAs become allies to the Indigenous plight for justice in their homelands, they are then culturally safe to Indigenous children, families, and communities. It is in this space that effective learning assistance thrives. This chapter will guide readers through a learning journey that will stir emotions. You may be feeling some already. Please know that deep learning is always accompanied by emotion. May your spirit of alliance awaken and yearn to know more.

SELF: WHAT DO YOU KNOW ABOUT YOUR ANCESTRAL BACKGROUND?

People are often curious about the culture of Indigenous Peoples. Many Canadians seek out Indigenous cultural expressions like totem poles, arts and crafts, drum songs, performances, and museum exhibits. But beneath the surface of those cultural expressions lies the dark history of the dispossession of land and self-governance and the ongoing oppression of Indigenous Peoples' rights. There is much to know about the beauty and salvation of Indigenous worldviews. But this interest in examining cultures cannot be one way. Settler Canadians should have knowledge of their own culture to understand how it has impacted the culture and well-being of Indigenous Peoples.

Cultural safety theory asks Canadians to understand the dispossession of Indigenous land, culture, and self-determination from the perspective of Indigenous people and their allies. This work is personal, and it is political. In the foreword of settler Canadian Paulette Regan's book *Unsettling the Settler Within* (2010), Indigenous scholar Taiaiake Alfred uses a no-holds-barred approach to name the issue of Canadian indifference to the Indigenous struggles in our country:

> Canadians grow up believing that the history of their country is a story of the cooperative venture between people who came from elsewhere to make a better life and those who were already here, who welcomed and embraced them....
>
> Canadians like to imagine that they have always acted with peaceful good intentions towards us by trying to fix "the Indian problem" even as they displaced, marginalized, and brutalized us as part of the colonial project. Canadians do not like to hear that their country was founded through frauds, abuses and violence perpetrated against the original peoples of this land....
>
> Writing from a settler perspective primarily for other settlers, the author [Regan] avoids the trap that so many non-Native scholars fall into—telling Native people how we must live. Instead, she homes in on what settlers must do to fix "the settler problem." (Alfred, 2010, pp. ix, x)

Regan and Alfred adjust the lens so that an examination of settler culture can come into focus. For example, regarding the public education system, there is clear acknowledgement that Indigenous students are less successful than their settler counterparts; however, a focus on Indigenous children and families as the "problem" is evidenced when school staff identify school readiness, attendance, student learning and behaviour challenges, and lack of parental involvement in the school as the reasons for this lack of success. In contrast, a culturally safe perspective points out that the public education system perpetuates settler standards and norms without acknowledgement of our colonial history and its impact, and consciously or unconsciously teaches a fundamentally foreign worldview. A cultural safety paradigm invites one to consider another viewpoint.

Many Canadians have been socialized in mainstream Canadian culture, where Indigenous perspectives are missing and colonial myths are perpetuated. While there are many Canadians who have some knowledge and respect for Indigenous ways of knowing, others may not have any knowledge or interest. For example, some staff in schools may understand that acknowledging traditional territory is protocol and acting on that protocol is a sign of respect for local First Nations; however, other people seem perplexed by the idea of acknowledging traditional territory and can't even name the larger First Nation let alone the local Bands. A culturally safe EA acknowledges local territory whether they have Indigenous students in their class or not. Ramsden makes the point that "Cultural Safety is a lifetime experience and the basic education programs can only provide the beginning tools for the growth and development of attitude and behaviour change" (Ramsden, 2002, p. 163); therefore, cultural safety for Indigenous people is an outcome that will be reached only when Canadians have increased their own awareness and understanding of colonial history and then taken steps toward acts of reconciliation.

Ramsden (2002) affirms that "Cultural Safety is about the nurse rather than the patient" (p. 6) or, in this case, about the EA rather than the student. Education assistants acting as allies to Indigenous people could not only increase cultural safety in the classroom for students with Indigenous ancestry, but could also raise the awareness of students with settler ancestry and contribute to reconciliation and building a more just society.

To understand Indigenous culture, individuals should first understand their own culture; they can begin by asking themselves the following questions: What is my ancestral background? Where did my family originate? What is my ancestral culture? What do I know about my own family and culture? How long has my family been in Canada? Why did my ancestors leave their ancestral homelands? And, what is Canadian culture? By breaking down the key components of culture—language, music, art, dance, architecture and housing, land base, religion, history, medicines, science and technology, food, governing structures, values, beliefs, and so on—one can see that Canada's "multicultural" society closely resembles the cultures of the colonizing nations of England and France; however, when one looks at the individuals living in our society, one sees a broad makeup of ancestral backgrounds from all over the world. So, we are Canadians by nationality, but our ethnicity or ancestry comes from other places on the planet. A key point for all Canadians to consider is that when those with settler ancestry want to look to their ancestral homelands for a cultural connection, even if they never visit that place, they know it exists. They know that there is a land base that holds their ancestral culture, where people look like them, speak their language, and eat their traditional foods, a place that holds their history, their museums, art, architecture, and music. This is a connection to a part of one's identity. It's important.

For Indigenous people, this is the only place on the planet for that connection. It is where their people have lived for thousands of years, where their entire culture and history resides. We need to reconsider the story that has long been told: Indigenous people were primitive and needed settler culture to "help" them become civilized; Indigenous people had choices about what happened to them. We need to acknowledge that imperializing nations were scouting the globe for lands and resources to take, strategically removed authority, colonized their new-found lands with settlers, and used assimilation strategies that have had terrible consequences for Indigenous Peoples. We also need to understand that there has been resistance to this dispossession by Indigenous Peoples since the beginning; there will always be resistance to assimilation. Indigenous worldview will always exist, here in the homelands of the Indigenous people. We need to reconcile this relationship with honesty, courage, and good intentions. The very best qualities of our multinational society can create a place to be proud of, where all people benefit from our democracy and rich natural resources. We simply must all see ourselves in the quest for reconciliation from our shameful history and ongoing subjugation of Indigenous Canadians.

SOCIETY: WHAT DO YOU KNOW ABOUT CANADIAN AND INDIGENOUS HISTORY AND CULTURE?

A distinct strategy of imperialistic nations is to dispossess Indigenous Peoples from their land (colonization), and to impose their worldview (cognitive imperialism). If the intentions of these nations had been anything other than colonization, there may have been an opportunity for two distinctive and vastly different cultures to explore each other's worldviews. As pointed out by Indigenous scholar Vine Deloria Jr., "the opportunity existed during the first several centuries in which the two groups encountered each other" (2004, p. 4). Instead of the portrayal of Indigenous Peoples as inferior or primitive beings (Cote-Meek, 2014, p. 47), if the opportunity had been taken to discuss philosophical worldviews, the basic principle of Indigenous thought would have been clearly identified: that we are all related to all things. From this principle, family and community relations, environmental and economic perspectives, could have been shared and much learning could have occurred.

So, what happened? How did it come to be that Indigenous Peoples in Canada are the most disadvantaged in society? Why is there such a disproportionately high number of Indigenous people represented in literally all negative social statistics? It all started in Europe some 500 years ago. The Catholic Church held tremendous power and issued papal bulls, official documents sanctioned by the pope. One of these papal bulls was the Doctrine of Discovery, which stated that any lands found by "explorers" could be taken if the lands were not occupied by Christians. The term *explorers* is used with caution because these were not anthropological explorations to see what was out there in the world. On CBC's *Tapestry*, Roxanne Dunbar-Ortiz (2017) summarized that "both Church and state were colonizers with purely economic interests. The exploration of the 'New World' was not a search for Christian converts but a quest for domination, looting, taking the wealth." Add to the Doctrine of Discovery the Terra Nullius decree that means "nobody's land" and you have the mindset of the people who "discovered" North America. The TRC is asking for these doctrines to be denounced (in Calls to Action 45, 46, and 49):

> We call upon all religious denominations and faith groups who have not already done so to repudiate concepts used to justify European sovereignty over Indigenous lands and peoples, such as the Doctrine of Discovery and *terra nullius*.

This historical information counters what many Canadians have believed—that the country was founded by people who negotiated in good faith. There needs to be an examination of how it came to be that the Indigenous Peoples in Canada now have just 0.2 percent of their traditional territory, while Canada claims 99.8 percent of the land (Manuel & Derrickson, 2017). Without a significant land base, culture is at risk. It is important to remember that the slight land base attributed to Indigenous Peoples is largely controlled by Indigenous and Northern Affairs Canada with the authority of the Indian Act.

An Indigenous perspective of Canadian history is that Canada and Canadian society were created at the expense of the Indigenous Peoples. Discussions about Indigenous rights can be uncomfortable at times, as they often include a range of subtle to blatant racist attitudes. It doesn't take long before defences are raised, and people speak of their family's long history in Canada. Anger replaces fear as settler people may feel the threat of their own dispossession as Indigenous Peoples continue to fight for reclamation of lands and self-determination. This is the worst-case scenario that shuts down an empathetic connection to Indigenous self-determination. For many Indigenous people, it can feel culturally unsafe to engage in conversations with co-workers, friends, and some family about Indigenous issues.

Colonization is a tricky thing. It not only dispossesses the Indigenous population from their land and resources, but it also colonizes stolen land with a new population and can "colonize the minds" of both the Indigenous and settler populations so that the process can be carried on unconsciously until it is considered normal. There needs to be an examination of dispossession: Why was it done? How does it continue? How can it stop? Assimilation was never the desire of the Indigenous Peoples. Resistance movements need to be highlighted. It is a fact that wherever anyone stands in North America, they are on the traditional territory of Indigenous Peoples. How do you understand the change from Indigenous self-determination to Indigenous dispossession?

Many researchers acknowledge, irrefutably, that colonizing nations have dispossessed and disadvantaged all Indigenous groups in their own homelands (Berger, 1991; Miller, 1996; Milloy, 1999; Regan, 2010; York, 1989). This dispossession also occurred in other areas of the globe where colonizing nations landed: Australia, New Zealand, and Africa, as well as North and South America. Ironically, many early settlers to Canada were escaping injustice in their own homelands, where religious persecution and lack of opportunity for land ownership left many people oppressed and, at times, unsafe. Deborah Chansonneuve (2005) highlights some of the social conditions in Europe during the time when Europeans were arriving on the shores of what would become Canada between the late 1200s and the end of the 1800s:

> From 1257 to 1816, 500 years of terror were decreed by Papal authority under the "Inquisition" in which over one million people, mostly women and homosexuals, were brutally murdered. Written by a priest, the Inquisitor's handbook entitled *Malleus Maleficarum* recommended that heretics (non-believers in Christianity) and witches be "often and frequently exposed to torture" before burning them alive. (p. 10)

The social conditions in Europe, for anyone who was not Christian, wealthy, white, heterosexual, able-bodied, and male, were incredibly oppressive. Why else would droves of people leave their ancestral homelands to go somewhere they had never been, many with no plans to ever return? Of course, imperialistic nations were invested in encouraging immigration to their "new-found lands," as populating is a key strategy of colonization. Colonists came to Canada from across the Atlantic Ocean with the promise of land ownership. How unfortunate that consideration was not given to the fact that they were being given Indigenous land and would be imposing foreign standards and norms. The opportunity to exchange the best of each other's culture, which existed at the time of contact, was missed.

Imagine the healing that can take place if Canadians can seek to understand an Indigenous perspective of Canadian history. How would it help Indigenous children in their classrooms to have their perspectives presented in a mainstream classroom? How would it benefit the Indigenous struggle for self-determination to have all students, Indigenous and settler, learn the truth about colonization and its impacts? We have the power to settle land claims, to return self-determination, to share in the richness of our country. It begins with a commitment to learning what happened and listening to proposed solutions from Indigenous voices.

CLASSROOM: HOW DO YOU SUPPORT THE INDIGENOUS STUDENTS IN YOUR CLASSROOM?

Nella Nelson has been the coordinator of Greater Victoria School District's Aboriginal Nations Education Division for over 30 years. She is a Kwakwaka'wakw woman who is rich in cultural teachings and a skilled administrator. One of her key messages with regards to working with Indigenous students is to understand the diversity within this population. There are 615 First Nations across Canada, comprising 10 distinct larger Indigenous language families and speaking at least 60 different Indigenous languages. The west coast Nations are as different from the prairie Cree as Germans are from the French in Europe, with different languages, foods, music, art, and so on. On Vancouver Island, there are three Island Nations (the Coast Salish on the south and southeast coast, the Nuu Chah Nulth Nation on the west coast, and the Kwakwaka'wakw Nation on the north and northeast coast) with dozens of Bands within each Nation. Each of these Nations has its own language, songs, art, traditions, and so on. Headdresses are not local. Totem poles do not exist on the Prairies. So, it is important for Canadians to learn the cultural nuances of the local Indigenous Peoples where they live.

Nelson also teaches that students with Indigenous ancestry may be from very traditional communities where culture is still vibrant, or they may have very little understanding of their indigeneity. There are students who speak traditional languages, participate in cultural activities, and take great pride in their heritage. And, there are students whose families have been distracted by the impacts of colonialism and who might have less awareness of their indigeneity and of colonial history. Some students may not want to be identified as different, so speaking to them about their ancestry might not be welcome. Adaptability is key when educators are building relationships with students in their classrooms.

Allies seek out authentic Indigenous voices to learn what is needed to support Indigenous self-determination. There will often be Indigenous staff working in schools who can be very helpful as team members for supporting Indigenous children and for providing clarification on issues. School districts often have an Indigenous department with resource people and countless books, games, puzzles, curriculum, and other resources for enhancing learning in the classroom. It is helpful for EAs to know the Indigenous serving agencies in their area (like Friendship Centres) that offer resources for supporting Indigenous students and their families. These agencies are often involved with students for social, emotional, recreational, and cultural supports.

Education assistants who acknowledge the local First Nations and territory act as allies to Indigenous students in the classroom and help educate all students to acknowledge territory. This builds cultural safety and trust with Indigenous students and supports a working relationship. It is important for EAs to learn as much as possible about the local First Nations to be able to highlight current events and opportunities for the class to increase their understanding of Indigenous Peoples, land, and culture. For example, if an EA finds out that the local First Nations are involved in Longhouse Culture, they will learn that this is a highly important educational experience for those students, and their families and communities. This might mean that students are occasionally or frequently away from school during this time, depending on their family's involvement. An EA does not have to know what happens in the Longhouse to understand that this is important learning. Culturally safe EAs support students to stay involved in key classroom learning, while giving them space to transition between the two worlds of mainstream education and cultural education. Connection with family is important so that both family and school can mitigate the changes experienced by students as they shift from one culture to the other.

Before meeting new students, it can be helpful for the EA to find some background information by looking at student files and talking to teachers and former assistants to learn what might be helpful to know about the student. For example, a student might find it confusing when someone asks what Band they are from, but if the EA has already learned through their own research that the student is from the local First Nation, they would then have an understanding that this student has a broad support system with many relatives, as opposed to a student whose ancestry is from out of province or district. Other information can be learned about Indigenous students' communities and perhaps similarities to the EA's culture can be highlighted. This supports relationship building between the two, and hence a more effective learning assistance environment.

The cultural safety framework asks EAs to understand the history of our country from the perspective of Indigenous Peoples. It reframes our colonial paradigm to ask how the settler culture of our country has displaced Indigenous Peoples and the consequences that have followed. This chapter is largely a plea for EAs to engage in this learning because it is the foundational knowledge that will open the doors to culturally safe practice, which, in turn, draws Indigenous students and their families into a working relationship with students' educational support system. This is the goal. As a cognitive shift (mental) recognizes the injustice (emotional), students engaging in a cultural safety framework (physical) make moves toward reconciliation (spiritual). This is not easy work.

We need great courage to address injustice and sometimes it is emotionally exhausting. Please do not give up trying. Many times, Canadians will feel offended by an Indigenous person's reprimand and take it as evidence that they should stop trying. You will make mistakes in your quest to become culturally safe, but please do not give up trying. It demonstrates a commitment to social justice and Indigenous people welcome your alliance.

Voices from the Field

Donna Sinclair has been an Aboriginal EA for over 30 years in the Greater Victoria School District. One of her key messages for anyone working with Indigenous students echoes that of Nella Nelson: understand that there is a spectrum of indigeneity and awareness of indigeneity. There are students from families or communities where culture is strong, and these students are balancing two worlds. There are also students who have some understanding of their culture, and others who know little to nothing. Donna and Nella ask that education staff check assumptions about what students might know about their ancestry and understand that kids do not want to be "put on the spot" to talk about Indigenous issues. Donna builds relationships with students and says that the key place to do that is on the playground before and after school and during breaks. She lets students know that they are part of a school family, and that other students are their school brothers and sisters and she is like a school auntie or mom. She reminds students of the school rules, so that the children see consistency with directions. Donna also believes that getting to know parents after school when they are picking up their children helps to build the relationship between student, school, and her role as a classroom helper. She can remind parents of their child's permission forms or learn about upcoming changes in the family through casual conversation. She speaks from many years of experience and being very comfortable about her role, but she also truly loves children and finds a way to help any student who may be in need of assistance. She is a strong advocate for "raising the bar" and insisting that students do their best work.

CRITICAL THINKING QUESTIONS

1. What does Donna mean by developing a relationship with children and what would be the benefit of that to an EA?
2. Why do some Indigenous students have little knowledge of their indigeneity?
3. How would an EA know that they are considered culturally safe by Indigenous students?

REFERENCES

Alfred, T. (2010). Foreword. In P. Regan, *Unsettling the settler within: Indian residential schools, truth telling, and reconciliation in Canada* (pp. ix–xi). Vancouver: UBC Press.

Berger, T. R. (1991). *A long and terrible shadow: White values, Native rights in the Americas*. Vancouver/Toronto: Douglas & McIntyre.

Deloria Jr., V. (2004). Philosophy and the tribal peoples. In A. Waters (Ed.), *American Indian thought* (pp. 3–11). Boston: Blackwell.

Dunbar-Ortiz, R. (2017, June 30). Reclaiming Indigenous spirituality. *Tapestry* [Radio program]. CBC Radio.

Chansonneuve, D. (2005). *Reclaiming connections: Understanding residential school trauma among Aboriginal People*. Ottawa: Aboriginal Healing Foundation.

Cote-Meek, S. (2014). *Colonized classrooms*. Halifax/Montreal: Fernwood Publishing.

Manuel, A., & Derrickson, Grand Chief R. (2017). *The reconciliation manifesto: Recovering the land, rebuilding the economy*. Toronto: Lorimer.

Miller, J. R. (1996). *Shingwauk's vision: A history of Native residential schools*. Toronto: University of Toronto Press.

Milloy, J. S. (1999). *A national crime: The Canadian government and the residential school system 1879 to 1989*. Winnipeg: University of Manitoba Press.

Ramsden, I. (2002). *Cultural safety and nursing education in Aotearoa and Te Waipounamu*. Doctoral thesis, Wellington University, New Zealand.

Regan, P. (2010). *Unsettling the settler within: Indian residential schools, truth telling, and reconciliation in Canada*. Vancouver: UBC Press.

Truth and Reconciliation Commission of Canada. (2015). *Honouring the truth, reconciling for the future: Summary of the final report of the Truth and Reconciliation Commission of Canada*. Winnipeg: Author.

York, G. (1989). *The dispossessed: Life and death in Native Canada*. Toronto: Lester and Orpen Dennys Publishers.

Intercultural

CHAPTER 11

Response-able Pedagogy: Fostering a Culturally and Linguistically Responsive Educational Environment

Greg Ogilvie

THREE KEY IDEAS

1. Response-able pedagogy creates a supportive, inclusive learning community.
2. Response-able pedagogy builds bridges to learning.
3. Response-able pedagogy promotes a rich linguistic environment.

Canada is a multicultural nation that prides itself on its diverse demographics. The continued commitment of the Canadian government to immigration and refugee resettlement means that the diversification of the population will continue. As demographics in schools inevitably reflect trends in the broader population, cultural and linguistic diversity will continue to characterize Canadian classrooms as well. This is significant because language and culture act as mediators of educational experiences, facilitating (or potentially inhibiting) classroom interactions and the exploration of subject matter. Therefore, educators who treat learners as culturally homogeneous and ignore the linguistic resources students bring to the classroom will inevitably inhibit the learning opportunities created for all students, but most significantly those who come from culturally and linguistically diverse backgrounds. To create an environment that recognizes and values heterogeneity and builds on learners' backgrounds and experiences to facilitate learning, educators must engage in pedagogy that is linguistically and culturally responsive, or what is referred to in this chapter as *response-able pedagogy*.

Response-able pedagogy is grounded in intercultural education, relational pedagogy, and second-language acquisition research. It applies a strength-based approach that not only recognizes the value of cultural and linguistic heterogeneity, but also draws on diversity as a resource within the classroom. As the name predicates, response-able pedagogy facilitates relational connections (with peers, with content) within the classroom that enable students to engage with and respond to material in a meaningful manner to foster learning and personal growth. This chapter explores how response-able pedagogy (1) creates a supportive, inclusive learning community, (2) builds bridges to learning, and (3) promotes a rich linguistic environment. It examines each of these areas associated with response-able pedagogy by elaborating on associated principles and highlighting numerous strategies that can be utilized in the classroom. In order to enhance connections to the classroom, the voices of education assistants (EAs) working with diverse populations have been included throughout the chapter.

RESPONSE-ABLE PEDAGOGY CREATES A SUPPORTIVE, INCLUSIVE LEARNING COMMUNITY

When children enter the classroom, they do not check their social, emotional, spiritual, or cultural selves at the door. On the contrary, students' identities and lived experiences greatly impact not only the learning that takes place, but all aspects of classroom life. When students' needs are unmet or they are struggling with conditions in their lives, participating in the learning process becomes less of a priority. This poses a challenge for many students, but in particular students from immigrant families who have had to deal with significant transitions in life, such as relocating to a new country or adapting to a new language and culture. For refugee families, the transition is even more difficult, as they often have to deal with trauma and a sense of displacement associated with forced migration (typically due to war or political and economic instability). Moreover, when children are exclusively exposed to classroom practices and materials that do not resonate with their lived experiences or identity, it makes it difficult for them to feel like valued members of the learning community. In such contexts, it is difficult for culturally and linguistically diverse students to thrive. In response, classrooms based on response-able pedagogy (1) promote holistic growth, and (2) value diversity.

Principle 1: Promote Holistic Growth

Educators bring a considerable amount of expertise to the classroom in the form of pedagogical content knowledge—knowledge about subject-specific content and instructional strategies to support learning. Nonetheless, if educators do not obtain knowledge about their students, it will be difficult for them to cater to individual needs in the creation of a productive learning environment. That is why it is important to adopt a relational approach to pedagogy—one in which pedagogical decisions are grounded in relations rather than fixed notions of teaching. In order to adopt a relational approach, it is essential for educators to get to know students, not just as learners, but also as human beings. One EA, Abigail, stated, "Instead of right away wanting to help them to learn the content, have an attitude of let me get to know you and I am going to let you know me too." Establishing rapport with students who speak limited English can be difficult, but EAs can use non-linguistic means to support the process. For example, Sabina explained, "With one of my students who doesn't speak English at all, it is just smiling. That is how I started a relationship with her.... She started coming and communicating with me more, like just by actions or drawing a picture of something, but she started to communicate." By demonstrating interest in the student and creating opportunities for communication, Sabina was gradually able to establish rapport with her. The process of establishing relationships is different with each student and requires patience and cultural sensitivity. For example, Sofia explained how a newly arrived student was inducted into her classroom in a gradual, supportive manner. This entailed "slowly trying to help her. Just maintaining our distance and being respectful of her boundaries because her culture is so different than our culture.... It is a lot of trial and error. What works with one student, doesn't work with all the other students." Sofia understood the influence of culture on relationship building, but she also recognized that many students have had traumatic experiences leading up to their arrival in Canada. As a result, she understood the importance of gradually building trust over time.

Establishing a trusting relationship is critical to the work of educators, as it facilitates identifying learners' actual needs. When students enter the classroom, we make assumptions about their needs based on previous experiences; however, we cannot truly understand their needs until we have established a trusting relationship based on open communication. Abigail commented, "We need to get to know them as individuals, know what they need, where they are at, their background, where they are coming from too, to advocate for their individual needs." This is particularly significant when working with immigrant or refugee students because their needs will often expand beyond academics. Sofia relayed a story about a student whose basic needs were not being met. Although the student seemed to be adjusting well to life in Canada, Sofia learned that her family was struggling to put food on the table. Similarly, a number of the EAs provided examples of culture shock and the influence of traumatic experiences associated with forced migration on student adaptation. According to Maslow's hierarchy of needs, basic needs (such as physiological and safety needs) and psychological needs (such as a sense of belonging) need to be met before self-actualization will be possible. In the context of the classroom, this means that students' needs associated with their relocation and adaptation to Canada need to be met in order for substantive academic learning to take place.

Understanding this, Abigail commented, "We need to understand what they are going through and make sure that the expectations in their learning don't conflict with their emotional wellness." Abigail was not downplaying the importance of academics, but rather highlighting how learning can only take place when students' holistic needs as human beings are attended to.

Once relationships have been established and learners' actual needs identified, educators can begin to attend to them. Abigail articulated, "If we as teachers and EAs know what is happening, that this is a true struggle, then we can address it with the student in a loving and caring way." For her student whose family was struggling to meet their basic needs, Sofia addressed the situation by finding funding to support the purchase of groceries. In other contexts, adaptation was supported through community-building activities (e.g., circle talks while sharing tea), field trips, grief counselling, and communication books where educators and students could communicate about their general well-being.

Principle 2: Value Diversity

Feeling safe and supported in the classroom not only involves addressing students' basic needs, but also being a part of a community that values the diversity they represent. Supporting diversity can be done in very overt, tangible ways, such as with the rules established for the classroom. Rules that prevent students from bringing their cultural identity into the classroom inhibit the participation of those students. For example, English-only policies require students to renounce their mother tongue in order to be accepted in the classroom. Although English-only policies are often grounded in a pedagogical rationale, they create an untenable situation for students by eliminating diversity from the classroom. That is why Sofia stated, "We do obviously teach in English and we try to make them [the students] use English as much as possible, but … there are no rules about them speaking their language in the class—they are encouraged to do so." In the classrooms in which the EAs worked, students' heritages were welcomed through the rules established.

Valuing diversity can also be achieved through representation in classroom materials. If the resources present in the classroom (e.g., posters, books, artifacts) are ethnocentric, it relays a clear message about the value of additional cultures. To combat this, educators can decorate the classroom and include learning materials that represent the values and accomplishments of various cultures. For example, when exploring the concept of democracy, educators could introduce learners to the ideas of the Iroquois Confederacy. This would not only challenge Eurocentric notions about the origins of modern governments, but would also help to foster an appreciation for the contributions of different societies from around the world. Abigail noted the benefits of incorporating students' cultures into the fabric of the classroom: "There is just so much richness that can be shared when students come from different countries and I think it really bridges understanding our humanity." For her, the inclusion of diverse cultures in the curriculum both supported the creation of an inclusive environment and enhanced the learning experience for all students. She explained, "We are a multicultural society and we need to see how valuable and how rich other cultures are … and to foster a classroom that is open to learning about new cultures and new ideas and new ways of thinking and living and experiencing the world."

While diversity can be promoted in tangible ways, such as through the rules and materials utilized in the classroom, it can also be supported in more tacit ways, for example through the creation of co-operative classroom structures (Sapon-Shevin & Schniedewind, 1991). When competitive structures are utilized in a classroom, a hierarchy is created based on desired skills and knowledge. As the acquisition and demonstration of such knowledge is tied to linguistic and cultural norms, those who are not familiar with these norms are inevitably disadvantaged and labelled as deficient. In an environment characterized by struggle between students to acquire rewards (whether in the form of marks, recognition, or some other tangible benefit), support for and interaction with those labelled as deficient is unlikely to occur. Hence, classrooms that track and reward individual achievement based on comparisons with others not only devalue the contributions of linguistically and culturally diverse students, but also isolate them from peer support and interaction that could significantly enhance the adaptation process. In contrast, Sapon-Shevin and Schniedewind (1991) highlight that co-operative classroom structures "foster interpersonal communication, creative conflict resolution, and the valuing of differences" (p. 174). A co-operative ethos, thus, can enhance cross-cultural empathy and understanding, and help to highlight diversity as a strength, leading to new ways of viewing the world, rather than a deficiency. Co-operative learning has the additional benefit of closely resembling the cultural values and learning styles of many minority groups (Gay, 2010).

RESPONSE-ABLE PEDAGOGY BUILDS BRIDGES TO LEARNING

In addition to requiring that students feel safe and welcomed in the classroom, response-able pedagogy also requires that supports be provided to enhance learning. Some newly arrived immigrant students will have experienced limited formal schooling and, inevitably, many of them will feel a disjuncture when entering Canadian classrooms. Creating optimal learning conditions requires educators to build bridges between learners' cultural backgrounds and lived experiences and the learning environment in which they find themselves. Scaffolding learning by engaging with learners where they are at has a cognitive dimension, as well as an affective dimension. In order for substantive learning to take place, students need to feel that their knowledge is valued and that they can make contributions to the learning environment. As a result, response-able pedagogy creates scaffolds for learning by attending to the following principles: (1) adopt a strength-based approach, and (2) make instruction relevant and relatable.

Principle 1: Adopt a Strength-Based Approach

Research has demonstrated that teacher expectations have a significant influence on student performance (Good & Brophy, 2003). When teachers do not demand excellence from learners based on perceptions of their ability to perform tasks, it can influence interactions between the student and teacher, eventually leading the student to internalize the expectations and adjust their learning behaviours. According to Gay (2010), one of the factors that influences teacher perceptions is the level of coherence between school and home cultures. In other words, teachers may unintentionally demonstrate lower expectations for learners based on their heritage and ethnic identity. To combat this, teachers need to adopt a strength-based approach grounded in the belief that all students can succeed with hard work and proper support.

The first step in adopting a strength-based approach is to critically analyze the perspectives we bring to the classroom as educators. Sabina intimated this when she stated, "Don't be biased. Like for me, I love all the kids. They are kids. Think of them as kids, not what their background or what their religion is. Come with a mentality of open-mindedness." Getting to the point where kids can be viewed as unique individuals does not involve pretending that we do not have any biases, but rather critically analyzing the prejudgments we bring to our interactions. Each individual has unique prejudgments based on one's identity and lived experiences; however, societal norms also have an impact on thinking. For example, Canada has a long colonial history. As written by the Truth and Reconciliation Commission of Canada (2015), "Residential schools were a systematic, government-sponsored attempt to destroy Aboriginal cultures and languages and to assimilate Aboriginal peoples so that they no longer existed as distinct peoples" (p. 107). Residential schools were grounded in the belief of white superiority and the sentiment that the "savage ways" of the Indigenous population needed to be eradicated. Although the last residential school closed in 1996, the remnants of this widely held belief still permeate discourses in the country.

Similarly, language carries historical meanings (including culturally based connotations) that influence how we think about and discuss particular topics (Moore, 1976). For example, the term *developing* is commonly used to describe less affluent countries, while *developed* is used to describe more affluent countries. The use of these terms creates the perception that affluent countries such as Canada have reached the zenith of development, while other countries are still finding their way to be more like us. Hence, a subtle hierarchy is created that can cause people to devalue the achievements of some societies and the people associated with them. Without critically analyzing our beliefs and perceptions, we may unintentionally perpetuate negative attitudes that can influence how we perceive and treat learners.

Another important step in adopting a strength-based approach is recognizing the knowledge and skills students bring to the classroom. A number of the EAs outlined how they did this by engaging in reciprocal teaching. Tigist relayed a story about a student who was very passionate and knowledgeable about the *Titanic*. She recalled, "We looked at books about the *Titanic* and the student taught me how many lifeboats were on the *Titanic* and what time they sailed off and what time they hit the iceberg." Olivia engaged in a similar exchange of knowledge, but in relation to language. She turned classroom learning into a mutually supportive activity in which the student would teach her Spanish while she helped the student to develop her English skills. The approach adopted by the EAs in these instances gave students confidence and a sense of pride by validating their knowledge. Acknowledging students' knowledge and skills does not have to be restricted to accomplishments in the classroom. Ladson-Billings (2009) highlighted a teacher, Dupree, who regularly recognized student achievements unrelated to school. In this way she was able to foster a strength-based mentality in the classroom based on a broader conception of students' talents. By valuing students' knowledge and skills and maintaining high expectations for learners, educators are able to build a bridge to further learning.

Principle 2: Make Instruction Relevant and Relatable

While it is important to adopt a strength-based approach, it is also critical to scaffold learning by making instruction relevant and relatable. Most contemporary theories of learning recognize that knowledge is not acquired in a simple, linear fashion, but rather in an idiosyncratic manner based on lived experiences and previously established knowledge. As a result, the effectiveness of teaching hinges on the ability of educators to create bridges between students' understanding and desired learning. When learners have had limited formal schooling or come from dissimilar cultural backgrounds, creating meaningful connections with academic content can be challenging, but it is imperative to the learning process.

One simple strategy to scaffold learning is to use learners' interests as the beginning point of instruction. By drawing on students' interests, educators can not only build meaningful connections with content, but also enhance students' intrinsic motivation for learning. For example, Ming talked about working with a student who was very passionate about video games. She used this interest to establish rapport with the student, and regularly connected the work they were doing in the classroom back to the video game. She explained the benefits of the approach: "He was able to make connections to the outside world more easily when he could make comparisons to his computer game." Similarly, Tigist sought to use the interests of a young learner to foster linguistic growth. As the boy was unable to speak English, Tigist used observations to ascertain his interests. She articulated, "We would kind of go around the classroom and I would follow him and I noticed he was gravitating toward yellow crayons and yellow blocks, so I determined that yellow was probably his favourite colour." As a result, colours became the initial focus of vocabulary development, followed by the toys found around the classroom.

Another strategy to make content more relatable is to use different modalities. When working with culturally and linguistically diverse students, educators have the dual responsibility of supporting linguistic development and promoting academic growth. As a result, students' mother tongue can be an important tool in enhancing content knowledge. The EAs commonly used translation apps or native-speaking peers to support learners in exploring difficult concepts. In addition to adjusting the language, educators can also adjust the modality to make the concepts more concrete. Abigail commented, "Making it as relevant as possible, you know. If we are talking about learning science and they are learning about the environment, well then let's go and touch it … and experience it as much as possible." This meant using experiments, manipulatives, visuals, and other tools to bring the concepts to life for students. One of my colleagues, Josh Markle, applied this principle to teaching math. He had students who had struggled learning in a classroom setting apply mathematical concepts in the construction of a canoe. The utilization of the concepts in a tangible application made them more relevant and relatable for the students and led to academic success.

A final strategy that is particularly relevant for new immigrants is the use of funds of knowledge to guide instruction. Moll, Amanti, Neff, and Gonzalez (2005) define *funds of knowledge* as "historically accumulated and culturally developed bodies of knowledge and skills essential for household or individual functioning and well-being" (p. 72). The authors advocated that this community-based knowledge could be used to help learners make connections between their lived experiences and the classroom. The authors acquired this knowledge by visiting students' homes and communities and inquiring about their family history (including work history), common household activities, and parenting practices. Several EAs engaged in this practice with the immigrant students in their classrooms and universally expressed the importance of the visits in learning valuable information about their students. Sofia explained, "We learned a lot about students by going on these home visits.... I think we have a better understanding about what each family expects of their kids and how it affects them at school." Understanding students' community-based funds of knowledge helps educators to bridge learner understanding and incorporate cultural mediators into instruction. For example, Kanu (2002) explained how storytelling mediated the learning of Indigenous students who were very comfortable with the approach, as it was commonly utilized in their community.

RESPONSE-ABLE PEDAGOGY PROMOTES A RICH LINGUISTIC ENVIRONMENT

Language serves an important role in creating response-able learning opportunities for students. Language is essential to learning, as it enables sharing and exploration of ideas and makes dialogue about content possible. Moreover, language facilitates internal thought processes or what renowned psychologist Lev Vygotsky (1962) termed "inner speech." As such, language cannot be separated from the learning process, but rather language development must be considered a precursor and complement to learning. This means that all classrooms should be rich linguistic environments, but in particular classrooms with learners of English as an additional language need to be responsive to learners' linguistic needs. Drawing on second-language acquisition research, the following section will outline how a rich linguistic environment that fosters linguistic development can be created based on two central principles: (1) optimize language exposure, and (2) encourage varied language usage.

Principle 1: Optimize Language Exposure

Research has demonstrated that exposure to rich linguistic input promotes language acquisition (Lightbown & Spada, 1999). Anyone who has learned a second language, though, knows that not all forms of input are equally beneficial. The type of language that is most beneficial to acquisition is what Stephen Krashen (1981) labelled "comprehensible input"—language that can be understood because it is at or just above the linguistic competence of a learner. Simply exposing second-language learners to authentic language is not adequate, as care must also be taken to ensure that the language is at the appropriate level.

Numerous strategies can be applied to enhance the comprehensibility of input provided to students in the classroom. One strategy is to use consistent, simple language. This means that colloquialisms should be limited and explained in depth when utilized, and routines of language usage should be promoted (this is one situation where a thesaurus is not beneficial). This does not mean that learners should never be exposed to colloquial or more complex forms of language, but rather that these forms of language should be introduced in a gradual, scaffolded manner. Closely associated with the use of simple language is adjusting speech so that words are clearly enunciated and the cadence of speech is adjusted to a more comfortable pace for learners.

Another strategy to enhance comprehensibility is to use supplements, such as actions and pictures, to reinforce word-meaning connections. In explaining how she supports comprehension, Sofia stated, "Lots of charades and breaking the language down. Just making sure we repeat ourselves as often as possible and draw—we use pictures to help us explain." Abigail explained how she takes learners on exploration walks around the school. She asks learners to point to things they cannot name in English and then provides them with the word and encourages repetition. She also takes a picture of the student with the item and prints it off with the word of the item written below to act as a reference for the learner.

Optimizing language exposure also involves creating diverse opportunities for engaging with language. Once a baseline of literacy skills has been established, textual language can be an important impetus for acquisition. Day and Bamford (2002) advocated for extensive reading as a means to promote linguistic development. Extensive reading involves reading simple texts (readers should understand 95 percent of the words they encounter) of interest for pleasure. This approach has the benefit of promoting reading as an enjoyable activity, which may encourage students to do it more often inside and outside school, and providing an additional source of comprehensible input.

Similarly, interaction with other individuals in the classroom can provide meaningful opportunities for engaging with language. Willis (1996) highlighted that learners in predominantly teacher-led classrooms have minimal opportunities to speak, averaging less than 80 minutes of language production during a 36-week course. This is significant not only because it inhibits the development of speaking ability, but also because dialogue serves an important function in acquiring language. Long (2015) noted that in interactions between a native speaker and non-native speaker, the native speakers would adjust their speech (e.g., using repetition, comprehension checks, and clarification requests) to make the language more comprehensible, which he labelled "negotiation." In a similar vein, Swain (2000) articulated that language production facilitates awareness about gaps in linguistic knowledge and enables learners to test developing language hypotheses. Creating opportunities for learners to engage in meaningful dialogue is an important practice in fostering language development. Educators can organize opportunities to engage in one-on-one interaction with language learners in the classroom; however, structured, meaningful interaction with peers in the classroom is also important. Olivia noted: "Basically allowing [an English language learner] to spend time with the other students and letting him learn from the other students [is important] because I feel that is a huge way that he actually learns English—interaction with other kids." Peer interaction can be facilitated through regular peer or group work, think-pair-share activities, peer tutoring, or any co-operative learning strategy.

Principle 2: Encourage Varied Language Usage

By the time children enter into the school system, they will have experienced approximately five years of linguistic development. As a result, they enter into the classroom with a strong linguistic foundation and the ability to communicate comfortably in social situations, what Cummins (2000) refers to as basic interpersonal communication skills (BICS). During these formative years, they also begin to develop the foundations of more formal forms of language, known as cognitive academic language proficiency (CALP). This is significant when considering the education of newly arrived immigrants with diverse language backgrounds, as their linguistic trajectory, which is closely associated with the ability to develop academic skills and content knowledge, will be quite different. According to Cummins (2000), immigrant children will acquire peer-equivalent conversational fluency in approximately two years, while academic language proficiency comparable to native-speaking peers will take between five and ten years to develop. This is important for a number of reasons. First, it highlights the importance of not making assumptions about students' language development based solely on conversational fluency. Cummins (2000) warned that this practice has resulted in English language learners being erroneously labelled as lazy or diagnosed as requiring non-linguistic learning support. In reality, it is simply a manifestation of the fact that learners have developed the ability to communicate effectively in cognitively undemanding, context-embedded situations (for example, face-to-face interactions), whereas their ability to use language in cognitively demanding, context-reduced situations (academic language usage) is still evolving.

Second, it reinforces the importance of supporting variable linguistic growth encompassing social and academic contexts. As previously mentioned, BICS is developed relatively easily due to the contextual cues (e.g., concrete situations, gestures, immediate feedback) present in face-to-face interaction. Nonetheless, it is important to recognize that students who come from a non-English-speaking community may not experience significant exposure to communicative language in English outside of the school; therefore, it is important to build opportunities for social language engagement into the classroom routine and make students aware of the appropriacy of language usage in different social contexts. Bolitho (2011) highlighted that this requires moving away from traditional classroom interaction that is teacher dominated by encouraging different functional uses of language and the exploration of language in different contexts.

Of course, this must coincide with instruction to scaffold the development of learners' academic language proficiency. One way to do this is to adjust the cognitive complexity or contextual cues associated with pedagogical tasks to make them more accessible for learners until their language proficiency has advanced. A more sustainable form of scaffolding, suggested by Gibbons (2015), involves exploring concepts in decreasing degrees of concreteness and increasingly difficult forms of language. The four-stage model involves (1) engaging with the concept in an experiential manner (e.g., doing an experiment), (2) introducing related vocabulary, (3) making sense of concepts through teacher-guided oral reporting/discussion, and (4) responding in writing to a prompt. Experiencing the concept first helps to contextualize the vocabulary introduced and reinforce word-meaning associations. Moreover, exploring the concept through oral speech with teacher guidance supports the eventual completion of the more linguistically complex written task. Gibbons (2015) articulated that the third stage creates an opportunity for learners to rehearse language and vocabulary that is more closely associated with written discourse, what has been labelled "literate talk."

Naturally, the effectiveness of scaffolding is dependent on educators' ability to model and guide appropriate language usage. This means that subject-specific vocabulary needs to be introduced and reinforced and the structure of genre-specific writing modelled. This is particularly important for English language learners, as the organization and expression of ideas is culturally dependent (Gibbons, 2015). Educators must also provide consistent feedback to highlight areas of growth, while still maintaining learner confidence and the flow of communication. Using recasts, a feedback strategy where the incorrect student utterance is repeated with the correction inserted, can be an effective strategy to achieve this balance.

Encouraging varied language usage in English is important to facilitate linguistic growth, but so is promoting the development of learners' mother tongue. Cummins (2000) advocated that common underlying proficiency is developed when learning a language that can be transferred across languages. Moreover, multilingual competence facilitates cross-language comparisons, which results in a deeper understanding about both languages. As a result, encouraging learners to continue to foster their mother language competence is important to achieving success in the new academic context.

The goal of education is to create opportunities for meaningful exploration resulting in the development of knowledge, skill, and personal growth. Engagement with content and interaction with other learners is highly dependent on language and culture. Therefore, the goal of educators working with linguistically and culturally diverse students is to create a learning community that enables them to respond to educational episodes in a meaningful way. This chapter has outlined several principles that will facilitate a response-able learning environment that (1) creates a supportive, inclusive learning community, (2) builds bridges to learning, and (3) promotes a rich linguistic environment.

Voices from the Field

Tips for new EAs working with linguistically and culturally diverse students:

It is very important to come into this profession knowing that we can do so much for [students] and that we can help them to succeed, but first for that success to happen, there has to be a relationship and there has to be an attitude of empathy and compassion. —Abigail

They should let their teacher know that they are interested in professional development sessions that will help them improve their abilities to work with linguistically and culturally diverse students. They could also ask their teacher about her own ideas about how she intends to work with linguistically and culturally diverse students and together come up with a plan of action. —Ming

You just have to remember that they are students, that they are kids and they should be expected to do as much and have the same expectations put on them as everybody else.... If you treat them differently, then they will see themselves as different and they won't ever reach that same potential that you put towards everybody else. —Olivia

Build relationships, first thing.... Come with that mentality of open-minded-ness that they are all kids and they have experienced things in their lives but now we can make a change. —Sabina

To first start off, just establish a relationship with the students. Have no expectations about any academics, academics is always second in here. I would tell them to first establish that relationship and to work with the teacher too to make sure you are on the same page. —Sofia

Be open to learn everything you can, would be my suggestion. Because if you are expecting to help someone to be in a linguistically and culturally rich environment, you need to expand your knowledge on their culture that they are coming from and understand their perspective. You are going to

Continued

have people coming from a different culture who might have a different way of understanding the world and if you are going to go in and try to help them learn about yours, you have to be open to have that give and take. —Tigist

CRITICAL THINKING QUESTIONS

1. What school or classroom structures inhibit the participation of linguistically and culturally diverse students? How could they be adjusted to be more inclusive?
2. How is learning connected to one's cultural heritage? How can this be used to enhance learning for all students?
3. In what ways can we foster language development in the classroom?

REFERENCES

Bolitho, R. (2011). Teacher talk and learner talk. *European Centre for Modern Languages*. Retrieved from archive.ecml.at/mtp2/grouplead/results/lucru/4/rod.pdf

Cummins, J. (2000). *Language, power and pedagogy: Bilingual children in the crossfire.* Clevedon, UK: Multilingual Matters.

Day, R., & Bamford, J. (2002). Top ten principles for teaching extensive reading. *Reading in a Foreign Language, 14*(2), 136–141.

Gay, G. (2010). *Culturally responsive teaching: Theory, research, and practice.* New York: Teachers College Press.

Gibbons, P. (2015). *Scaffolding language, scaffolding learning: Teaching English language learners in the mainstream classroom.* Portsmouth, NH: Heinemann.

Good, T. L., & Brophy, J. E. (2003). *Looking in classrooms* (9th ed.). Boston: Allyn and Bacon.

Kanu, Y. (2002). In their own voices: First Nations students identify some cultural mediators of their learning in the formal school system. *Alberta Journal of Educational Research, 48*(2), 98–121.

Krashen, S. (1981). *Second language acquisition and second language learning.* Oxford: Pergamon Press.

Ladson-Billings, G. (2009). *The dreamkeepers: Successful teachers of African American children* (2nd ed.). San Francisco: Jossey-Bass.

Lightbown, P. M., & Spada, N. (1999). *How languages are learned* (2nd ed.). Oxford: Oxford University Press.

Long, M. (2015). *Second language acquisition and task-based language teaching.* West Sussex, UK: Wiley Blackwell.

Moll, L., Amanti, C., Neff, D., & Gonzalez, N. (2005). Funds of knowledge for teaching: Using a qualitative approach to connect homes and classrooms. In N. Gonzalez, L. C. Moll, & C. Amanti (Eds.), *Funds of knowledge: Theorizing practices in households, communities, and classrooms* (pp. 71–87). New York: Routledge.

Moore, R. B. (1976). *Racism in the English language: A lesson plan and study essay.* New York: Racism and Sexism Resource Center for Educators.

Sapon-Shevin, M., & Schniedewind, N. (1991). Cooperative learning as empowering pedagogy. In C. E. Sleeter (Ed.), *Empowerment through multicultural education* (pp. 159–178). Albany: State University of New York Press.

Swain, M. (2000). French immersion research in Canada: Recent contributions to SLA and applied linguistics. *Annual Review of Applied Linguistics, 20,* 199–212.

Truth and Reconciliation Commission of Canada. (2015). *What we have learned: Principles of truth and reconciliation.* Retrieved from http://nctr.ca/reports.php

Vygotsky, L. S. (1962). *Thought and language.* Cambridge, MA: Massachusetts Institute of Technology Press.

Willis, J. (1996). *A framework for task-based learning.* Harlow, UK: Addison Wesley Longman.

CHAPTER 12

The Role of Education Assistants in Helping "Young Ambassadors" Form Self-Determined Identities

Jeffrey MacCormack and Lindsay Morcom

THREE KEY IDEAS

1. Identity formation is complicated for students who embody "differences" in the classroom.
2. Exceptional students and Indigenous students may need some support developing self-determined identities.
3. Education assistants can support students' development through a critical theory perspective.

While those starting out as EAs are launching into a unique and generative career, they are also starting in a field that is in the fits of transition and re-vision. For decades, EAs were hired and trained based on a few assumptions about how they might contribute to classroom spaces (e.g., EAs improve struggling students' academic progress). Unfortunately, those long-held assumptions about how EAs support the academic development of struggling students have been challenged by comprehensive longitudinal studies. For reasons that will be unpacked in this chapter, it can no longer be assumed that proximity to EAs leads to enriched and improved student learning. In fact, substantial evidence has suggested that EAs are poorly positioned to do the thing that is expected, which is to facilitate and support academic learning of students.

Prior to 2009, the literature on EAs was uneven, with some studies showing that EAs offer a positive academic contribution (Alborz, Pearson, Farrell, & Howes, 2009; Slavin, Lake, Davis, & Madden, 2011) and others suggesting a negative or null academic contribution (Farrell, Alborz, Howes, & Pearson, 2010; Gerber, Finn, Achilles, & Boyd-Zaharias, 2001). Ambiguity around the contribution of EAs for academic learning may have been why the troubling results of the Deployment and Impact of Support Staff project (DISS; Blatchford et al., 2007; Blatchford, Russell, & Webster, 2012) rang through the industry like a sounding brass. The robust data collection method used by DISS included 700 pupil observations and 100 EA observations, 17,800 survey responses, and 470 interviews. According to the findings of DISS, the contribution of EAs to pupils' academic attainment is significantly negative. Many felt that the results were bizarre and troubling. Even the researchers who conducted the study said that they considered the findings "disappointing and counter-intuitive" (Blatchford et al., 2012, p. 20). So, what does this mean for someone entering the field? Since those challenging findings have become part of the academic conversation around the implementation and deployment of EAs, this chapter is designed to reflect on what EAs may do to contribute to the classroom.

Irrespective of what has been learned in the last 10 years about the contribution of EAs to the classroom, the fact remains that the field of education continues to rely on EAs. In fact, school boards across the country and beyond are relying on EAs more now than ever before—numbers of EAs in England tripled between 2000 and 2016. So, what then is the role of EAs? EAs are well-positioned to support students as they move toward identities that are *self-determined* (Deci & Ryan, 1985), which means EAs can help students be the best version of themselves. To do that, EAs should examine their conceptions of neurodiversity and disability and move from a medical or deficit approach to neurodiversity and disability to an approach informed by critical disability theory where neurodiversity and disability are important parts of a person's identity.

Identity formation tends to be a sticky, often undignified, process. Reflect for a moment on your own path of identity formation. Perhaps you wore dark, gothic clothing for the summer going into grade 10; perhaps you joined the swim team and only drank protein shakes. Individuals try on different roles as they develop a sense of self. Knowing oneself is difficult and, while this is true for nearly everyone, it can be especially true for students with differences. Students with diverse emotional, cultural, social, and cognitive characteristics tend to face extenuating challenges when it comes to understanding themselves in relation to others. For many students with differences, framing their identities within a cultural marker or medical diagnosis means that they form identity within those boundaries. In essence, students embody a representation of their difference and, whether they want to or not, they become young ambassadors of their lived experiences.

We are using the phrase *young ambassadors* to describe the experience of students with differences who are put in a position of representing their life experience to others. For example, a student with muscular dystrophy may be the only person with muscular dystrophy in her grade 4 class. Answering questions about the condition may be a regular part of her daily life. In many ways, she is an ambassador for her lived experiences. We, the authors, are particularly interested in the ways that EAs can contribute positively to the processes these young ambassadors utilize to form healthy identities during childhood and adolescence. This chapter incorporates two case studies to help describe the unique situation of young ambassadors. The first case study is Lowen, an eight-year-old with autism spectrum disorder (ASD). The second case study is Brody, an eight-year-old Anishinaabe student.

CASE STUDY 1: LOWEN

Lowen first heard about ASD from his grade 3 teacher. One of the storytime books was about a child with ASD who was having a hard time making friends. Lowen's teacher finished the book by saying, "And, you may not know this, but we have someone in the class who has autism spectrum disorder; can anyone guess who?" Lowen looked around the room, as surprised as his classmates to hear that someone in the class had ASD. "Lowen does!" his teacher announced. All faces turned to Lowen. From the look on his face, his teacher knew that this was the first Lowen had heard of his own diagnosis. "Oh gosh, Lowen. Didn't your parents tell you about autism?" No, they had not. As it turned out, they had been waiting until the summer to talk to him about his diagnosis. Lowen looked around the classroom at his wide-eyed classmates. A moment ago, he was just another kid in grade 3. Now, there was something that made him different from everyone else. Just then, a classmate of Lowen's leaned over to him and whispered in his ear, "What does autism feel like?"

CASE STUDY 2: BRODY

Brody comes from a tight-knit Anishinaabe family. He spent the first years of his life in a fly-in First Nation community in Northern Ontario. Brody's mother became ill when he was in grade 2, and his family moved to a city in Southern Ontario so that she could receive treatment. Brody started grade 3 there. Brody's first language is Anishinaabemowin, and he is used to learning in a classroom with five other children in a mix of English and Anishinaabemowin. In his new school, he is the only visibly Indigenous child in a multi-ethnic classroom with 25 other students. During a social studies class, his teacher is talking about First Nations communities in the 1800s; his focus is on plains Indigenous Peoples and he refers to buffalo hunting and life in teepees. At the end of the class, the teacher says, "And there are still Indigenous people today. Brody is Indigenous!" Brody feels shy; he doesn't like to be singled out. His teacher in his old school never singled any child out. He is afraid to answer when several children turn to him and ask, "What is it like to live in a teepee?" He knows that his experience in his First Nation community bears no resemblance to what the teacher has talked about, and he doesn't know how to explain that he lives in a house like everyone else.

IDENTITY FORMATION

As suggested in Lowen's and Brody's case study situations, identity formation is a complex process that includes the interplay of factors such as status, self-evaluation, and social comparison. While we hone our perceptions of self throughout our lives, the heavy lifting of identity formation happens during school-aged years. Constructing a sense of self is an uneasy and volatile process, as recognized by Erikson (1969) and Deci and Ryan (1985), and much of it is done in school spaces. Beyond the clanging, sharp-edged challenges that come along with identity construction of all students, developing a healthy sense of self can be uniquely effortful and wrought with tension for students with intellectual, emotional, social, or cultural differences. An EA may work with a middle-grade Blackfoot student who is dyslexic as she navigates the complexity of grade 7 social spaces; along with the additional challenges of representing indigeneity to her mostly white classmates, she must navigate the academic difficulties that her learning disability presents. Or an EA may meet a grade 4 student with low hearing and support him while he shares all of the hitches developing a sense of self that are typical of that age group, while explaining his life with audio technologies.

There is not enough space in this chapter to fully discuss the complex construct of identity formation; however, it is important to recognize the influence of group membership, especially in classroom spaces, as a component of development of identity. Identity is not discovered in isolation. As described by Neisser (1997), understanding oneself requires seeing the self as "embedded in its environment, ecologically and socially situated in relation to other objects and persons" (p. 19). It can be a harsh lesson but knowing where one does *not* fit is an essential step in knowing where one does fit. Unpleasant as the process can often be, social exclusion and boundary maintenance are steps in the process of understanding oneself. It will likely be no surprise to the reader that students can be singularly brutal when it comes to identifying differences in peers, as noted by Erikson (1969):

> Young people can become remarkably clannish, intolerant, and cruel in their exclusion of others who are "different," in skin color or cultural background, in tastes and gifts, and often in entirely petty aspects of dress and gesture arbitrarily selected as the signs of an in-grouper or out-grouper. (p. 132)

Classmates are not the only ones who identify out-grouper students with external labels. Educational institutions also designate and categorize students with labels that may be perceived as something undesirable (e.g., learning disabilities, attention deficit) or something benevolent (e.g., giftedness). Winzer (2008) argued that labels that are used in educational settings reflect the social need to align student needs with educational supports and do not necessarily suggest pejorative or discrediting meaning. Regardless of the purpose or intention of the use of educational labels, explicit labels made by psychologists and educators affect the perspectives of self as they are developed by children and adolescents during formative school-aged years (Lo, 2014). As with any label (e.g., race, culture, gender), labels related to ability often come with stereotypes. In short, during identity formation, students with differences face the additional challenge of being told who they are by peers and institutions. In consideration of the time children spend in classrooms while navigating issues of identity, it falls on educators to help. Children need to be active participants in their identity formation; for children who labour under the weight of explicit labels, the need for self-determination is perhaps even greater.

WHAT CAN BE LEARNED FROM CRITICAL THEORY?

Supporting identity development of students is where EAs can benefit from learning about intersectional critical theories. In current educational circles, neurodiversity and disability tend to be pathologized; that is, people with neurodiversity or disability are diagnosed using formal medical or psychometric testing and then assigned a label, much like an illness. For example, think about the description that someone *suffers from* autism or cerebral palsy. The word *suffers* is important here because it suggests that the lived experience is something negative that must be endured. Neurodiversity and disability are treated as problems to be solved, and it is made the EA's job to solve the problem and help the child perform more like their typical peers. The goal in that way of thinking is to get rid of the person's condition of neurodiversity or disability to let their "real" self come through. In reality, however, from a critical disability standpoint, neurodiversity or disability are integral parts of people's identities. At the same time, they are not the individual's *whole* self—for example, Lowen's autism is a part of who he is, but autism is not all that Lowen is. While neurodiversity and disability certainly present challenges to people who live with them, they also present strengths and opportunities, and they inform the development of an individual's concept of self.

This is where the worlds of critical disability theory and critical race theory intersect. Historically in many colonial contexts, the same approach that is often applied to individuals who are neurodiverse or have disabilities was applied to Indigenous Peoples. That is, indigeneity was seen as a deficit, and education was heralded as the path forward to assimilating Indigenous people into colonial society. For example, in a Canadian context, Indigenous children were removed from their families and forcibly placed in residential schools for the purposes of assimilation (Truth and Reconciliation Commission, 2015). In recent years, Canadian society has come to realize the consequences of that approach: not only has it produced tragic outcomes for Indigenous families and communities that were robbed of their heritage, languages, and cultures, it has also robbed Canadian society of the richness of Indigenous knowledges and a full understanding of the land on which we live and the history of the places we call home. Luckily, the resilience of Indigenous communities and the courageous commitment of generations of knowledge keepers means that Indigenous cultures, languages, and knowledges are alive, and we can now use education to pass them on to future generations.

To that end, all school boards in Ontario are required to include Indigenous perspectives in their classrooms (Ontario Ministry of Education, 2007). Many school boards have hired Indigenous education experts (IEEs). Like EAs, IEEs are educators who work in schools but who do not tend to work as classroom teachers. Instead, they are tasked with supporting Indigenous students in their academic success and their development of healthy and proud cultural identity. IEEs also support teachers' professional development and help them indigenize content and pedagogy. Finally, they visit classrooms and work with students of all heritages to help them understand the beauty of Indigenous cultures and celebrate the diverse contributions of Indigenous people (Morcom, 2017). For children like Brody, they are an anchor and a bridge. On the one hand, they can help Indigenous children connect their school and home cultures, help them deal with challenges, give access to important cultural teachings, and make school feel more familiar and more relevant. On the other hand, they can work with whole classes to answer the questions that these children do not want to or cannot answer. They can also work with teachers to help include and celebrate children's heritage in a way that is appropriate to and reflective of their specific culture. That means that a child like Brody no longer has to be a young ambassador whose role it is to teach his classmates and teachers about being Indigenous. The IEE can free Brody from that responsibility while at the same time giving him support to figure out who he is and how he fits into his classroom and communities.

WHAT IS SELF-DETERMINATION?

Just as everyone has the physical need for food, water, and shelter, according to Deci and Ryan (1985), everyone has basic psychological needs: competence, relatedness, and autonomy. As students learn to fulfill those basic needs, they move toward living self-determined lives. Where do these fundamental needs fit into the classroom? Do teachers actually teach that? Very rarely, actually. The majority of educators do not use formal instruction programs for self-determination and only one in five educators report feeling prepared to teach those skills (Wehmeyer, 2007); therefore, there is a great need for EAs to support students' self-determination. Unfortunately, supporting the fundamental needs of students is not an easy task and, the evidence has shown, EAs are not always well positioned to provide that support. The following sections describe the classroom applications of the needs that are integral for self-determination: (1) competence, (2) relatedness, and (3) autonomy.

Competence

What does the word *competence* bring to mind? Possibly the development of skills? Fulfilling the fundamental need for competence requires more than the development of skills. In this context, competence actually means *effectance*. Effectance is a constant interaction with our environment by which we can have an *effect* on our world (Deci & Ryan, 1985; White, 1959). According to White (1959), humans are healthiest when they are "alive, active, and up to something" (p. 315). People do not shy away from challenging tasks; in fact, evidence from decades of behavioural and empirical psychology demonstrates that, from early years throughout our lives, we seek out difficult puzzles because we want to accomplish them! The desire to engage with one's environment begins in infancy and lasts throughout life. That desire to be *up to something* means that, as humans and as students, people do best when they can interact with their world. How can EAs help students improve their effectance?

Learn the Content

Education assistants are commonly asked to teach content outside their expertise and comfort zone. Blatchford et al. (2012) described an EA who incorrectly taught a student how to round numbers. When it comes to supporting young ambassadors, EAs should do some homework of their own. They should find out more about the lived experiences of the student. They may also find that the teacher is a good resource. Even though pupils' learning experiences are directly affected by how much the EA knows (Farr, 2018), many jurisdictions do not include paid hours for EAs to plan and collaborate. Without meaningful opportunities to understand the context and salient features of the content, EAs are often left responding to lessons in reactive rather than proactive ways.

Ask Open, Generative Questions

Interactions that students have with EAs tend to be of lower quality than those students have with teachers; they tend to be more focused on task completion than learning (Webster et al., 2011). Teacher prompts are often designed to enhance student thinking, whereas prompts from EAs tend to give the answers without requiring creative or intellectual effort (Blatchford et al., 2012). Education assistants must avoid the temptation to prompt the right answer as they help students solve problems. This may be a faster way to get the work completed, but it can seriously harm students' sense of competence in the long run.

Relatedness

As mentioned earlier, identity formation is a subjective process. That means that we develop our identity in terms of the perspectives and actions of others. We get to know ourselves through a process of self-rumination during which we understand ourselves in terms of "constant comparison between [one]self and others" (Lo, 2014, p. 289). Recognizing oneself in relation to a social biome is only the first step in identity formation. Students must also find the balance between community membership and singularity as they reconcile conflicting needs for group assimilation and differentiation (Brewer, 1991). Optimally, students seek easy membership in a larger group while demonstrating individuality. Finding the balance between sameness and differentness can be difficult for young ambassadors for whom the process of getting to know oneself tends to be completed under the banner of difference. How can EAs help them find this balance?

Be Approachable

Student interactions with EAs tend to be more personalized and less formal than student interactions with teachers (Webster et al., 2011). Education assistants "bring a wealth of experience, creativity and passion to the classroom" (Harris & Aprile, 2015, p. 160) and see their roles as "supporting the pupil, the teacher, the curriculum and the school" (McVittie, 2005, p. 28). In fact, if the EA is well liked by the class, EA interactions can improve social networks among the children (Giangreco, Edelman, Luiselli, & MacFarland, 1997).

Be Aware

Additionally, students see EAs as a (more or less) constant presence in classrooms (Eyres, Cable, Hancock, & Turner, 2004), and as occupying an important role of "significant other" (Fraser & Meadows, 2008). Education assistants have a role in ensuring that all students have the ability to communicate their needs in the classroom (Mason, 2008). Students reported that they preferred to have at least one EA in their classroom, if not more (e.g., one per "group") (Eyres et al., 2004; Fraser & Meadows, 2008). Students were able to make the distinction between teachers and EAs, seeing EAs as "helpers" they could go to and as an important resource in their classrooms to help them get their work done (Eyres et al., 2004).

Autonomy

Having an EA hovering around can make students feel like they are less capable than other students. Students can *learn* to be helpless when they rely too much on an EA in the classroom. Some research suggests that direct access to an EA may actually harm student learning because the student is separated from the teacher's direct instruction (Webster et al., 2011). As time spent with EAs increases, student interaction with the teacher decreases (Blatchford et al., 2012; Farr, 2018; Giangreco, 2012). Helping students be autonomous should be a central goal for EAs— EAs need to work to put themselves out of a job. The job of the EA is not to help students work through their math problems, but to help students know how to work through their math problems on their own. Autonomy is particularly important when it comes to the role of EAs in the classroom. When children feel autonomous, they feel able to make volitional decisions about their lives. Students need to find resources, stick up for themselves, and make their own decisions. Unfortunately, there are few opportunities for students to make decisions and educators do not feel equipped to teach decision making (Wehmeyer, 2007). How can EAs support student autonomy?

Stand up for Students

An EA is positioned to construct their role as "an advocate whose relationship with the pupil is accepting and supportive" (Farr, 2018, p. 118). As described by Worrall and Steele (2008),

> [EAs] have a vital role to play in helping to create a culture in schools and early years settings, where all levels of ability can be identified and nurtured, where social and emotional needs can be addressed and where exceptional achievement can be celebrated without the youngsters themselves feeling the need to hide their potential because of possible negative reactions from their peers and others. (p. 109)

Teach Students to Stand up for Themselves

Self-advocacy refers to the ability to "stand up for oneself and to advocate on one's own behalf" (Wehmeyer, 2007, p. 60). To be successful self-advocates, students need deliberate support (Lehman, Davies, & Laurin, 2000; Test, Fowler, Wood, Brewer, & Eddy, 2005; Wehmeyer, 2002). Teaching students to self-advocate is a relatively nascent approach, which has roots in women's suffrage, labour movements, and the civil rights movement. Self-advocacy is not something that comes intuitively to students.

WHAT CAN EAs LEARN FROM THE WORK OF IEEs?

Like EAs, IEEs also play an important role in helping students develop in the areas of competence, relatedness, and autonomy.

Competence

Indigenous education experts understand that children growing up in Indigenous families may come to school with ways of knowing, teaching, and learning that are different from their non-Indigenous peers. Their job is to understand those aspects of a child's culture, and then work with the child to help them learn in a way that works for them. They must also help teachers to understand how to integrate culturally appropriate content and pedagogy. That way, the child does not have to change an important part of their identity to fit into the classroom environment or feel like a failure when they find they do not learn through the same pedagogies as their peers. By doing this, IEEs can help Indigenous children understand and celebrate their gifts while still holding strong to their cultural identity. Similarly, EAs can celebrate that students who are neurodiverse or have disabilities are still competent learners—they just learn in different ways from some other people. They can also help peers and teachers learn to interact more effectively and celebrate students' strengths. Finally, many IEEs are themselves Indigenous people, which allows them to relate to students, be role models, and speak with an authentic voice to students and teachers. While most EAs are probably not individuals who are neurodiverse or have disabilities, it is worth increasing efforts to train people who do have these identities as EAs. Imagine what it might mean for a child's developing concept of competence to find out that their EA also learns differently! Imagine what a difference it makes for Indigenous learners to see Indigenous professional role models, and for those who are neurodiverse or have disabilities to get to work with professionals who are also neurodiverse or have disabilities!

Relatedness

Indigenous education experts play a very important role for Indigenous students. First, by organizing Indigenous-focused events and programming, they create opportunities for Indigenous learners to meet other students who may have similar backgrounds and experiences. For students like Brody, who might be the only visibly Indigenous or openly self-identifying child in their class, those opportunities let them experience cultural sameness in a world where they are bombarded by difference. In addition, they can work with students and teachers to dismantle negative stereotypes, share authentic Indigenous knowledge, and understand the diversity of Indigenous individuals and communities.

Education assistants can do similar work. They can provide opportunities for children who are neurodiverse or have disabilities to make friends with others who have similar experiences. They can also help bridge the gaps of difference that might exist between these children and other students and help them find ways to relate to one another.

Autonomy

Indigenous education experts work with Indigenous students to develop autonomy in a culturally appropriate way. For many Indigenous people whose cultures are community-oriented, doing things for their own benefit seems selfish, but doing things for the good of the community is a noble pursuit. Indigenous education experts can help students identify their strengths to seek ways to serve the community. Similarly, EAs can help students who are neurodiverse and have disabilities find ways to use their strengths to contribute meaningfully to their communities. They can then make choices to help them reach their goals of contributing. To do that, however, both Indigenous students and students who are neurodiverse or have disabilities need to have the freedom to focus on the future, rather than being overwhelmed by the challenges of the present. Since these children are often different from their classmates, they might experience bullying, prejudice, or marginalization. In their position, IEEs can fight racism against Indigenous students by educating teachers and other students, and by teaching Indigenous students how to respond to occurrences of racism on their own. Education assistants can take much the same approach in their work.

Historically, EAs have been tasked with working with students who are neurodiverse or have disabilities to help them succeed academically; however, recent studies, particularly the DISS, have suggested that the approach EAs sometimes take can actually have a detrimental effect on student success (Blatchford et al., 2012). One cause for that might be in the approach EAs are taking in relation to working with students who are neurodiverse and have disabilities—namely, trying to get these diverse students to fit into a mainstream mould. This ties into societal concepts of neurodiversity and disability more broadly. Historically, neurodiversity and disability have been placed in a medical context, and people living with neurodiversity and disability have been seen as having, or being, a problem that needs solving; however, critical disability theory teaches us that neurodiversity and disability, while not encapsulating a person's identity, are a critical part of their identity. Children who are neurodiverse and children with disabilities progress through their formative years like anyone else, having to figure out who they are as people, and also having to take into account that they are different in a significant way from those around them. At the same time, they are often placed in the position of a young ambassador who must explain to peers, and even to teachers and other adults, about their lived experiences as a person who is neurodiverse or has a disability.

While we are still working to find new ways for EAs to support learning, EAs are extremely well situated to help when it comes to supporting young ambassadors and catalyzing safe, inclusive spaces (Farrell, 2000; Moran & Abbott, 2002). They are deeply embedded in the culture of the classroom and play a "gluing, quilting and genuinely cementing role in the frequently poor communication between other staff" (Dyer, 1996, p. 191). Teachers overwhelmingly agree that EAs positively affect students' attitudes, social skills, and self-efficacy (Blatchford et al., 2012). The presence of an EA was positively associated with the amount of student engagement in the classroom: an increase in on-task behaviour and a reduction in off-task behaviour (Blatchford et al., 2012). Students also see EAs as important members of their school community (Fraser & Meadows, 2008), in part because students were nine times more likely to have sustained interactions with an EA than with a teacher (44 percent with EAs, 5 percent with teachers) (Webster et al., 2011).

Their unique position means that EAs can play a critical role in identity formation for students who are neurodiverse or have disabilities. To do that effectively, they must move from a deficit model of disability and toward a model where neurodiversity and disability are viewed as elements that contribute to human diversity. In so doing, they can learn a great deal by also understanding other critical approaches, such as critical race theory, and the work of other educators, such as IEEs. Both EAs and IEEs support specific groups of students who may be marginalized in schools. They help them to develop belief in their own competence, build identity in the light of relatedness, or similarity and difference to others, and gain autonomy by advocating for them, helping them learn to advocate for themselves and guiding them in making positive choices for a meaningful future. They also give these students space to grow by removing the burden of acting as a young ambassador, since the EA can take on the role of educating peers and teachers. By approaching their work through a critical disability lens, EAs can help children move beyond a pathologizing, medical, deficit-based approach and into a place of self-determination where neurodiversity or disability, much like culture, form a critical part of personal identity.

Voices from the Field

Revisiting Case Study 1: Lowen

When Lowen started grade 5, a new EA, Claire, was assigned to his classroom. The previous EA used to walk him through his math assignments and, sometimes, kind of slip him the answers. That made it easier, but he didn't always know how to do the assignments alone. When he asked Claire for help with his math, he was surprised to find out that Claire's favourite saying was, "you can DO IT!" The letters in "DO IT!" represented a process with steps for making decisions. Claire explained that the first step to solving any problem is to define the problem. Figuring out our options, she told Lowen, means we have to know what we have and what we need to have. Over time, Lowen learned to think about his strengths and difficulties, and he became less self-conscious of the difficulties he experienced understanding the meaning of other people's statements. It was in November when he started telling people about his diagnosis. At first it felt awkward, but the more he did it the more comfortable he became. One day, Lowen didn't understand something that the substitute teacher said to him as he was about to go for recess: "Oh, it sounds like a great idea that you leave your desk like that!" Lowen told the teacher, "I have autism so sometimes I miss the meaning of what you are saying. I think you are being sarcastic. You don't actually think it is a great idea, do you?" The teacher seemed a little startled, but was quick to clarify: "No, Lowen, I think you should tidy up a bit more before you leave."

Revisiting Case Study 2: Brody

Brody's teacher noticed how embarrassed he seemed when he was singled out in class. The teacher had meant to celebrate Brody's culture and make him feel welcome, but his approach was clearly not successful. The teacher went to see Ms. Wesley, the school board's IEE. Ms. Wesley met with Brody and his family to talk about his home community and his educational experience. Ms. Wesley is Anishinaabe, too; she shared stories about her own school experience with Brody, and she met with him one-on-one on a regular basis to help him understand what he was learning in class and relate it to his experience and culture. She also helped him prepare answers for some of the questions his classmates were asking him. She invited Brody to join in activities with other Indigenous young people. The teacher asked Ms. Wesley to look at his lesson plans and talk about his teaching style. She helped him include more content that was relevant to Brody's culture and to local Indigenous Peoples and taught him more about Indigenous pedagogies. When the teacher started including more local Indigenous content and pedagogy, three more children in the class started talking about their own Indigenous heritage, and Brody felt less alone than he had before. Ms. Wesley also helped the teacher connect with local knowledge keepers to teach content that he felt uncomfortable teaching himself. Brody beamed with pride when the knowledge keeper who came into their classroom greeted everyone in Anishinaabemowin. After the teacher introduced them to each other, Brody chose to stay in at recess and chat with the knowledge keeper in his own language.

CRITICAL THINKING QUESTIONS

1. What biases about ability and ethnicity do I bring to my work as an EA?
2. How might I support young ambassadors as they navigate issues of identity in the classroom?
3. What classroom factors support student self-determination?

REFERENCES

Alborz, A., Pearson, D., Farrell, P., & Howes, A. (2009). *The impact of adult support staff on pupils and mainstream schools: Technical report*. Research Evidence in Education Library. London: EPPI-Centre.

Blatchford, P., Bassett, P., Brown, P., Martin, C., Russell, A., & Webster, R. (2007). *Deployment and impact of support staff in schools: Report on findings from the second national questionnaire survey of schools, support staff and teachers (Strand 1, Wave 2, 2006)*. London: Department of Research and Skills.

Blatchford, P., Russell, A., & Webster, R. (2012). *Reassessing the impact of teaching assistants*. New York: Routledge.

Brewer, M. B. (1991). The social self: On being the same and different at the same time. *Personality and Social Psychology Bulletin, 17*(5), 475–482.

Deci, E., & Ryan, R. M. (1985). *Intrinsic motivation and self-determination in human behavior*. New York: Springer Science and Business Media.

Dyer, H. (1996). Where do we go from here? Issues in the professional development of learning support assistants. *Research in Post-Compulsory Education, 1*(2), 187–198.

Erikson, E. (1969). *Identity, youth and crisis*. New York: W. W. Norton and Company.

Eyres, I., Cable, C., Hancock, R., & Turner, J. (2004). "Whoops, I forgot David": Children's perceptions of the adults who work in their classrooms. *Early Years, 24*(2), 149–162.

Farr, J. (2018). Between a rock and a hard place: The impact of the professionalization of the role of teaching assistant in mainstream school physical education in the United Kingdom. *Sport in Society, 21*(1), 106–124.

Farrell, P. (2000). The impact of research on developments in inclusive education. *International Journal of Inclusive Education, 4*(2), 153–162.

Farrell, P., Alborz, A., Howes, A., & Pearson, D. (2010). The impact of teaching assistants on improving pupils' academic achievement in mainstream schools: A review of the literature. *Educational Review, 62*(4), 435–448.

Fraser, C., & Meadows, S. (2008). Children's views of teaching assistants in primary schools. *Education 3–13, 36*(4), 351–363.

Gerber, S. B., Finn, J. D., Achilles, C. M., & Boyd-Zaharias, J. (2001). Teacher aides and students' academic achievement. *Educational Evaluation and Policy Analysis, 23*(2), 123–143.

Giangreco, M. F. (2012). Teacher assistant supports in inclusive schools: Research, practices and alternatives. *Australian Journal of Special Education, 37*(3), 93–106.

Giangreco, M. F., Edelman, S. W., Luiselli, T. E., & MacFarland, S. Z. (1997). Helping or hovering? Effects of instructional assistant proximity on students with disabilities. *Exceptional Children, 64*(1), 7–18.

Harris, L. R., & Aprile, K. T. (2015). "I can sort of slot into many different roles": Examining teacher aide roles and their implications for practice. *School Leadership and Management, 35*(2), 140–162.

Lehman, J. P., Davies, T. G., & Laurin, K. M. (2000). Listening to student voices about postsecondary education. *Teaching Exceptional Children, 32*(5), 60–65.

Lo, C. O. (2014). Labeling and knowing: A reconciliation of implicit theory and explicit theory among students with exceptionalities. *Journal of Educational Research, 107*(4), 281–298.

Mason, M. (2008). The inclusion assistant: Young people with high-level support needs in mainstream schools, colleges and universities; Developing good practice. In G. Richards & F. Armstrong (Eds.), *Key issues for teaching assistants* (pp. 62–71). New York: Routledge.

McVittie, E. (2005). The role of the teaching assistant: An investigative study to discover if teaching assistants are being used effectively to support children with special education needs in mainstream schools. *Education 3–13, 33*(3), 26–31.

Moran, A., & Abbott, L. (2002). Developing inclusive schools: The pivotal role of teaching assistants in promoting inclusion in special and mainstream schools in Northern Ireland. *European Journal of Special Needs Education, 17*(2), 161–173. doi:10.1080/08856250210129074

Morcom, L. A. (2017). Self-esteem and cultural identity in Aboriginal language immersion kindergarteners. *Journal of Language, Identity and Education, 16*(6), 365–380.

Neisser, U. (1997). The roots of self-knowledge: Perceiving self, it, and thou. *Annals of the New York Academy of Sciences, 818*(1), 19–33.

Ontario Ministry of Education. (2007). *Building bridges to success for First Nation, Métis and Inuit students.* Toronto: Aboriginal Education Office.

Slavin, R., Lake, C., Davis, S., & Madden, N. (2011). Effective programs for struggling readers: A best-evidence synthesis. *Educational Research Review*, *6*(1), 1–26.

Test, D. W., Fowler, C. H., Wood, W. M., Brewer, D. M., & Eddy, S. (2005). A conceptual framework of self-advocacy for students with disabilities. *Remedial and Special Education*, *26*(1), 43–54.

Truth and Reconciliation Commission of Canada. (2015). *Honouring the truth, reconciling for the future: Summary of the final report of the Truth and Reconciliation Commission of Canada*. Winnipeg: Author.

Webster, R., Blatchford, P., Bassett, P., Brown, P., Martin, C., & Russell, A. (2011). The wider pedagogical role of teaching assistants. *School Leadership and Management*, *31*(1), 3–20.

Wehmeyer, M. (2002). Riding the third wave. *Focus on Autism and Other Developmental Disabilities*, *15*(2), 106–116.

Wehmeyer, M. L. (2007). *Promoting self-determination in students with developmental disabilities*. New York: Guilford Press.

White, R. W. (1959). Motivation reconsidered: The concept of competence. *Psychological Review*, *66*(5), 297–333.

Winzer, M. A. (2008). *Children with exceptionalities in Canadian classrooms* (8th ed.). Toronto: Person Education Canada.

Worrall, M., & Steele, J. (2008). Inclusion, extension and enrichment: Personalized gifted and talented provision. In G. Richards & F. Armstrong (Eds.), *Key issues for teaching assistants* (pp. 108–119). New York: Routledge.

SECTION IV

SUPPORTING ALL STUDENTS

This section provides an overview of key issues that are important for education assistants (EAs) to consider in the generalized classroom context. The educational team works together to create an inclusive classroom, a safe, collaborative learning environment. Downing, Ryndak, and Clark (2000) note that the EA role has evolved from being an assistant to the teacher to a key member of the education team. The EA is now a support in the areas of instruction, tutoring, management of classroom behaviours, and other activities that correspond with the activities of the classroom teacher (Pickett, 1997). Chapter 13 identifies the importance of inclusive leadership as an education assistant. The education assistant provides opportunities for support in course content, and for students to share their learning with others. In an inclusive classroom, the belief is that all students have something valuable to share.

Chapter 14 focuses on supporting academics; although there is a commitment within the education assistant's role to supporting social interaction, we cannot ignore that academics are a major pillar of practice. In an inclusive classroom, the student is supported to learn and engage with all learning opportunities, and while this may not happen in the same way as it does for other learners, challenging students to learn as much as possible is always the goal (Downing, 2010). Chapter 15 highlights excellent resources and strategies for work in the classroom, providing user-friendly tools to build an inclusive and supportive classroom environment. Chapter 16 examines students' transitions and how important it is for education assistants to work toward the goal of transition well before students are ready to either move on to secondary school or transition out of secondary school into community or post-secondary education. Without effective and thoughtful planning, students with diverse needs may have difficulty with effective career/education transitions. Planning needs to include understanding the issues inherent for students with diverse needs and developing supporting activities to explore transition needs.

REFERENCES

Downing, J. (2010). *Academic instruction for students with moderate to severe disabilities in inclusive classrooms*. Thousand Oaks, CA: Corwin.

Downing, J., Ryndak, D., & Clark, D. (2000). Paraeducators in inclusive classrooms: Their own perceptions. *Remedial and Special Education, 21*(3), 171–181.

Pickett, A. (1997). Paraeducators in school settings: Framing the issues. In A. L. Pickett & K. Gerlach (Eds.), *Supervising paraeducators in school settings: A team approach* (pp. 1–24). Austin, TX: PRO-ED.

Classroom Inclusion

CHAPTER 13

Education Assistants as Inclusive Leaders in Classrooms

Linda Hill

THREE KEY IDEAS

1. Inclusive education assistants help create relaxed learning environments that bring out the best in everyone's differences.
2. Inclusive education assistants are role models and mentors for communicating with compassion.
3. Inclusive education assistants are allies and advocates who are prepared to stand up for inclusion.

What if you arrive in your classroom one morning to find that everything is the same as it has always been except for one change? What if no one in your classroom (absolutely no one) is reacting to disabilities and other differences as problems? What if everyone (absolutely everyone) is now welcoming and accepting diverse abilities and all other differences as valuable gifts that enrich the classroom, the school, and the wider world? For about 50 years now, these kinds of what-if questions have been inspiring a global movement toward welcoming and valuing diversity. As schools and the wider world have shifted from exclusion to inclusion, education assistants (EAs) have been leaders in bringing these inclusive ideals to life in classrooms by developing their own inclusive leadership skills and by sharing inclusive leadership with students, families, and other educators.

Families and educators began asking these kinds of what-if questions in the 1960s and 1970s. Before that time, there were few, if any, EAs working in public schools, and schools mostly dealt with diversity by excluding the children who didn't fit in. Children with disabilities, children with differences in appearance and behaviour, children from ethnic minority groups, Indigenous children, gifted children, poor children, children who were ill, and many other children were routinely sent away from their local schools, their neighbourhoods, and sometimes even from their families to special classes, special schools, training programs, treatment centres, hospitals, institutions, and other segregated settings. Students who were segregated commuted long distances each day or stayed in residential schools, hospitals, and other facilities for days, weeks, months, and years at a time. As the Law Commission of Canada (2000) points out, the intent may have been to improve the lives of these children, and there are success stories; however, the fact remains that the policies and systems that required children who were different to be singled out and sent away were unfair. The impact of excluding children from home, school, and community was always disconnecting and often devastating for the individual children involved, their families, and their communities (Hill, 2001, p. 146; Law Commission of Canada, 2000, pp. 1–3).

Beginning in the 1950s, and continuing to the present day, there have been numerous waves of civil rights movements advocating for equal rights and equal respect for all the diverse identities that make up our multicultural communities. Canada has led the world in a progressive movement toward inclusive education that has gone from segregated schools, to special classes, to integration based on normalization, to inclusion based on respect for diversity (Andrews & Brown, 2014). Parents and other leaders of the educational inclusion movement united with leaders of other civil rights movements to create a powerful force for change that eventually led to a legally binding paradigm shift in Canada. In 1982, the Canadian Charter of Rights and Freedoms recognized that "every individual is equal before, and under the law, and has the right to the equal protection, and equal benefit of the law without discrimination and, in particular, without discrimination based on race, national or ethnic origin, colour, religion, sex, age or mental or physical disability" (Canadian Charter of Rights and Freedoms, 1982, s 15(1)).

The outcome of this paradigm shift is that in Canada and many other parts of the world children and youth are growing up during the first generation in history when exploring, sharing, and celebrating differences has become part of our everyday lives (Hill, 2001, p. 3). Canada has also led the world in exploring and discovering the incredible potential EAs have to share leadership with students, teachers, other EAs, and families in supporting students of diverse abilities to be included in ways that are safe, respectful, equal, and joyful (Wasykowski, 2001). Inclusive education has not only transformed the lives of individual children and their families, but is also shifting entire classrooms, schools, and communities in inclusive and welcoming directions (Inclusive Leadership Co-operative, 2015).

Implementing Canada's legal commitment to the inclusion and participation of persons with disabilities in Canadian society is a challenge that is being met through ongoing research, inclusive practices, professional development, guidance, and support for educators, students, and families. In the same way that the training of teachers is increasingly focused on learning about inclusion (Hutchinson, 2017), training programs and professional development for EAs also focuses on inclusive educational practices (Wasykowski, 2001). Education assistants have vital roles to play in providing inclusive guidance, support, and leadership to the students they are hired to assist, as well as the students' peers, their families, and their classroom teachers (Hill, 2001; Inclusive Leadership Co-operative, 2015).

Education assistants who are practicing inclusive leadership in their classrooms are mindfully and skilfully doing the following three things over and over again:

1. Creating relaxed learning environments that bring out the best in everyone's differences
2. Being role models and mentors for compassionate communication
3. Being allies and advocates who are prepared to stand up for inclusion

By learning and practicing these sets of skills for embracing diversity, EAs can help guide individual students toward safety, respect, equality, and joy within their learning environments, and can help guide entire classrooms to become inclusive learning communities where all students experience acceptance and belonging (Inclusive Leadership Co-operative, 2015).

INCLUSIVE EAs HELP STUDENTS RELAX ABOUT DIVERSITY

Relaxing about diversity is the foundation skill involved in creating learning environments that bring out the best in everyone's differences. On the surface, this seems so simple because everyone knows how to relax; however, EAs who are inclusive and welcoming in their leadership know that students do not naturally relax about differences. Unless children are guided to learn to relax about diversity, they tend to automatically group themselves according to commonalities and react to differences with their fight/flight/freeze survival instincts (Inclusive Leadership Co-operative, 2015, p. 14–19). Fortunately, when inclusive leadership is available, students (and adults) easily open up to learning about diverse identities, including differences in ability. In the short term, classrooms that are made up of teachers, EAs, and students who are developing skills for relaxing about diversity become calm places for everyone to learn and thrive. In the long term, students who learn to relax in response to differences become happier, kinder, more compassionate lifelong learners (Greenland, 2010).

Education assistants (and all the educators and mentors in students' lives) who are aware of the relationship between diversity, inclusion, relaxation, and learning can easily guide students to learn to relax in response to differences. All relaxation techniques involve taking long, deep breaths that bring air into the diaphragm. Deep breathing increases the supply of oxygen; the heart beats more slowly, blood pressure lowers, muscles loosen, and the brain literally opens up to learning (Greenland, 2010). Some of the ways to guide students to relax are to lead activities that promote stretching and deep breathing, as well as smiling and laughing. Education assistants can lead activities such as meditating, running, singing, art, drama, and other creative pastimes, co-operative games, blowing bubbles, and any kind of play. Early childhood educators have a saying, "Children's play is children's work" (Best Start Resource Centre, 2018, p. 4). This is because playing is what children of all ages do naturally to keep their relaxed nervous systems open for learning (Greenland, 2016; Joseph, 1994).

Here is a story, from the author's experience helping to build inclusive classrooms, that illustrates the power of guiding students to relax about differences in ability. From the time she was a young child, Melissa (not her real name) had always loved art, music, books, and animals. Sadly, by the time she was 10 years of age, she often felt too unwell to draw, sing, read, or study nature. Medication that prevented her from having seizures caused headaches, fatigue, sore muscles, ringing in her ears, and other side effects. Melissa was often absent from school. Each time she arrived back in the classroom she seemed to be a little more disconnected, a little more fragile, and a little more hopeless. One day she confided to her EA, "I stayed home from school because my brain just doesn't work anymore." When Melissa was referred to a school psychologist, things began to turn around. After a session with Melissa and her parents, the psychologist came to Melissa's school to spend a morning guiding Melissa and all the students in her grade 4 class in relaxation techniques. What a calming, enjoyable, and bonding morning this was for students, staff, and Melissa's parents! The session began with breathing exercises and ice-breakers, and then proceeded to a co-operative art project focused on relaxing about Melissa's seizure disorder. During the art project, the psychologist guided the class to continue to breathe deeply while collaboratively creating a big picture book of poster-sized pages showing what students and adults appreciated about Melissa, what Melissa appreciated about school, what was known about epilepsy, and pages that showed ideas for helping Melissa feel better. The two immediate outcomes of making the book were as follows:

1. Everyone became more appreciative of Melissa as a person with many strengths and interests.
2. Everyone felt more comfortable and relaxed about Melissa's health challenges.

The long-term outcome of making this book was that the class now had a valuable tool for maintaining this shift toward appreciative and relaxed interactions with Melissa. Each morning for the rest of the year, Melissa's EA was responsible for supporting Melissa (or another student if Melissa was away) to lead the class in a few minutes of thoughtful, deep breathing. Once the class was relaxed, students would select one page from the Melissa picture book to review and discuss. This daily routine of breathing deeply and sharing meaningfully together helped Melissa and the other students feel relaxed and comfortable instead of stressed and scared. Melissa became an approachable and valued member of her classroom community. Now that she felt relaxed and supported in class, Melissa began coming to school almost every day, even when she felt unwell. As she told her parents, "My friends at school know lots of ways to help me feel better."

INCLUSIVE EAs COMMUNICATE WITH COMPASSION

Education assistants spend a large amount of time each day listening to students, parents, and teachers. As a result, it is not surprising that so many EAs become highly skilled compassionate communicators. Education assistants who listen and share with compassionate acceptance can make such a difference in shifting relationships toward mutual respect, reciprocity, and equal inclusion. In her qualitative research on EAs' perspectives on inclusive education, Wasykowski (2001) found that EAs are often the first people students choose to receive their personal, private confidences. She also found that EAs develop an uncanny ability to listen to and understand students with diverse learning needs, as well as their parents, classroom teachers, and consulting teachers (Wasykowski, 2001, p. 111).

Compassionate communication between EAs and the students they support often involves bridging differences in language, vocabulary, facial expressions, body language, and other behaviours (Hill, 2001, p. 79). Inclusive EAs know that all behaviour is communication. The key to compassionate understanding is to open one's senses, mind, and heart to these diverse ways of communicating. Inclusive EAs support teachers and classmates to understand students who communicate differently, and they also support students to make sense of what their teachers and classmates are saying. They often become compassionate interpreters, guides, and role models for everyone in the classroom community. The outcome is that all students experience ongoing opportunities to learn to listen compassionately, acknowledging, empathizing, accommodating, and understanding diverse ways of communicating (Faber & Mazlish, 1980; Inclusive Leadership Co-operative, 2015; Rosenberg, 2004).

In their pioneering book about supporting and encouraging inclusive friendships between people with diverse abilities, Perske and Perske (1988) contrasted relationships based on fixing people to relationships based on accepting people as they are:

> Somehow, when you don't qualify as "normal," you often become the centre of a wide array of interventions with words such as these attached to them: teach, heal, correct, supervise, prepare, monitor, evaluate, manage, direct, drill, order, guide, shape, modify, discipline, persuade, coach, instruct, enlighten, train, advise, control. After an overfull schedule of such relationships, try to sense how you might feel if you suddenly found a friend who became attracted to you exactly as you are, just liked being with you, and never—repeat never—felt the need to fix you. (Perske & Perske, 1988, p. 71)

One way to shift a classroom from a focus on fixing to a focus on compassionate acceptance is to bring together diverse groups of students for small-group compassionate listening circles. A circle of students who are focused on listening compassionately to each other is very different from a group in which the special education students are being assisted by peer mentors, peer counsellors, peer intervenors, or peer tutors because, in a compassionate listening circle, no one is trying to correct any problems. Instead, students of diverse abilities are invited to gather together in a circle of equally magnificent people to compassionately listen to each person's stories about their individual struggles and celebrations (Hill, 1998). The outcomes are inclusive and welcoming heart-to-heart connections.

Sometimes the stories that are shared are full of pain. During one heart-to-heart circle, David (not his real name) described his experience in his previous school:

> Ninety percent of the kids in the school didn't know me and didn't want to know me. Five percent of the kids in my school knew me and hated me. There were five percent who would play with me but I hated them…. They treated me like I was an outsider. It was insulting when kids wouldn't play with me, or called me names. But it was even worse when they planned parties right in front of me as if I were invisible. Sometimes I would do things on purpose to provoke a fight because the physical pain was preferable to the emotional blocks…. I guess I've let all this stuff that I've gone through get me down to the point that I don't trust too many people. (Hill, 2001, p. 6)

In the circle, David found that he felt safe and respected within a compassionate listening environment focused on inclusion. As he shared his past struggles with his peers, he began to rebuild his trust in others. As his needs for acceptance, acknowledgement, and respect were met, he no longer tried to provoke fights. He settled into learning, growing, and enjoying social and academic success.

Other times, the stories shared in a compassionate listening circle are full of wonder. During one magical circle, Pam (not her real name), who has low vision, shared about the first time she saw a star. She described how her camp counsellor took her and some other campers outside one dark night to a huge field, far away from the city lights. The camp counsellor helped Pam point a pair of binoculars up to the heavens: "The star I found was bright and beautiful and it shone right into my eye." As she shared with her heart, each person in the circle who was compassionately listening to her story experienced the joy Pam felt when she looked through those binoculars and saw a star for the very first time (Hill, 2001, p. 84). Students began offering to help her see other natural phenomena that she had never seen before such as fish, insects, and birds. Pam eventually became an enthusiastic participant in the school's outdoor club and a strong advocate for the environment.

INCLUSIVE EAs ARE PREPARED TO STAND UP FOR INCLUSION

The third theme in this chapter is that EAs who are helping to build inclusive and welcoming classrooms need to be prepared to be allies and advocates who know how to respond effectively when exclusion happens. The first aid metaphor presented here helps everyone understand the importance of becoming skilled at responding to situations of exclusion by standing up for inclusion. Begin by considering all the education and practice involved in learning to drive a car. Eventually, after hours and hours of instruction and training, the skills involved in driving come to feel automatic, easy, and natural; however, even with all this defensive driving education and practice, driving a car is still risky. Therefore, many people take additional emergency first aid training in case they are on the scene of a motor vehicle accident. Complete the metaphor by thinking about the skills involved in becoming an EA. Eventually, after hours and hours of education and practice, the many skills involved in assisting students and teachers come to feel automatic, easy, and natural; however, no matter how carefully EAs cultivate the skills involved in assisting in classrooms, navigating the complexities of diverse learning environments is still risky. Therefore, many EAs take additional emergency first aid training in case they are on the scene of an incident of exclusion.

Hill and other trained and experienced members of the Inclusive Leadership Co-operative teach anti-discrimination first aid through workshops, manuals (Inclusive Leadership Co-operative, 2013), and courses (Inclusive Leadership Co-operative, 2018). The purpose of anti-discrimination first aid training is to prepare EAs and other inclusive leaders to shift away from being bystanders to being active witnesses who are prepared to notice and respond to situations that appear to be unsafe, unfair, inequitable, or otherwise hurtful. The goals are to prevent exclusion from escalating; reduce harm; restore respect, fairness, and dignity; repair damage; and re-open hearts and minds to possibilities for healing and reconciliation.

Remembering what to do is as easy as reciting the alphabet. A is for *assessing* the situation with a focus on deciding how to respond. A is also for being an *ally and advocate in asserting access rights* because all students have equal rights to participate fully in their classroom communities. B is for *breathing* deeply to re-open one's relaxed nervous system. B is also for taking a *break* from stressful, hurtful, and confusing situations in order to de-stress, calm down, and start thinking again. C is for *communicating calmly, compassionately, and courageously.* D is for *debriefing, defusing, discussing* and taking steps toward *doing things differently.* E is for *educating* the world through *ethical witnessing.* F is for *forming* circles of support that provide inclusive sanctuaries of *fairness, fun and freedom* from exclusion (Inclusive Leadership Co-operative, 2013).

These steps are illustrated through another story from the author's personal experience helping to build inclusive and welcoming classrooms. The hero of this story is Alicia (not her real name). Alicia always felt like a champion when she returned from an empowering summer at a CHAMP Camp for child amputees and their families (War Amps, 2018); however, the year she and her classmates entered middle school, her confidence was short-lived. She spent her first week of middle school struggling to survive the painful reality that her friends from her elementary school were avoiding her and several students from other elementary schools were making fun of her. She confided in her EA who responded with anti-discrimination first aid:

A is for *assess.* The EA's assessment of the situation was that the problem of Alicia's peers reacting negatively to her differences was only the tip of a very large iceberg of negative interactions. Everyone in the grade 7 class seemed to be reacting to the many changes involved in transitioning to middle school with fight/flight/freeze survival instincts.

B is for *breathe* and also for taking a *break.* The EA took some deep breaths and invited Alicia to take some deep breaths too. They took a break from class and went together to consult with the school counsellor, who was also well-trained in anti-discrimination first aid.

C is for *communicate* and D is for *debrief, defuse, and discuss.* Alicia, the EA, and the counsellor listened to each other's perspectives as they made a plan for how to support Alicia to assert her right to belong to her school community.

E is for *educate* and F is for *forming* circles of support. Alicia, the EA, and the counsellor planned a workshop for Alicia's homeroom class called "How to Be a Champion." During the workshop, Alicia shared her story of how children and youth who were amputees went to CHAMP Camp each summer to learn how to become champions of their own lives. The information she shared helped everyone shift from reacting with alarm to her physical differences to responding to her with interest and admiration. After sharing her story, Alicia demonstrated to her classmates how she used her elbows to do things most people do with their hands. When the EA encouraged all the students to follow Alicia's lead, the room filled with sounds of laughter and excitement. Sandra discovered she could put chalk between her elbows and draw bouquets of flowers on the blackboard. Toby managed to turn the door handle with his elbows, and the students all went outside to play a game of elbow-ball. As students opened up to exploring the skills Alicia had developed through her life of living with her very different arms, Alicia's middle-school classmates began to view her in the same way she had been viewed by her peers in elementary school: as an interesting, approachable role model for how to be a champion at home, at school, and in the community. They left the workshop with a sense of excitement about the possibilities for becoming champions of their own lives (Hill, 2001, p. 30).

Becoming an inclusive EA involves intentionally practicing leadership skills for relaxing about differences, communicating with compassion, and being prepared to stand up for inclusion. By combining these inclusive leadership skills with all the skills involved in their position, EAs are playing vital inclusive leadership roles in guiding entire classrooms to become inclusive learning communities where students with diverse abilities and all students experience safety, respect, fairness, joy, and belonging.

Voices from the Field

Janice Maxwell, Inclusive Leadership Co-operative participant, Victoria, British Columbia

If there is a movement afoot to build more inclusive and welcoming communities, then my husband, Robert, our daughter, Melanie, and I are pioneer founders of that movement. Our journey began in 1979, when Melanie was born 10 weeks premature and developed cerebral palsy. For 39 years our focus has been on trying to get Melanie included. It was called *integration* at first. I remember the days when we asked people to "tolerate" our daughter's disabilities. In 1985, she was the first student with multiple disabilities to go to regular public school in a typical classroom in Victoria, British Columbia. It seemed like we should be grateful that our daughter was allowed to attend. She even received a special award at BC Government House for being special enough and brave enough to go to school. We didn't want Melanie to be *special*. We wanted her to be included, which is to feel important, respected, and valued. Thank goodness we have moved to inclusion and valuing diversity. We have lived through it all!

Through participating in the Inclusive Leadership Co-operative, I have learned that building inclusive classrooms is only part of a much larger question of how to build communities that promote inclusion for all human beings regardless of age, ethnicity, gender, sexual preference, physical/mental ability, health status, and more differences. Because it turns out that it is not only people with ability differences who tend to feel excluded. Many people experience exclusion in mainstream settings.

Inclusive leaders learn to look behind behaviour to identify the causes of the pain of exclusion. Behind the pain of exclusion is aggression. Behind aggression are feelings of hurt, helplessness, and fear. In many cases the causes of hurt feelings can be remedied by identifying, recognizing, acknowledging, empathizing, making adjustments, making amends, and reconciling.

The outcome is inclusion. Inclusion makes us feel like we belong. We feel comfortable and included when others notice us, welcome us, listen, empathize, respect, accept, encourage, value, and support us. We feel valued and heard. It feels safe to ask for what we need. Our human differences are accommodated, understood, and accepted. Our creativity and best performance comes forth. Inclusion is contagious. There is a ripple effect. A few inclusive leaders can change the tone and improve quality of life in their families, schools, communities, workplaces, and beyond.

CRITICAL THINKING QUESTIONS

1. What is a story from your own life experience that illustrates the impact of learning to relax about ability differences?
2. What are the compassionate communication skills involved in encouraging and supporting students to develop mutually respectful, accepting, and non-judgmental relationships?
3. What is an experience from your own life when you or someone else noticed and responded to a situation of exclusion in ways that prevented exclusion from escalating; reduced harm; restored respect, fairness, and dignity; repaired damage; and re-opened hearts and minds to possibilities for healing and reconciliation?

REFERENCES

Andrews, J., & Brown, A. R. (2014). Special education. *The Canadian Encyclopedia.* Retrieved from www.thecanadianencyclopedia.ca/en/article/special-education/

Best Start Resource Centre. (2018). *Learning to play and playing to learn: Getting ready for school.* Toronto: Author. Retrieved from www.beststart.org/resources/ hlthy_chld_dev/pdf/school_readiness_english_fnl.pdf

Canadian Charter of Rights and Freedoms, S. 15. Constitution Act, Schedule B, Canada Act (UK). (1982). c 11.

Faber, A., & Mazlish, E. (1980). *How to talk so kids will listen, and listen so kids will talk.* New York: Scribner.

Greenland, S. (2010). *The mindful child: How to help your kid manage stress, and become happier, kinder, and more compassionate.* New York: Free Press.

Greenland, S. (2016). *Mindful games: Sharing mindfulness and meditation with children, teens, and families.* Boulder, CO: Shambhala Publications.

Hill, L. (1998). *Discovering connections: A guide to the fun of bridging disability differences.* Duncan, BC: Inclusive Leadership Co-operative.

Hill, L. (2001). *Connecting kids: Exploring diversity together* (2nd ed.). Duncan, BC: Inclusive Leadership Co-operative.

Hutchinson, N. (2017). *Inclusion of exceptional learners in Canadian schools: A practical handbook for teachers* (5th ed.). Upper Saddle River, NJ: Pearson Education.

Inclusive Leadership Co-operative. (2013). *Anti-discrimination first aid.* Duncan, BC: Author.

Inclusive Leadership Co-operative. (2015). *Inclusive leadership adventures: Guidebook for exploring, sharing, and celebrating diversity* (24th ed.). Duncan, BC: Author.

Inclusive Leadership Co-operative. (2018). *Discover your inclusive leadership potential.* Retrieved from https://inclusive-leadership-global-village.thinkific.com/courses/self-guided-inclusive-leadership-potential

Joseph, J. (1994). *The resilient child: Preparing today's youth for tomorrow's world.* New York: Perseus.

Law Commission of Canada. (2000). *Restoring dignity: Responding to child abuse in Canadian institutions; Executive summary.* Ottawa: Minister of Public Works and Government Services.

Perske, R., & Perske, M. (1988). *Circles of friends: People with disabilities and their friends enrich the lives of one another.* Burlington, ON: Welch Publishing.

Rosenberg, M. (2004). *Teaching children compassionately: How students and teachers can succeed with mutual understanding.* Nonviolent Communication Guides. Encinitas, CA: Puddle Dancer Press.

War Amps. (2018). Ways we help. Retrieved from www.waramps.ca/ways-we-help/child-amputees/

Wasykowski, J. (2001). *Perspectives of teacher assistants working with students with diverse learning needs.* Lethbridge, AB: University of Lethbridge Institutional Repository.

Academics

CHAPTER 14

Supporting Academics

Heather Wik and Barbara Eckersley

THREE KEY IDEAS

1. Academic support begins by knowing students.
2. Academic support incorporates the use of diverse strategies for supporting literacy and numeracy across the curriculum.
3. Academic support requires working and communicating as a team.

FOCUSING ON STUDENT LEARNING

Each province and territory in Canada has a mission statement about education. It is a public declaration that describes their originating principles, including what they do and why they do it. At the very core, schools are about academic learning. Today, students face many challenges and barriers that impact their learning, and education assistants (EAs) are often the ones who spend the most time supporting the students who have the greatest needs (Konza & Fried, 2012). Education assistants play a vital role in equipping students to meet their academic goals.

The goal for students is to become independent learners who know and utilize a variety of strategies and who can advocate for their learning needs. Some students become independent learners quickly, while others need more scaffolding. For educators, the keys to supporting academic success are to know their students, to teach and reinforce using various learning strategies, and to communicate and work with others as a school-based team.

Every student comes to school with a history: a family history, a school or learning history, and a medical history. These are important pieces that make up the essence of each student. It is essential that an EA has knowledge of these histories in order to develop a deeper understanding of how to best support a student's academic learning. The first place to start learning about a student is in the student's file.

Every student who enters the public school system will have a student file. Its purpose is to document the history of a student's education program over time. If a student is receiving additional government funding, there will usually be a second student file that contains the individual education plan (IEP) and the ministry of education's required documentation to support the additional funding.

When working with specific students, an EA needs to know the goals for each student, as well as the recommended adaptations and suggested strategies as outlined in the student's IEP. This is critical information to have before working with any student.

Another excellent source of information is previous staff members who have directly worked with the student. Education assistants should take time to talk with past teachers, other EAs who have worked or are currently working with the student, and, of course, the student's current teacher(s). It is important to ask about the student's history in the three key areas: school, family, and medical. An open-ended question often works best; for example, "I am working with (student's name) this year in grade 3. Can you tell me a bit about him/her?"

After reading the student file and talking with other staff members who have worked directly with the student, the next step is for the EA to compile the information they have gained. This could include the following:

1. Strengths, weaknesses, and current grade levels in reading, writing, and math

2. Supports in place for reading, writing, and math (including what strategies have worked in the past)

3. Strategies that have worked best to support this student's work habits (e.g., alone, with a partner, check-ins, direct support)

4. Strategies that have worked best to support behaviours (e.g., focus, distractions, transitions, new people)

5. Social considerations to be aware of while supporting the student

Supporting student learning is a relational practice. As Pierson (2013) states, "students don't learn from people they don't like." To be an effective EA, one needs to develop a positive rapport with students. When they first sit down to work with a student, an EA should take a moment to connect with them, starting with eye contact, a smile, and a nod (Emerson, 2010). They can ask the student about their day, or what they did last night or on the weekend, or plans they might have after school. This is teaching through relationships and it is a critical step in learning. After the EA has taken time to connect, the EA and the student will be ready to begin the academic work.

WHAT SHOULD THE STUDENT LEARN TODAY?

Once an EA knows the learning history of the student they will be supporting, it is time to look at how to best support their academic learning. Education assistants work under the direction of the teacher, and the teacher will assign various tasks to all students. Classrooms are busy places and the EA will often need to ask the classroom teacher for explicit instructions for the student they are supporting. While all team members try to always be cognizant of short- and long-term learning goals for individual students, sometimes teachers, EAs, and students get focused on work completion and forget to focus on the learning. That is, task completion becomes more important than learning. When asking a teacher for clarification about an assignment, the difference can be discerned simply by asking the right question. Instead of asking the teacher, "What would you like (student name) to complete today on this assignment?" the EA can ask, "What would you like me to focus on with (student name) in terms of his/her learning with this assignment?"

It is important that students have ownership of their tasks. Education assistants are there to support, but the responsibility of task completion, learning, and working hard belongs to the student. To begin, EAs can talk about the expectations and have the student set a clear goal. The EA can ask the student, "What do we need to accomplish for this task? What are you learning about?" This will encourage the student to restate the teacher's directions. If the student cannot answer, the EA will need to remind the student of the directions. Once the expectations are understood, it is time to start working.

STRATEGIES

A learning strategy is the student's approach to completing a task. Strategies give EAs different ways of working with different students and, as the EA learns to work in different ways, they are better able to recognize and respond to students' different learning styles. The ultimate goal is the independent use of strategies for independent learning (Brownlie & Schnellert, 2009).

Before selecting strategies to use with students, it is important for EAs to remember that these students are working tirelessly. Value the energy and effort that students with diverse learning needs put into their learning. Recognize that there is a reason why they often feel frustrated and defeated.

When supporting students, there are some general strategies that work across the curriculum, with almost every student. Some of the most common strategies include the following:

1. Expectations/goals for today: "Let's make sure we understand the teacher's directions before we start. What did you hear the teacher say about this assignment?"

2. Readiness to learn (is the student ready to learn or is there a preliminary need for a drink, snack, change in the environment, specific supplies, a wiggle cushion, etc.?): "How are you feeling? Are you ready to tackle this assignment?"

3. Giving choices: "How would you like to begin?"

4. Technology: "What technology could we use to help with this?"
5. Connection to prior knowledge: "What do you already know about this topic? Remember yesterday when …" "What does this remind you of or make you think about?"
6. Chunking: "Let's cover up the rest of this paper and focus only on the first section. Does that sound like a good idea?"
7. Increasing wait time after asking a question or making a request
8. Celebration of successes: Often students are not quite capable of seeing their progress, so they need us to show them how much they have grown and learned. Success is motivating (Wormeli, 2003)

Reading

Reading and writing skills are fundamentally important, and their development can be supported in virtually every activity throughout the entire school day. Reading is a complex process that involves seeing the words on a page and then using many parts of the brain to make sense of the visual message. Reading is divided into three areas, all of which require distinct supports: pre-reading, during-reading, and after-reading.

The pre-reading stage is about getting ready to read. Education assistants can encourage students to become engaged with and excited (as much as possible) about the text they are going to read. To do this, they can take time to just look through the text with the student. This is often referred to as a picture walk or a text walk. The EA can ask the student to make predictions and connections and ask questions. This creates a purpose for reading.

There are two important processes that happen in the during-reading stage. The first is the actual reading or sounding out of words. This is called decoding. The second is comprehension. This is where students make meaning and understand what they are reading. To help a student with decoding, the EA and the student can agree to try choral reading, where they read the words together, or echo reading, where the EA reads the words and the student echoes the EA to read the same passage aloud. The EA and the student can also take turns reading the text aloud. Vocabulary checking is necessary. When a student struggles with a word, the EA can ask the student to stop reading and they can then talk about the word and make sure the student understands any new vocabulary. This helps with decoding and comprehension.

To build comprehension, it is important for the EA to continuously monitor the student's understanding by asking questions about the text or having the student provide a brief summary. Talking about the text with the student also builds understanding. The EA can ask the student about their favourite parts, what they would change, and what pictures or images were vivid as they read or listened. They can also ask if they have any questions or if there are things they are wondering about at that point. The EA must do their best to engage the student in reading.

Finally, the post-reading stage involves demonstrating learning and understanding of the text. This usually takes the form of assignments. Before beginning the assignments, the EA should take time to talk to the student about the text, asking what they liked or disliked, if there were parts that did not make sense, and, if it was fiction, if they would read another book/poem/short story by the same author. After this discussion, the EA and student can begin the assigned task.

Writing

Writing is similar to reading in that it is also a highly complex process that is divided into stages, with different types of support for each stage. Because writing is a process, it is often slow and students can easily get discouraged. Writing requires students to read and comprehend, synthesize information, put their thinking into words, and to have the fine motor skills to record their thoughts while they retrieve previous knowledge of spelling, sentence structure, and grammar rules. And it is expected that each of these processes works together instantaneously to produce writing! It is a high-level skill that is academically, physically, and emotionally demanding.

Pre-writing is the first stage of the writing process. Students explore as many ideas as possible and then decide on a main idea. To support students, EAs can use graphic organizers, offer to write while the student talks, use different coloured markers on large sheets of paper, and encourage ideas to be shared with peers.

The drafting stage is next. Students decide on a main idea from the pre-writing stage and develop an outline and rough copy. The EA can encourage students to focus on one main idea and then group the details together to create a rough outline for their writing. They can also offer sentence starters and reinforce that it is okay to make mistakes—it is a first draft.

Once the draft is complete, it is time for the revising stage. At this stage, students will self-edit for content, organization, and clear communication of ideas. This is where a lot of the learning takes place. The EA can start by explaining that revising is messy, and then ask the student to choose a coloured pen to make changes and notes. Another useful strategy is to have either the student read their work aloud or the EA read the student's writing aloud. As the student or EA reads, the listener can correct errors as they are heard. The EA can then ask the student reflective open-ended questions; for example: "Are you happy with this paragraph?" "Is there anything more you would like to add?"

Then comes the "picky" editing stage. This is the final check for grammatical errors and the structure of the writing. Together the student and EA should check for correct spelling and punctuation, full sentences, and paragraph structure. Students should be encouraged to add or delete and make changes. They can then share the writing with a trusted peer or another adult in the school and ask for feedback.

Publishing is the final stage of the writing process. It is when students will create the final copy and celebrate their writing. Students who struggle with the writing process will often be tired at this point, and their motivation may be decreasing. Education assistants must be sensitive to this. The EA can offer to write/type as the student reads the words aloud, taking lots of breaks and setting goals. Once the final copy is completed, students can be encouraged to share their writing with "important people" like the principal or a teacher of a higher grade. The student can then participate in the classroom celebrations of the writing.

Numeracy

Math is one of the most feared subjects in school, but students will need the skills developed in this subject for the rest of their lives.

Math is integral to every aspect of daily life, and "[numeracy] skills can be used to solve problems related to time, sports, travel, money management, science, and art, to name a few" (Government of British Columbia, 2018). Today, students need to understand both the procedural and conceptual foundations of math, as well as the language of math. They need to be able to solve complex problems by making connections between prior learning and new knowledge (Mink, 2010).

To support student numeracy development, EAs need to have a deep understanding of math. They need to see the sense of math, understand connections between different math concepts, and present a positive attitude and growth mindset. When working with students, there is a need for EAs to promote understanding using real-life problems, conversations, manipulatives, technology, modelling, problem solving, and more. The goal is to help students develop math understanding, not just rote memorization. Before trying to support students, EAs must first understand the math concepts. This often requires spending extra time with the math teacher to review concepts, taking home a math textbook and doing the assignments ahead of time, or finding resources on the Internet to help further understand the concepts and processes.

Education assistants play an important role in helping students become deliberative thinkers about math. They can encourage students to ask themselves if they understand what is being asked of them, if they have shown all their work and thinking, and if they can see other strategies to use to answer the same math questions.

Manipulatives are one of the best resources for math. They are effective teaching tools that can be used to help students understand key mathematical concepts (Mink, 2010). Manipulatives include almost any physical object used to represent an abstract concept; common manipulatives and math tools found in classrooms include base ten blocks, Cuisenaire rods, fraction circles and strips, hundreds charts, number lines, games, and multiplication tools.

Supporting numeracy takes resourcefulness, patience, repetition, enthusiasm, and a belief that all students can "do math."

CONCLUDING AND TRANSITIONING

Part of supporting students academically is assisting them with navigating through transitions. Each school day is structured, with multiple designated start times and end times. It is important for EAs to conclude the current activity with students and prepare them to move to the next activity. Taking time to effectively conclude each work session will help solidify the learning and set up the next session for success. Education assistants should be sure to plan for 5 to 10 minutes to engage in the transitioning process. They can help students in this process by guiding them with questions or prompts.

When supporting a student with transitioning, the EA can ask them what they need to do to end the current task and get ready for the next class/task/subject. Some students will require direct step-by-step instructions, while others will know the routines of the classroom. The EA can check to make sure the student is ready for the next subject or task, both physically (the student has the necessary supplies and knows what is coming next) and emotionally (the student is calm, feeling confident about the task they just completed, and ready to move on). The EA should always conclude with a specific positive comment about the student's work, thank them, and restate the plan for the next day when returning to the task.

DOCUMENTATION/COMMUNICATION

An important step for EAs in supporting academic learning involves communicating with the classroom teacher. It is the teacher's responsibility to assess and report on the academic progress of all students in the class, but often the EA will have important information to contribute. It is necessary for the EA to communicate with the teacher after working with a student, especially if they are not working in the classroom with the student. Communication can be verbal or written. Written information for the teacher should include the following:

1. Student's full name, date, subject, and task
2. What the student accomplished

3. The amount/level of support given
4. Adaptations
5. General comments about the student and their learning
6. The EA's signature, date, and job title

It is important for the EA to be succinct, objective, and professional in written communications to the teacher. An EA's notes can become part of the student's school file and could even be subpoenaed for legal proceedings.

CHALLENGES OF SUPPORTING ACADEMIC LEARNING

Education assistants are part of a team that includes administrators, student services teachers, classroom teachers, counsellors, and other support workers. All these individuals must work together to support students with diverse learning needs and their education. Each party has their own specific role and responsibilities, as outlined by the ministry of education. When working in a classroom, the EA and the teacher are the immediate team, tasked with supporting the learning of all students. Working as a team is critical, and the end goal is always the same—student success.

In a perfect world, teachers and EAs would work as a unified team to support academic learning, and students would come to school ready to work and learn, but that is not always the reality. Sometimes there are challenges. For example, there will be times when the teacher asks the EA to persevere with a student who is struggling on an assignment. This can be especially problematic if the EA is working with a student outside the regular classroom. What should the EA do if the student is shutting down, behaviour is escalating, or the student is refusing to complete the assignment? Sometimes EAs need to make decisions that are in the best interest of the student, in that moment. This might look like going for a brief walk, listening to music for a short time, or getting a drink of water, or it could mean putting the assignment away for the time being. Whatever the decision, the EA must remember to communicate or document it for the teacher.

There will also be days when the student the EA is working with has little to no motivation, which can be another challenge to supporting academic learning. They will not want to begin, will not want to work, will not want to pick up their pencil or turn on the computer. What then? The EA must remember to always look behind and beyond the behaviours, asking, "What could be the reasons for this lack of motivation?" Maybe the student does not know how to start, or they are afraid of doing it "wrong," so they do not even want to begin. Maybe the student is hungry, tired, or distracted by something that happened before school or last night. Maybe the student is failing the course and no longer sees the point of doing any more work.

The EA can talk with the student: "You seem to be distracted today and struggling to get started on this assignment. Is everything okay?" After listening to the answer, the EA and student can problem solve together. This is how to look beyond the behaviour and move toward support and solutions. If the student is hungry, the EA can ensure that they get a snack. If they are tired, the EA can ask them to go for a walk to get some fresh air, or to the bathroom to splash some cold water on their face. If they are upset about something other than school, the EA can offer the services of a school counsellor or another support person in the school. If the student is upset about the work, the EA must make use of their toolbox of strategies, rely on previous information they have gathered about the student, then decide on the best way to proceed. It is always best to start with the smallest task, which will allow the student to have the most success. That is the first step to motivation. The EA can then build on that, one small successful step at a time, with lots of task-specific positive feedback.

Supporting the academic needs of students begins and ends with relationships. Education assistants need to know their students well. This includes knowing their educational goals and recommended strategies, strengths, history, and learning preferences. It requires an investment of time, energy, teamwork, genuine care, and purposeful relationship building. Only when EAs really know their students will they be equipped to support their academic growth.

Wormeli (2003) suggests that EAs ask themselves daily, If I had been the student working with me today, would I want to come back tomorrow? This is a valuable concept on which to reflect. Education assistants must ask: Have I established a relational practice that encourages students to strive for success?

Voices from the Field

Mary Hennig

I was an EA working in a high school in British Columbia. Matt was a grade 11 student who had a history of physical violence against school staff and students, lived in many different foster situations in many towns, and, due to some very profound gaps in learning, had about a grade 4 reading level. He struggled with drug and alcohol use and came to class on several occasions injured from the various physical altercations he was in while under the influence. The quintessential "tough guy," he used a lot of profanity and my token protests over its use became my "in" when I was given the task of supporting him in some text-heavy classes.

A sense of humour definitely helped in this situation ("Hey dude, perhaps the 'F' word you are looking for is fabulous?!?"), as did slipping him a granola bar and juice box when I presented him with an adapted version of the texts. I would check on his physical condition, offer to facilitate medical assistance when necessary, and then offer academic support.

By becoming his "go-to" trusted adult, I could read those good days when I could push a little harder in academic areas. I could see the rough days when the place he was in only allowed me to offer a snack or a break, so that he could leave the classroom to get some pain medication from his locker. Because I read his non-verbal cues accurately, he could trust that I wouldn't engage him in activities beyond what he could handle. My existing relationships with the classroom teachers meant that my judgment regarding Matt's physical, emotional, and academic condition were respected and honoured while we worked together to keep him engaged and help him find academic success at school.

Connection is key.

CRITICAL THINKING QUESTIONS

1. Explain why "connection is key" when supporting students' academic needs?
2. How can the implementation of specific strategies impact a student's ability to acquire and integrate learning? Discuss and provide several examples.
3. What are several ways in which an EA can foster teamwork and communication in order to better support students?

REFERENCES

Brownlie, F., & Schnellert, L. (2009). *It's all about thinking: Collaborating to support all learners in English, social studies, and humanities.* Winnipeg: Portage & Main Press.

Emerson, J. (2010, November 25). Collect before you direct [Blog post]. *Connecting with children.* Retrieved from www.connectingwithchildren.blogspot.ca/2010/11/collect-before-you-direct.html

Government of British Columbia. (2018). BC's new curriculum: Mathematics. Retrieved from www.curriculum.gov.bc.ca/curriculum/mathematics

Konza, D., & Fried, L. (2012). Maximising the contribution of paraprofessionals in schools: A win-win-win story. *International Journal of Interdisciplinary Social Sciences, 6*(9), 115–123.

Mink, D. (2010). *Strategies for teaching mathematics.* Huntington Beach, CA: Shell Education.

Pierson, R. (2013, May). Every kid needs a champion [Video file]. *TED Talks.* Retrieved from www.ted.com/talks/rita_pierson_every_kid_needs_a_champion

Wormeli, R. (2003). *Day one and beyond: Practical matters for new middle-level teachers.* Portsmouth, NH: Stenhouse Publishers.

CHAPTER 15

Collaborative Strategies and Resources for the Classroom

Kyla Cleator

THREE KEY IDEAS

1. Working with curriculum goals and understanding the physical environment, intellectual, social, and behavioural barriers to learning are important to building a collaborative classroom.
2. Understanding students in terms of their strengths, needs, and learning styles helps to identify connection to the strengths and areas of interest of educators and parents, which supports a comprehensive learning plan.
3. Having and using a variety of supports, tools, and resources can support students' active participation and ultimately the achievement of their goals.

Classrooms are now more diverse than ever and many education assistants (EAs) and teachers face significant challenges in meeting the needs of such diverse groups of students. There is so much for EAs and teachers to consider when it comes to planning and setting up their classroom. Teachers and EAs are expected to keep up with new curriculum and resources, as well as what were formerly known as classroom management strategies. Universities don't often teach courses in classroom management and, if they do offer courses in challenging behaviour, it is difficult for education students to fit them into their schedules in addition to their many required courses.

Teachers and EAs are often challenged (by a lack of time) to look ahead and plan out what the school year will look like for each of the subject areas and what their students' needs are. Thompson (2002) suggested that "teacher/teacher assistant teams should have more time to converse, clarifying roles and discussing responsibilities" (p. 30). In her research study, one EA noted that "her concern, and one which is shared by teachers and teacher assistants alike, is that it is difficult for teachers and assistants to find time in their hectic daily schedules to meet and plan collaboratively" (p. 31). This planning often does not account for students who unexpectedly register on the first day, especially if they have significant or complex needs. Given today's diversity in classrooms, planning for various learners needs to be at the forefront of any teacher's or EA's mind. There are so many things to think about: Who are these students? What are they all about? How can EAs and teachers build and nurture relationships that support all the students in the class? This chapter provides some concrete collaborative strategies for EAs and teachers to help facilitate those relationships, as well as plan what students will learn throughout the year and the resources and knowledge needed to ensure that all students are successful.

One important idea to consider is setting aside time to collaborate and plan at the very beginning of the year. It is especially important that a meeting be set up early in the year or shortly after an EA is hired to enable the teacher and the EA to clarify their respective roles and establish clear channels of communication. School boards should provide time for teachers and their EAs to confer on a regular basis throughout the year to engage in planning, exchange feedback, and discuss individual situations (Alberta Teachers' Association, 2016, p. 7). This is often difficult because start times for the teacher and EA can be different, and teachers often have many meetings in the first few days back in the classroom before students arrive. With classrooms being so diverse there is a more critical need for teachers and

EAs to work collaboratively to support students in proactive ways. Research studies demonstrate that issues pertaining to communication, clear expectations, and collaborative planning time all affect the development of effective relationships between teachers and EAs (Thompson, 2002, p. 37).

There are, of course, many definitions of collaboration, depending on the context. For the purposes of this chapter, *collaboration* will be defined as the classroom teacher and the EA working together to plan for all students' success. In addition to defining collaboration, it is also important to determine how to actually be collaborative. Teachers and EAs can decide together how to collaborate to plan for students. This chapter offers many ideas and resources to support the EA and teacher in becoming a strong team. To set up the teacher and EA for a successful collaborative partnership, it is important to have a "framework to clarify the roles, responsibilities, and shared duties of teachers and educational assistants, and a process to facilitate communication" (Elk Island Public Schools, 2013, p. 1). Using a framework or template, rather than relying only on a conversation, can also ensure a commitment to collaboration. Writing a plan can provide something tangible for the teacher and EA to check, revise, and update as needed. The more clearly defined the roles and responsibilities of both the teacher and the EA, the better the relationship between the two. The better the relationship, the more positive the classroom environment is for everyone, especially the students.

UNIVERSAL DESIGN FOR LEARNING: BACKGROUND KNOWLEDGE

Before proceeding to explore some solutions, it is important to develop a slightly deeper understanding of universal design for learning. Universal design for learning (UDL) is a set of evidence-based principles that can be used by teachers and EAs to help make the classroom environment accessible and effective for all students. It has become a leading framework in many districts in terms of guiding school staff in their collective knowledge of supporting the wide range of students in the classroom (CAST, 2018). The overarching goal of UDL is to plan for the diversity of student needs at the start of a lesson, rather than modifying or adapting it in the moment. One of the best resources for learning about UDL is the CAST website, developed by Dr. David Rose. The big ideas of UDL came from the field of architecture. Buildings that include ramps and elevators allow people with wheelchairs, parents with strollers, and so on, access to buildings that in the past they would not have been able to access. The ideas featured on the CAST website will help both teachers and EAs understand more fully what UDL means and how to implement meaningful UDL strategies into their classroom environment. Another resource that can help develop a deeper understanding is the website for the National Center on Universal Design for Learning.

WHOLE CLASS PLANNING

First and foremost, it is important for educators to know what curriculum topics are included in all subject areas within the grade being taught. The teacher is legally and professionally responsible for delivery of the curriculum. The EA's role is to assist the teacher with their instructional responsibilities. Collaborative best practices suggest that it is imperative that the teacher and EA take the time to sit down together and explore the topics that need to be taught and explore available resources. It is important to examine these in the provincial context in which the school is located. In Alberta, these topics are referred to as the "programs of study" for each curricular area (Alberta Education, 2018). Generally speaking, each curricular area includes a lot of content to be covered over the course of the year. Because there are so many concepts to teach, it may be necessary for teachers and EAs to narrow down concepts to the big ideas for some students (who have complex needs), by thinking about what is absolutely critical or key for students to know. The key questions to ask are: What are the essential learning outcomes for each subject and are there any possible areas of cross-curricular study?

In addition to exploring the curriculum and essential learnings, it is important for educators to determine what resources will be used to support the curriculum goals. Having a solid knowledge of the curriculum, including what comes before and after certain concepts, helps with thinking about and planning ahead for the needs of the class as a whole. Knowing the linear progression of learning the concepts helps to identify the gaps in student learning and what concepts should be targeted for individual or small group instruction/intervention. One example of this idea of the progression of learning is found in an Alberta Education document entitled "Literacy and Numeracy Progressions" (n.d.b), which outlines the progression of learning concepts across the divisions. Using this resource can help educators understand where students have gaps or get "stuck" in their learning and then identify what concept to begin teaching to bridge that gap. Teachers and EAs can examine this resource and ask themselves what specific interventions they will use to teach the concepts that are missing. Alberta Education also offers an online resource called "Instructional Strategies and Supports" (n.d.a) that provides some essential and necessary learnings as well as optimal resources that can be accessed for the full range of student learning needs. Using UDL, it is much easier to differentiate activities and create options for student learning ahead of time, rather than being reactive or playing catch up when students are struggling.

Creating a Class Profile

When teachers and EAs are working together at the start of year to plan how they will support all the students in the class, it is important that they gather information about who their students are. Students will have a wide range of abilities, backgrounds, personalities, learning styles, and learning needs. This is true in all classroom environments; this is simply human nature. There are a variety of tools or frameworks that the teacher and EA can use to gather information about the students who will be part of their class. This information can be used to create a document called a "class profile." The class profile would be filled out at the start of the year to allow the educators to gain a big picture understanding of the class as a whole. (Building more individualized student profiles for students with significant needs is discussed later in the chapter.) This understanding helps the collaborative team plan lessons throughout the year that take into consideration the wide range of needs of students in their care. The class profile could include the following information:

- subject area and cross-curricular concepts
- competencies
- class strengths
- class challenges
- individual need-to-knows (sensory, social emotional, language, medical)
- differentiated strategies/activities/tasks (relevance); also consider Revised Bloom's Taxonomy question starters (2016) to help differentiate activities or tasks
- choice to demonstrate learning (flexibility/options/learning styles)
- an area for class observations (by who, when, which subject area, define purpose)
- student learning styles and preferences

To support creating a class profile, there are several resources that teachers and EAs can use to help identify how students learn best and how they demonstrate their learning. Texas Education Agency's "Learning Styles for Multiple Intelligence" (2018) is one document that outlines different ways students can demonstrate their learning.

Shelley Moore, an educator and author working in British Columbia, has developed another possibility for a class profile, based on the following ideas:

- classroom strengths
- classroom stretches
- teacher- and class-identified goals
- decisions
- individual concerns (medical, language, learning, social emotional, other)

Whatever information the teacher and EA choose to include, the most important factor is taking the time to complete the class profile at the beginning of the year. This means, again, collaborative time spent by the teacher and EA to explore, discuss, observe, review, and then, ultimately, implement.

The EA can be particularly helpful in supporting the teacher to create the class profile by gathering information from student files and talking with parents and even previous teachers and EAs. Report cards, individual education plans, learner profiles, formalized assessment reports, and multidisciplinary reports all hold key information about students, including knowing what grade level they are working at, their learning needs, speech and language needs, and medical history. Edmonton Public School District (2018) has created a Learner Profile and Intervention Plan that is an excellent tool for teachers and EAs to help gather what they know about a particular student.

Classroom observations made by the EA may also support completing a class profile. For greatest insight, accuracy, and effectiveness, it is important to dedicate time to make observations and take notes and ask the question, "What do I notice?" Making observations during different subjects, at different times of day, in different environments, and, if possible, with different teachers (when the EA is supporting in a different teacher's class, for example, physical education, music, art) is key to building a complete picture about what the class strengths and challenges are. Time permitting, the EA could also connect with the teacher who taught a majority of the students last year and ask questions about what strategies worked well in terms of teaching the entire class. When completing class profiles or class planning templates, in terms of supporting what will be taught, it is important to look at what resources are available both in the actual classroom and school environment and online. When exploring resources and reflecting on what has worked well during past teaching experiences, one needs to consider planning the lessons around differentiated strategies/tasks and the ways that students will demonstrate their learning. What is the learning goal for *all* students? What are the learning goals for students at both ends of the range of student needs? Will the students have access to technology?

Does the entire class come together to start the lesson to learn what *all* students will be expected to know? What will this look like? Where will the learning take place? Is this an activity that can best be done by dividing the class into smaller groups? What resources need to be in place at the beginning of the learning activity?

Classroom Environment

Important considerations for lesson planning also include the physical set-up of the classroom and any barriers to learning that may exist within it. For example, students who struggle with attention and focus can greatly benefit from flexible seating options such as giving them a choice about where and how they sit. A standing workspace can be a great support for students with attention or focus issues. There is much research on the topic of flexible seating options for students. Uncomfortable students may be distracted and unproductive. Flexible seating encourages students to find their best spot to stay calm, focused, and productive. Stephen Merrill (2018) summarizes a study completed in 2015 in the United Kingdom by researchers at the University of Salford on the effect of classroom design on academic achievement. The researchers found that personalization of classroom space, which included flexible seating (defined as student choice within the space), accounted for a full quarter of the improvements, alongside naturalness and stimulation.

In addition to flexible seating options in terms of supporting engagement, students who struggle with reading could benefit from options for different levels of text. Technology (for example, Google Read and Write) can be used to support students to read more independently. It is extremely important for both the EA and the teacher to be aware of, understand, and seek out the variety of tools and strategies that can be used/applied as supports in the classroom. Having these available from the start and teaching all students about these tools allows students to choose what works best for their individual learning style.

Many resources are available to support teachers and EAs with planning effective educational programming for all students. Paula

Kluth (2018) is an author who focuses on differentiation/UDL/supporting all learners. Her resources emphasize collaboration amongst school staff, outside partners, and parents to create environments, lessons, and experiences that are inclusive and respectful of, and accessible for, all learners. Another excellent resource to help teachers and EAs create a calm and supportive classroom environment for all students is Jennifer Katz's (2018) "The Three Block Model of UDL." This offers an effective approach to classroom management, planning, instruction, and assessment that can be used to create a compassionate learning community for K–12 classrooms.

Whole classroom planning also includes establishing expectations for how students, teachers, and EAs treat each other. A respectful classroom environment where all students are accepted and everyone respects themselves and those around them is critical to the success of all students. Teachers and EAs can be proactive in their thinking and planning as to what they will do to prepare students for learning, and what modifications or adaptations are needed if things don't go according to plan. What are the routines, rules, and expectations for learning and behaviour? Do students know what is expected of them? Are the expectations/rules posted and clearly understood by all? Do parents know what these expectations are? If parents as partners are also aware of and know the class expectations and rules, then they can support this same learning at home.

Establishing classroom routines at the start of the year is an important step to a collaborative classroom environment. Inviting students into a discussion about what they want the classroom environment to look like is also an important step in the process. Along with the teacher, EAs can facilitate this classroom conversation and create posters of the decided-upon classroom expectations. Once the expectations are posted around the classroom, EAs can remind students of the rules and support them in following these when they are struggling to do so. It is also beneficial for staff and students to reflect on and update the rules and expectations at several points throughout the year. If the rules and expectations are not working, the EA and the teacher can work collaboratively to figure out what needs to be changed in order to make the expectations effective and relevant for students again.

Developing a class profile and establishing a positive classroom environment creates a clear and straightforward system for dealing with challenging behaviours in the classroom. Implementing these, along with the other actions suggested in this chapter, will reduce challenging behaviour in the classroom. Students who have their social, emotional, and learning needs met in the classroom often have less need to act out in challenging ways. It is, however, impossible to address every single need in the classroom, and situations evolve and change in students' lives that can result in their acting out behaviourally. Someone close to them may be ill or have been in an accident. The student may have witnessed or experienced something that affects their learning in negative ways. What are the collaborative practices that the EA and teacher can utilize in the classroom to address these challenges when they arise? Dr. Ross Greene's website is an excellent resource for the EA, teacher, and, if possible, school staff in general to explore. Dr. Greene's philosophy is called collaborative and proactive solutions (CPS) and is a non-punitive, non-adversarial, trauma-informed model of care. The model is based on the premise that challenging behaviour occurs when the expectations being placed on a child/student exceed their capacity to respond adaptively, and that some students are lacking the skills to handle certain demands and expectations. The model focuses on identifying the skills the student is lacking and the expectations they are having difficulty meeting; in the CPS model, those unmet expectations are referred to as "unsolved problems" (Greene, 2018). The goal is to help kids and caregivers solve those problems rather than trying to modify kids' behaviour through application of rewards and punishments.

There are endless resources to support teachers/classroom staff in dealing with challenging behaviours. The series of books "Supporting Positive Behaviour in Alberta Schools: Individualized, Classroom and Schoolwide" (Learn Alberta, n.d.) is an excellent resource. The book one chooses depends on what specific behaviour is at issue, or how widespread challenging behaviour is. The most effective methods are typically successful when implemented on a school-wide basis.

EA Strengths and Challenges

When developing a class profile, the teacher and EA will learn many things about their students in terms of strengths and challenges. At the same time, it is important that the teacher and EA determine their own strengths, passions, and challenges. Which subjects are the most comfortable for them in terms of teaching and knowledge and which are a bit of a stretch? It is important for EAs to consider which areas they are strongest in and which have always been a struggle. Once they have identified these areas, the next step is to determine how to use this information. It is important for the teaching team to take advantage of individual strengths and preferences and to figure out how to leverage them to support everyone in the class. For example, an EA who is an excellent organizer could be given time to organize a cluttered/messy space in the classroom. An EA may have experience or completed coursework in an area that the teacher has not, so could supplement planning special activities in this particular area; for example, physical literacy, music, and art can be supported by someone who has strengths in these areas.

There are many different ways for EAs to investigate or explore their own strengths and challenges. Shelley Moore (2018) has two wonderful resources on her website—"Who Am I Profile?" and "Strength-Based Student Profile"—that can be used for this purpose. Either of these tools can be adapted or modified for the person who is filling it out (educator or student). An EA can also send this or a similar survey to parents and collect and organize the data to discover parents' strengths and passions. This knowledge can enrich and expand the way that students access the learning that will happen in the class throughout the school year. It is great for educators to know if a parent is working in a particular field or has a special interest or talent that ties into any of the curriculum areas, as the parent's experiences can be incorporated into classroom learning. Allowing students to see meaningful and engaging real-life examples enhances the learning of each individual student in the class, as well as the school and parent community.

EAs can ask themselves if there is a way of showcasing class, student, parent, teacher, and their own strengths: could there be an area of the classroom (or even a common area) allocated to sharing these strengths with the class or the school community? It is not only important for EAs to know the school and district big picture goals and instructional focus, but it is also critical to align these with students' strengths and the learning that is happening all year long. Relevant connections to the school, the district, and to each other are what make learning more engaging and interesting.

INDIVIDUAL STUDENT PLANNING

In addition to creating an overall class profile, it is important to really understand those students in the class with complex needs and how to support them. Some of the planning for these complex needs will develop when creating the class profile. While completing the class profile, the EA and teacher may learn that one or two students have significant learning needs. From that starting point, a learning plan can be developed for more complex learners. A learning plan is different from an individual program plan (IPP) or individual education plan (IEP). The focus of a learning plan is big picture lesson planning to include or reach students who are working at a vastly different level than the rest of the class. It may be useful to create a learning plan in the form of an individual planning template to outline expectations for students with more complex needs.

Some areas to consider including in an individual learning plan template are as follows:

- what is the class doing?
- what is the student doing?
- place or environment
- purpose or relevance
- competencies: personal, social, intellectual (and goals for each area)
- a place for teacher comments or anecdotal notes

The learning plan template could answer questions such as: What are other students doing and what is expected for this student? What are the goals for this student? How will these goals be achieved and what will this look like? Who will support the student (e.g., teacher, EA, parent, peer) and how and when? The planning template can be used as a guide in all curricular (and, if needed, extracurricular) areas throughout the year. The content and use of the template depends on the student, their needs, and the context.

If an EA is going to support implementing more targeted and direct strategies for complex students, what does that look like? When will this targeted support happen and when can the student work more independently or with the support of peers? Are there times when the teacher can work with a small group and the EA can directly observe and take note of what is working well and what needs to be changed? Could the EA also identify, with documentation, observations, and tracking, what strategies are working and what needs to be changed? Connecting with other multidisciplinary professionals and parents is crucial to supporting the overall plan for a complex student and helping to identify when changes need to be made. Depending on the district and the student's needs, a referral to a speech-language pathologist, occupational therapist, physical therapist, psychologist, or behavioural specialist could be an important part of the planning process. The more information EAs have about students with unique or complex needs, the better they can support and include them in whole class learning.

The following offers an example of how the individual inclusion planning template could be completed for a specific activity:

- what is the class doing? physical education class: learning about Canada's Food Guide
- what is the student doing? making a personal food choice between a healthy and unhealthy option (from visual options of two food items)
- place or environment: physical education class (gym or classroom)
- purpose or relevance (all students): to make healthy choices that influence physical, emotional, and mental well-being

- purpose or relevance (complex student): student will attend part of the class and participate in activities (participate in food guide stations, peer work, making a choice activity)
- competencies: social, intellectual
  - social: initiate check-in with teacher, participate in partner or group station, use communication tools as indicated in individual plan (IEP or IPP)
  - intellectual: participates in making a healthy choice and through an adapted activity related to overall class goal

To really understand the more complex learners in the class, it is important to review all the necessary documentation in the student's file. The EA can gather the various multidisciplinary reports, which often include excellent recommendations and strategies that address the areas of challenge with the student's learning. These reports, as well as the student's learning support plan (IEP, IPP), can provide incredibly valuable information about how they learn and what they already know. Gathering as much information as possible about these complex learners and presuming they are competent and can learn is the key to offering engaging and meaningful learning opportunities for all students, but especially complex learners.

If a student has communication challenges and there appears to be no system (such as a picture exchange communication system [PECS], iPad, visuals, signs, or gestures) in place to assist them, then it might be worth exploring a collaborative meeting with the inclusive support team or multidisciplinary specialists to determine next steps. Joy Zabala (2019) outlines such a meeting as a SETT (student, environments, tasks, tools) process. This collaborative process examines the student's areas of strength and challenge, the various environments in which the student is expected to learn, the learning tasks, and the tools (both low and high tech) that could be used to assist them. It is essential to include parents and the school-based team in such a meeting in order to fully understand the student's strengths, the environment, and the tasks the student is expected to do. An individual learning plan template is a very helpful tool to support the SETT process, and can be filled out before or after the meeting. To be able to support the complex learner, it is important to know what other students in the class are doing. Once the meeting and planning has been completed, it is important for the teacher and EA to collaboratively discuss how the plan will be implemented: What tools will be used for what task and in what environment? Who will be supporting the student and when? In what situations does the student need direct support and when can they, independently or with peers, work on the tasks outlined in their support plan or IEP?

One way to help determine levels of support (right time, right place, right support) is, again, by collaboratively planning beforehand. Causton-Theoharis (2018) outlines many ideas to help staff collectively determine levels of support, and discusses alternatives to side-by-side support and the range of available supports, from least to most intrusive. Causton-Theoharis outlines some alternative supports as follows:

- providing visual materials of the concept to reinforce or clarify understanding
- provide a visual "to-do list" or "checklist" rather than verbal reminders
- modify expectations or the task so that the student can work independently
- arrange for peer support

Peers are often underutilized in assisting students with complex needs; there is often not enough thought and structure put into how peers can work with these students. With regards to peer support, students who have their own challenges are often overlooked in favour of students who are already successful themselves. Research has shown that many teachers have found that students who struggle academically or socially often make great peer buddies (Carter, Cushing, & Kennedy, 2008). Being a peer buddy puts them into a leadership role that requires them to teach and be responsible. These experiences can help them build their own self-confidence and academic skills. Indeed, further research suggests that peer support programs are a "two-way street," boosting the academic outcomes, social skills, and self-esteem of both students with disabilities and the peers who support them (Carter, Cushing, & Kennedy, 2008).

Classrooms are diverse and EAs need to expect this diversity. It is challenging for teachers and EAs to be completely prepared for the extent and range of the diverse needs of students. In addition, needs are always evolving and issues and situations will suddenly present themselves; no matter how experienced or skilled the classroom team is, there will be stumbling blocks. Teachers and EAs, just like students, have a range of knowledge, skills, and abilities, *and* stressors that come along in their lives. In collaboratively planning beforehand and preparing for and reflecting on the needs of the whole class, EAs can set up all students for success. Some of the key areas of planning are as follows:

- knowing the curriculum and competencies, including the linear progression of learning concepts over time
- knowing the range of student needs/learning styles in the class and completing a class profile (by reviewing IEPs/IPPs, past report cards, multidisciplinary reports)
- understanding the more complex students at opposite ends of the range of needs and what tools/resources are available to plan to meet those needs
- having clear class expectations, routines, and rules (visually available) and including students in developing them. Having clear expectations and strategies (collaborative problem solving, social emotional strategies) in place is especially important for dealing with students with challenging behaviour
- using visual strategies to support overall communication, understanding, and learning
- knowing the strengths and challenges of not only the students in the room, but also the adults, and including parents as partners in their child's learning
- planning beforehand what teacher and EA support will look like in the classroom: When, where, how, and who will support? Keeping in mind "right place, right time, right support" for each student in a diverse classroom. It is important to have discussions around alternatives to side-by-side EA support. How do the EA and teacher plan beforehand to promote student independence?

Voices from the Field

In the span of my career (29 years) working as an occupational therapy (OT) consultant with Edmonton Public Schools I have noticed significant changes in the makeup of classrooms. Classrooms have become increasingly diverse and complex. Whereas 29 years ago I might have been called in to provide support for one student in a school, there are now many students identified for OT support in any given school and often more than one in a classroom. Additionally, supports are provided by those working in many other disciplines within the classroom (e.g., speech-language pathologists, psychologists, specialists in teaching English language learners, social workers, physical therapists, behaviour specialists). Some students receive the support of more than one consultant at a time, and some teachers and EAs receive this involved support for multiple students in the classroom. This support itself can become overwhelming for the teaching team, with many consultants providing multiple strategies to support students. A collaborative approach is more important than ever—to support the teacher and EA in a practical and meaningful way.

In an effort to streamline support for students and school staff, Edmonton Public Schools has adopted a system of "school linked teams" where a team of consultants is assigned to specific schools. This has allowed the consultants and school staff to work together on a more regular basis, facilitating the development of strong team relationships, a key component in collaborative practice. Two or more consultants may visit a classroom/observe a student together as a way of coordinating service. Another component of successful collaboration is time—time to meet and discuss concerns and issues in the classroom. This can be difficult, as classrooms, teachers, and EAs are busy and time is at a premium. In many schools, "collaborative team days" are scheduled regularly over the year and classroom coverage is arranged to allow teachers and EAs dedicated, uninterrupted time to discuss issues with various consultants. Through these rich collaborative discussions, priorities can be set, strategies suggested for classroom staff to implement, and plans can be made to provide follow-up and schedule specific treatment as appropriate.

CRITICAL THINKING QUESTIONS

1. How can we think differently about identifying barriers to learning?
2. How can building a class profile of student needs/strengths assist with inclusion and big picture planning?
3. How can we identify supports/tools/resources that are good for all students?

REFERENCES

Alberta Education. (n.d.a). Inclusive education library: Instructional strategies and supports. Retrieved from http://www.learnalberta.ca/content/ieptlibrary/lib08.html

Alberta Education. (n.d.b). *Literacy and numeracy progressions.* Retrieved from https://education.alberta.ca/media/3402192/lit-and-num-progressions.pdf

Alberta Education. (2018). Programs of study. Retrieved from https://education.alberta.ca/programs-of-study/?searchMode=3

Alberta Teachers' Association. (2016). *Teachers and educational assistants: Roles and responsibilities.* Edmonton: Author. (Original work published in 2000). Retrieved from https://www.teachers.ab.ca/SiteCollectionDocuments/ATA/Publications/Teachers-as-Professionals/MON-5%20Teachers%20and%20Educational%20Assistants.pdf

Carter, E., Cushing, L., & Kennedy, C. (2008). Promoting rigor, relevance, and relationships through peer support interventions. *TASH Connections* (March/April), 20–23. Retrieved from www.waisman.wisc.edu/naturalsupports/pdfs/Peer_Supports_TASH_Connections_2008.pdf

CAST. (2018). Universal design for learning. Retrieved from www.cast.org

Causton-Theoharis, J. (2018). The golden rule of providing support in inclusive classrooms: Support others as you would wish to be supported. *Teaching Exceptional Children, 42*(2), 36–43. Retrieved from http://www.inclusion-ny.org/files/GoldenRule-1.pdf

Edmonton Public School District. (2018). Learner profile and intervention plan. Retrieved from https://drive.google.com/file/d/1IxhrRcnTZ-W9XMKOYu7vqoqLZ8GnZKb2/view

Elk Island Public Schools. (2013). *Collaborative teams in the classroom.* Retrieved from https://www.erlc.ca/documents/collaborative_teams_in_the_classroom_2013-10-08.pdf

Greene, R. (2018). Lives in the balance: Fostering collaboration, transforming lives, inspiring change. Retrieved from https://www.livesinthebalance.org/

Katz, J. (2018). The three block model of UDL. Retrieved from https://www. threeblockmodel.com/

Kluth, P. (2018). Towards inclusive classrooms and communities. Retrieved from http://www.paulakluth.com/

Learn Alberta. (n.d.). Supporting positive behaviour in Alberta schools. Retrieved from http://www.learnalberta.ca/content/inspb1/html/introduction.html

Merrill, S. (2018, June 14). Flexible seating: Research is promising but scarce. *Edutopia*. Retrieved from https://www.edutopia.org/article/flexible-classrooms-research-scarce-promising

Moore, S. (2018). Templates [Blog post]. *Blogsomemoore: Teaching and empowering all students.* Retrieved from https://blogsomemoore.com/shout-outs/templates/

Texas Education Agency. (2018). Learning styles for multiple intelligences. *Texas CTE.* Retrieved from https://txcte.org/sites/default/files/resources/documents/Learning-Styles-for-Multiple-Intelligences.pdf

Thompson, D. M. (2002). *Teachers and teacher assistants: Building effective relationships.* Lethbridge, AB: University of Lethbridge, Faculty of Education. Retrieved from https://www.uleth.ca/dspace/bitstream/handle/10133/840/Thompson_Dawn_M.pdf?sequence=1&isAllowed=y

Wilson, L. O. (2016). Bloom's taxonomy revised: Understanding the new version of Bloom's taxonomy. Retrieved from https://thesecondprinciple.com/teaching-essentials/beyond-bloom-cognitive-taxonomy-revised/

Zabala, J. (2019, March 24). Sharing the SETT framework. Retrieved from http://www.joyzabala.com/

CHAPTER 16

Transition: The Journey to Adulthood

Asha Rao and Jane Litman

THREE KEY IDEAS

1. Transition to adulthood for students with complex learning needs is an important planning element for educators and education assistants.
2. Specific strategies and supports are identified as best practice in transition planning.
3. Education assistants play an important role for students with complex needs who are in transition to adulthood.

TRANSITION TO ADULTHOOD

Transitions involve significant changes in a person's life. In the context of education, there are many significant transitions: entering school, transitioning to middle or high school, and transitioning to adulthood, which may include further schooling or other community programs. Transitioning to adulthood is a significant challenge for all youth, and for youth with disabilities the transition is a complex journey (Young-Southward, Cooper, & Philo, 2017). It involves not only planning to make the journey but also developing the skills, abilities, and supports required to transition both independently and interdependently into the adult world. The Government of British Columbia (2009) asserted that transition is more than identifying skills or supports; transition also involves students exploring and making decisions for their future. For youth with disabilities, a coordinated, collaborative, and person-centred transition process is critical to assisting them in preparing for the multiple changes in their lives as they enter adulthood. This chapter explores the context of transition in school and community, the transition process, and the role of the education assistant (EA) in transition planning, and concludes with a discussion about working toward interdependence.

School

By age 14, students with exceptionalities need school teams to come together to support them for the upcoming transition from high school into the next stage of their lives (Ministry of Children and Family Development, n.d.). Gauthier-Boudreault, Gallagher, and Couturec (2017) noted that parents found that transition was often occurring too late in a student's life, especially in terms of getting important paperwork for funding and various types of community supports such as health care plans, programs, or post-secondary support. While students with exceptionalities are in school, there is a certain level of support and funding they are entitled to in order to support their inclusive access and rights to education. Services may include case management from a learning support teacher and access to other itinerant teachers and professionals such as speech-language pathologists, counsellors, and physical and occupational therapists. Students, throughout their time in school, experience opportunities for inclusive academics, social and emotional supports, and connections with peers in neighbouring schools. Wehman (2013) noted that schools that promote inclusive practice significantly affect how a student will transition into adulthood. Opportunities to be involved in school activities, academics, and graduation proved to have better outcomes for students transitioning into adulthood, as they had a sense of belonging and participation in community. Gauthier-Boudreault et al. (2017) noted that if EAs do not intentionally plan supports to aid students with transition, students could experience profoundly negative impacts. Examples of these impacts include a decline in community participation, access to social networks, and opportunity for choices, as well as compromised mental health. Schools play an important part in helping students develop the competencies to make transitions. Training to attain these competencies includes academic preparation, employment practice, self-advocacy, and social skills development and empowerment, so students can be active in decision-making processes. Education assistants must develop a community of support to help students develop daily life skills and academic, social, and community goals that prepare them to transition to adult life.

Community

The Convention on the Rights of Persons with Disabilities stressed the need for social inclusion and community participation (United Nations [UN], 2006). Gray et al. (2014) identified three key areas in this UN document: increased independence, access to employment, and improved participation in community. Education assistants must consider the values inherent in community living when determining the many elements required for a student to transition into a community. These values include the rights of an individual for full citizenship, choices, dignity, quality of life, inclusion, and meaningful participation. These concepts reveal that transition into community is not a linear process of gaining independence. While developing independence is a necessary element of transitioning into adulthood and community, an ongoing process around interdependence and connection with others in community is equally significant in order to experience a full life as a citizen.

Nguyen, Stewart, and Gorter (2016) articulated that the process must be person-centred, with full participation of the youth, their families, and the community partnerships who together create a planned, systematic, and shared model of support. This collaborative planning helps to develop creative ways to support students so that they continue schooling and find programs that suit their areas of interest, meaningful employment after they leave school, and housing that enables them to live and participate in their own communities. Gray et al. (2014) argued that students who were living with parents after high school were not necessarily participating in daytime activities or employment and that this negatively affected their participation in community and directly impacted their quality of life and mental health. Transitioning to adulthood requires building multiple partnerships in community with agencies such as local living organizations, health care supports, employment access, housing options, post-secondary resources, and ongoing family supports. To make the multiple decisions around transition, students, families, school personnel including teachers and EAs, and other professionals, groups, and agencies collaborate in this process called transition planning.

WHAT IS TRANSITION PLANNING?

From the time students walk in the door of their kindergarten classroom to the time they walk across the stage to receive a graduation certificate, they go through several transitions. Many students who are on an adapted program leading to graduation will not need extensive planning for the transition to adulthood. Students with a learning disability or a physical or medical condition that does not impair their cognition may require no more than the school counsellor's help in connecting with the office for students with disabilities at the college or university of their choice. Their individualized education plan (IEP) may include a transition goal, and the counsellor or EA may accompany the student on orientation visits to the post-secondary or work setting to which the student has applied.

However, transition planning for students who are complex learners with diverse abilities is a process, not a single event. Looking ahead to the future for a student with diverse needs and abilities requires a thoughtful team approach. The student may require support to prepare for additional schooling, employment, housing, being independent in their personal care, acquiring functional life skills, or becoming connected in the community for leisure and recreational activities.

What Is Best Practice?

In the report *Transition Planning for Youth with Special Needs: A Community Support Guide*, the Ministry of Children and Family Development (n.d.) suggested that person-centred planning, which involves the student, school team, family, community, and transition coordinator, is the key to a successful transition (p. 2). Person-centred planning for transition focuses on the "wants and needs of an individual and recognize[s] the importance of both formal and informal supports in assisting the person to achieve his or her dreams" (Wehman, 1997, p. 22). This approach to transition is a partnership.

At the school level, the personnel involved in the transition team could include an inclusive learning teacher or case manager, EAs, a school counsellor, a speech-language pathologist, or an occupational therapist. These professionals are members of the student's IEP team and will be aware of their needs and the accommodations that are in place in the school program. The student's school team will be integral to a person-centred approach in the transition of the student to adulthood. This approach, beginning in the last two years of the student's schooling, uses some or all of the following steps:

1. Build a transition team
2. Gather information
3. Develop the transition plan
4. Implement the transition plan according to established timelines
5. Update the plan as needed, over the period between ages 14 and 18
6. Hold a celebration or exit meeting (Ministry of Children and Family Development, n.d., p. 5)

Why Use Person-Centred Planning?

Person-centred planning often makes the most sense for the most complex learners. Students who have significant cognitive, communicative, or physical challenges and students who demonstrate challenging behaviour have been, for many years, served within a medical deficit model. Person-centred planning, particularly when it comes to life after high school, focuses instead on a student's strengths and wishes. The conversation becomes less "the person can't, isn't able to do this" and becomes more "the person wants to be able to do this." O'Brien and O'Brien (2000) noted that person-centred planning involves a change in how we view persons with complex needs: "seeing people first rather than relating to diagnostic labels; using ordinary language and images rather than professional jargon; actively searching for a person's gifts and capacities in the context of community life; and strengthening the voice of the person and those who know the person best" (p. 4). This focus on strengths and wishes can be a way of breaking down barriers in the community between complex learners and the larger normative culture.

BEING PART OF THE TEAM: THE ROLE OF THE EA

Students with complex needs and diverse abilities benefit from the skills and life experience of every member of their school team. Often, in the earlier grades, the focus is on including the student in the classroom while on a modified academic program, as well as providing any necessary support for personal care or life skill needs. The EA is often the team member who implements the modified program with the student. Doyle (2008) suggested that the role of the paraprofessional or EA could include the following:

> Provid[ing] certain types of support to individual students with disabilities, such as implementing specific instructional procedures developed by the special educator, assisting with physical management and positioning of the student as specified by the physical therapist, or using a specific feeding program designed by the occupational therapist. The paraprofessional also might be asked to assist individual students ... to review or practice skills under the direction of the general educator or the special educator. (p. 57)

As students progress through school, the goal is for them to achieve a degree of independence in managing aspects of their life, such as personal care.

The school team must have good communication skills. Creating the time for collaboration between the EA and the teachers or therapists working with the complex student will go a long way to helping the EA provide appropriate support. The team needs to implement a system for recording confidential information about students and their needs, as EAs often collect data on skill acquisition or the demonstration and frequency of specific behaviours. A clear system for communication with parents and outside agencies or professionals must also be in place. In addition, the EA and school team must be familiar with the province's and school district's guidelines on protecting students' privacy (Doyle, 2008, p. 111).

The role of the EA on the school team should be practical, appropriate to the complexity of student need, and understood by all members of the school team. The EA's role can be pivotal, as EAs can come to know the students well.

A Description of EA Support in Secondary Schools

The program for a secondary school student with diverse abilities may shift from the modified academics of earlier grades to a tighter focus on functional life skills, community opportunities including using public transit and carrying a personal ID card, social communication, and social behaviour. EAs are the support most likely to assist students in these program areas. Because EAs support students in a variety of high school and community settings, under the direction of teachers and therapists, the EA is often the team member who, aside from parents, is best able to "read" the student and identify their needs.

EAs support complex students with the transition to adulthood in a variety of ways. One way is to apply Causton-Theoharis's (2009) "golden rule" for support. Causton-Theoharis advocated that adults "ask and listen" (p. 40). The EA who is supporting a complex learner in secondary school may well be the team member in the best position to ask students about the *kind* of support they want and *how* that support is offered. Asking questions such as "Is it okay if I sit beside you?" or "Would you like me to remind you or give you a to-do list?" or "Do you need help with that job today?" gives students the opportunity to make their own choices about adult support. Students who are non-verbal can have these choices and questions loaded into their communication device or can be taught to use pictures and visuals to support the decisions they would like to make. This move toward self-advocacy will stand the student in good stead as an adult. Students who do not use conventional communication methods will tell EAs with their behaviour if they are too close or if their well-intentioned support is too invasive. According to Doyle (2008), EAs are often the ones who understand what the student is communicating through their behaviour: "People act in ways that communicate their experiences of the world. When their behaviours are unusual, disruptive, or challenging in some way, it is likely that they would prefer that those around them try to understand and respond" (p. 110). The EA will also be in the best position, in collaboration with the school team, to implement a careful plan to fade the adult support. The EA, as the team member who spends the most time with the complex student, will be able to recognize when to step away as appropriate and when to step back in as needed. Opportunities for complex students to work or be social without an adult at their shoulder play a large role in their ability to function as independently as possible as they approach the transition to adulthood. The information gathered from and about the student by the EA and the rest of the team is critical to supporting the complex student in becoming part of the larger community as an adult.

SELF-ADVOCACY: WHAT IS IT?

The key part of transition planning is for students to become involved in the process of decision making. Corbey et al. (1999) noted that many students with exceptionalities have not learned the skills to be more actively involved in their transition process. From an early age, students can start to learn the skills of self-advocacy, which will provide them with the tools to become engaged in their transition. Self-advocacy is a skill that can be taught in schools by helping students develop a knowledge of themselves and their rights, as well as communication skills (Prater, Redman, Anderson, & Gibb, 2014). It is also a movement.

Self-advocacy is a movement that says that people with disabilities have the right to control their own lives and make their own decisions. Families, friends, and advisors also have a role in supporting self-advocacy (Inclusion BC, 2018).

When students learn how to self-advocate, they are more likely to have successful transitions to community participation, post-secondary engagement, and employment (Carter et al., 2013). Learning self-advocacy skills gives students empowerment in that they have awareness and control over their own education and futures as they grow in their abilities to responsibly practice these skills. Prater et al. (2014) contended that when the larger community sees that students with exceptionalities can be a part of decision making, this new perspective can shape and change the way they perceive people with exceptionalities. In other words, there is the opportunity for all citizens to see that an inclusive community is one filled with diversity.

Key Strategies

Education assistants are critical members of the transition team and promoters of inclusive and collaborative practices. Whether working in a kindergarten or grade 12 class, an EA works with students and a team to create a supportive environment and opportunities to learn, develop, and practice key skills for self-advocacy. The goal with transition is to support students in gaining skills while also finding ways to fade out the support so that students gain their own sense of confidence and responsibility (Causton-Theoharis, 2009). Education assistants can teach self-advocacy in three strategy areas: accommodation and inclusion, strengths and needs, and communication skills and practice.

Accommodation and Inclusion

One of the best ways EAs can teach self-advocacy is by helping the student understand the IEP. When a student is involved in the IEP process, they become part of a person-centred planning and decision-making process. Roberts, Ju, and Zhang (2014) observed that when students learned how to speak up about their needs, there was increased participation in their IEP process as they had learned about their own strengths and areas of need in their exceptionalities. Accommodations in the school setting such as extra time, use of technology, separate setting, spell checkers, readers, and speech recognition software could also be beneficial to all students in an inclusive education system. Students with exceptionalities are entitled to these accommodations, and EAs are vital in implementing accommodations and helping students understand why they might benefit from them and how they link to their strengths and needs. Education assistants can provide verbal prompts and cues for how a student may ask for these accommodations during assignments, tests, and exams. They can also model and show examples of different tools and technology that may support these accommodations. In doing so, EAs can work with students on a strength-based approach to show them how to access their learning.

Strengths and Needs

Developing self-awareness and self-knowledge is a key step in building self-advocacy skills. Roberts et al. (2014) emphasized that self-awareness and self-knowledge are critical skills for achieving successful outcomes in school and in life. Often, IEPs identify students' strengths and needs; however, EAs can work with students to help them identify their own strengths and can acknowledge any strengths exhibited by students. Many students can also self-identify the areas in which they need support, which EAs can discuss further when working with students on assignments or supporting them in the classroom. Education assistants can also identify students' strengths through skill inventories and student-created lists. According to Moore (2017), strength-based student profiles allow students to identify for themselves what their interests are, how they show their knowledge, what they are good at, and what areas they may need to develop. Recognizing how strengths and needs link to the accommodations to which students are entitled is critical to implementing these accommodations and to lesson planning overall.

Communication Skills and Practice

To teach students that they have choice and control in their lives EAs can work with them to practice communication skills such as how to ask for support and accommodation (Lord & Hutchison, 2011).

Students need to be involved in learning the skills to make decisions, express concerns, identify strengths and needs, and practicing these skills in the school environment. By learning effective communication skills and practicing them in safe and supportive environments, students learn that, as they transition, building relationships with others is important for their lives in community.

EAs support communication development in many ways, including the following:

- working with small groups of students to develop empowerment and confidence (Anderson & Bigby, 2017)
- teaching students key words, phrases, and questions to ask verbally or to write down to identify their needs
- supporting students while they practice strategies such as video modelling role plays in real-life situations (Prater et al., 2014)
- developing scripts so students can generalize the skills of communication across multiple settings
- reflecting on what worked or did not work well in different situations in the school

IEP TRANSITION GOALS

It is important and necessary to include a transition goal in the IEP of all students who have been designated as having diverse learning needs. Teachers and case managers can write transition goal(s) as early as grade 10 and they should be in the IEP no later than grade 11. For all students with diverse abilities, a transition goal that reflects some aspect of self-advocacy is appropriate.

Students with a learning disability or with a physical or medical condition that does not impair their cognition and who are on a graduation path would benefit from goals and objectives that address the adaptations they require at school. While students may fully understand the need for specific adaptations, many adolescents find it difficult to speak to their teachers and expose themselves and their needs to the scrutiny of others, including adults and peers. This is where an EA can be of great assistance. Working with the student, the EA models and has students practice a respectful and quiet way to request the necessary adaptations. Under the direction of the student's case manager, the EA expands the acquisition of these advocacy skills to include meeting with a supervisor in a job placement, preparing for a job interview, or meeting with support staff in a post-secondary setting.

For many years, the education and medical systems have programmed and supported students with complex and diverse abilities within a medical deficit model; however, these students' IEPs and report cards can be written from the perspective of their individual strengths and abilities. Using the student's voice and "I" statements lend themselves very well to the creation of transition goals in the IEP. Complex learners who are on a modified program and a school completion path can have their transition goals built with this type of strength-based language. The following "I" statements are examples provided by the British Columbia Ministry of Education that could be incorporated into a transition IEP:

- "In a safe and supported environment, I respond meaningfully to communication from peers and adults. With support, I can be part of a group" (BC Ministry of Education, 2018b, profile 1).
- "I can participate in classroom and group activities to improve the classroom, school, community, or natural world" (BC Ministry of Education, 2018a, profile 2).
- "With support, I can show a sense of accomplishment and joy, and express some wants, needs, and preferences" (BC Ministry of Education, 2018c, profile 1).
- "I can recognize my value and advocate for my rights. I take responsibility for my choices, my actions, and my achievements" (BC Ministry of Education, 2018c, profile 3).
- "I make decisions about my activities and, with support, take some responsibility for my physical and emotional well-being. I can express my wants and needs and celebrate my efforts and accomplishments" (BC Ministry of Education, 2018c, profile 2).

In practice, these competencies could be written as objectives in the IEP and implemented with the following strategies:

- alternative, assistive, or augmented communication devices and apps
- participating in recycling programs or community newspaper routes, working in a school garden or cafeteria, and supervised volunteering
- visuals to support the steps in a task
- a visual or voice output "button" that states, "I need help" or "I can do it myself," which can be shown to an adult
- personal portfolios, certificates of accomplishments from teachers, job placements, and volunteer settings

Person-centred planning tools typically include the IEP transition goals as part of the process. Members of the complex student's team, which includes the student, teachers, EAs, parents, and therapists, will all have input into the content of the transition goals and the timelines for anticipated achievement of those goals.

While transitions foster independence and growth of skill sets, fostering interdependence is another way of looking at transition. The focus is on relationships and building connection in the community, thereby acknowledging that the student will require assistance with certain tasks in life in order to be truly independent and autonomous. This interdependence links to community living values and a person-centred focus in which the person's interests and goals are at the heart of this transition. Students learn that they are not in isolation in this process but rather surrounded by a community of supports. Students, given opportunities to explore interdependence during the transition years, gain experiences in how fluid their life is depending on their own goals and dreams. Further, they can discover that as they age and change, they can be engaged in creating their lifelong participation in community.

Voices from the Field

Andrea Hermanson, High School Inclusive Learning Teacher, Victoria, British Columbia

How Does an EA Work as Part of a Team?

Collaboration is critical. Constantly ask questions, actively listen and share ideas/thoughts/behaviour observations with classroom teachers and case managers about students.

Be flexible. Schedules can change often. Sometimes EAs are absent and they are not replaced—that means schedules need to be adjusted. Education assistants can also be redeployed when a new student arrives who needs support or when a student moves schools. Change can also happen on the fly and being flexible makes a team stronger.

How Can EAs Support Students to Be Self-Advocates for Their Learning Needs?

Form relationships. Get to know the students. Relationships are critical, as you need to know the student before you can support them. Ask students about what their passions are, what they are good at, what did they do on the weekend, and so on. As well, EAs should get to know as many students as possible. Getting to know students during your supervision breaks can be very beneficial.

Reinforce their strengths, understand what they need, and build resiliency skills. It's important to view student IEPs and talk to case managers so you are aware of each student's strengths, needs, and adaptations in class. If you know a student's strength is group discussion then you can make sure during a group activity that they can report back verbally to the class. Students will require reminders and modelling on how to ask the teachers for adaptations (for example, extra time on tests or a scribe) and it's best to refrain from asking the teacher on behalf of the student. After some reminders and prompting, the student must ask the teacher—if they are able. Once students become better at self-advocating their needs, you will see an improvement in their self-confidence. Also make sure the students have opportunities to make mistakes and build their resiliency skills. As we all know, EAs have big hearts and I know they want their students to be successful, but hovering and doing their work for them is not beneficial in the long term.

How Can EAs Best Support Students in Their Transition Goals?

To support students with academic transition goals like completing English 12, it's important you connect with the teacher and the case manager to understand your role. The student might not need an EA's support in these classes on a daily basis. You might be needed for the beginning of the course and then there can be a gradual release of responsibility. You might not even be needed in the class at all in some cases; however, the student knows where to find you if extra support is needed. It's important (especially as student go on to post-secondary) that they learn how to find their supports. For example, an English 12 student who doesn't require an EA in class can be left to work independently, knowing extra help is available in the resource room. That student knows where you are and learns to use their supports when needed.

To support students who have very complex needs, EAs must know the student's specific goals in the class. For example, a student who is in foods class might have a communication goal that they are working toward. Again, communication with the student's case manager is critical. Continue to collaborate, ask questions, and know that your directions should come from the student's teacher and case manager. And remember it's okay to make mistakes—that's how we all grow as learners.

CRITICAL THINKING QUESTIONS

1. Why should an EA be concerned with the transition to adulthood for students with complex needs?

2. Thinking about key ideas in this chapter, how would an EA support students in the transition process? What questions might an EA still have?

3. How are adult and community support and philosophy of inclusion involved in the transition to adulthood?

REFERENCES

Anderson, S., & Bigby, C. (2017). Self-advocacy as a means to positive identities for people with intellectual disability: "We just help them, be them really." *Journal of Applied Research in Intellectual Disabilities, 30*(1), 109–120.

British Columbia Ministry of Education. (2018a). Profiles: Communication competency (draft). Retrieved from https://curriculum.gov.bc.ca/sites/curriculum.gov.bc.ca/files/pdf/CommunicationCompetencyProfiles.pdf

British Columbia Ministry of Education. (2018b). Profiles: Personal awareness and responsibility (draft). Retrieved from https://curriculum.gov.bc.ca/sites/curriculum.gov.bc.ca/files/pdf/PersonalAwarenessResponsibilityCompetencyProfiles.pdf

British Columbia Ministry of Education. (2018c). Profiles: Social responsibility competency (draft). https://curriculum.gov.bc.ca/sites/curriculum.gov.bc.ca/files/pdf/SocialResponsibilityCompetencyProfiles.pdf

Carter, E. E., Lane, K. L., Cooney, M., Weir, K., Moss, C. K., & Machalicek, W. (2013). Self-determination among transition-age youth with autism or intellectual disability: Parent perspectives. *Research and Practice for Persons with Severe Disabilities, 38*(3), 129–138.

Causton-Theoharis, J. B. (2009). The golden rule of providing support in inclusive classrooms: Support others as you would wish to be supported. *Teaching Exceptional Children, 42*(2), 36–43.

Corbey, S., Boyer-Stephens, A., Jones, B., Miller, R. J., West, L. L., & Sarkees-Wicenski, M. (1999). *Integrating Transition Planning into the IEP Process* (2nd ed.) [Excerpt]. Arlington, VA: Council for Exceptional Children. Retrieved from http://www.ldonline.org/article/7757/

Doyle, M. B. (2008). *The paraprofessional's guide to the inclusive classroom: Working as a team.* Baltimore: Paul H. Brookes Publishing.

Gauthier-Boudreault, C., Gallagher, F., & Couturec, M. (2017). Specific needs of families of young adults with profound intellectual disability during and after transition to adulthood: What are we missing? *Research in Developmental Disabilities, 66,* 16–26.

Government of British Columbia. (2009, November). *Cross ministry transition planning protocols for youth with special needs.* Retrieved from https://www2.gov.bc.ca/assets/gov/family-and-social-supports/children-teens-with-special-needs/2012_ytpp_protocol.pdf

Gray, K. M., Piccinin, A., Keating, C. M., Taffe, J., Parmenter, T. R., Hofer, S., & Tonge, B. J. (2014). Outcomes in young adulthood: Are we achieving community participation and inclusion? *Journal of Intellectual Disability Research, 58*(8), 734–745. doi:10.1111/jir.12069

Inclusion BC. (2018). What is self-advocacy. Retrieved from http://www.inclusionbc .orf/what-is-self-advocacy

Lord, J., & Hutchison, P. (2011). *Pathways to inclusion: Building a new story with people and communities.* Concord, ON: Captus Press.

Ministry of Children and Family Development. (n.d.). *Transition planning for youth with special needs: A community support guide.* Victoria, BC: Government of British Columbia.

Moore, S. (2017). Strength based student profile. *Blogsomemoore.* Retrieved from https:// blogsomemoore.files.wordpress.com/2015/02/strength-based-student-profile.pdf

Nguyen, T., Stewart, D., & Gorter, J. W. (2016). Looking back to move forward: Reflections and lessons learned about transitions to adulthood for youth with disabilities. *Child Care Health and Development, 44*(4), 83–88. doi:10.1111/cch.12534

O'Brien, C. L., & O'Brien, J. (2000). *The origins of person-centered planning: A community of practice perspective.* Lithonia, GA: Responsive Systems Associates.

Prater, M. A., Redman, A. S., Anderson, D., & Gibb, G. S. (2014). Teaching adolescent students with learning disabilities to self-advocate for accommodations. *Intervention in School and Clinic, 49*(5), 298–305.

Roberts, E., Ju, S. L., & Zhang, D. (2014). Review of practices that promote self-advocacy for students with disabilities. *Journal of Disability Policy Studies, 26*(4), 209–220. doi:10.1177/1044207314540213

United Nations. (2006). *Convention on the rights of persons with disabilities and optional protocol.* Geneva, Switzerland: Author. Retrieved from http://www.un.org/ disabilities/documents/convention/convoptprot-e.pdf

Wehman, P. (1997). *Life beyond the classroom: Transition strategies for young people with disabilities* (2nd ed.). Baltimore: Paul H. Brookes Publishing.

Wehman, P. (2013). Transition from school to work: Where are we and where do we need to go? *Career Development and Transition for Exceptional Individuals, 36*(1), 58–66. doi:10.1177/2165143413482137

Young-Southward, G., Cooper, S. A., & Philo, C. (2017). Health and wellbeing during transition to adulthood for young people with intellectual disabilities: A qualitative study. *Research in Developmental Disabilities, 70,* 94–103. Retrieved from doi:10.1016/j.ridd.2017.09.003

CONTRIBUTOR BIOGRAPHIES

EDITORS

Mary Harber, MSW, has been a social worker and educator for the past 30 years, supporting individuals, families, and communities in the areas of substance use and prevention, trauma support, and creative intervention methods in practice. She has worked in the field of disabilities with a focus on healthy sexuality, social competence, and diverse learning needs. She teaches at Camosun College in Victoria, British Columbia, and believes in the capacity of innovation and creativity to facilitate change.

Asha Rao, MEd, has taught for over 16 years in elementary to post-secondary schools, locally and internationally. Her work is focused on inclusive education, mental health and wellness, and social justice principles. She is currently program lead and faculty in the Education Assistant and Community Support Program at Camosun College, Victoria, British Columbia, and faculty in the Community Family and Child Studies Department. She believes in collaborating to create engaging, inclusive, and accessible learning environments. She encourages analysis, critical thinking, and multiple means of representation and expression with students. She believes in fostering creativity and imagination in her work, in the classroom, and in the field.

CONTRIBUTORS

Joan Astren, MEd, has more than 30 years of experience in the field supporting individuals with diverse needs; she has had the privilege of supporting children and their families in a variety of contexts. Joan has worked as a child care consultant, early childhood educator, and child and youth care worker, and as an instructor at Camosun College in

Victoria, British Columbia. She is currently a behaviour consultant for families with children with autism.

Joanie Chestnut is an EA in School District 71, Comox Valley, and also provides behaviour intervention and support privately. She has a strong background of community engagement, volunteer work, and social justice activities. She is a graduate of Vancouver Island University's School and Community Support Worker Program.

Kyla Cleator, MEd, is a supervisor with Edmonton Public Schools in the Department of Inclusive Learning. She currently supervises a multidisciplinary team of consultants supporting students with diverse and challenging learning needs. She has a master's in educational psychology and has been an educator for almost 30 years. She is passionate about finding ways to support each and every student, no matter their disability or challenge.

Barbara Eckersley, MEd, taught in the K–12 public education system for over 25 years and continues to work part-time as a student services teacher. She is also an instructor at the College of the Rockies in British Columbia in the Child, Youth, and Family Studies Department, specializing in the Education Assistant Program. She is dedicated to collaborative and inclusive education where every student is a valued member of the classroom and school community.

Janine Fajenski, BEd, completed her bachelor of education degree at the University of the Fraser Valley in British Columbia, and is currently an elementary teacher in the Chilliwack School District. She also completed her community support worker certificate at the University of the Fraser Valley and was an education assistant in the Chilliwack School District for 10 years, supporting students with autism and severe behavioural challenges.

Lisa Gates, EACSW, CYFMH, has been in human services since 1989 and believes this is truly "good work." As a classroom and community support worker, she created cultural change for individuals with disability. She participates in person-centred planning, bringing groups of people together in support of individuals charting their own futures—some of the most rewarding work of her career. She currently teaches at Selkirk College, and is co-author of the Shelter Guides Respite Care and Home Share and Spectrum ASD curriculum.

Jane Green, MEd (Special Education), has been in service to people with differences and their families since 1980. As an education assistant and community support worker instructor/coach, she has invested heavily in stewarding inclusive community and is committed to practical skill building and encouraging respect, curiosity, and commitment to excellence. This shows up in curriculum development work: FLASH, ShelterGuides, and Spectrum ASD. A lifelong learner, she is intrigued by creative process, learning styles, and resilience. She has been described as a "weaver of possibility."

Dr. Linda Hill, PhD, coordinator of the Inclusive Leadership Co-operative, has been a passionate pioneer in Canada's inclusion movement since the 1970s, when she was an education assistant questioning segregated special education systems. She has travelled the world guiding educators, students, and family members to explore, share, and celebrate diversity and inclusion in schools and communities. She is the author of many articles, books, and courses on inclusive leadership, and received the Canadian Voice of Women Peace Education Award in 2018.

Victoria Johnston-Hatch, PgD, has been faculty and department chair at Kwantlen Polytechnic Institute, British Columbia, since 2012. She is currently completing her master's in intellectual and developmental disabilities (Kent) focusing on research into positive behavioural supports. Since 2005, she has been a behaviour consultant with CBI Consultants, working with agencies throughout British Columbia. She believes that all individuals have the right to a high quality of life and inspires others to feel the same.

Jane Litman, MA, is an educator with over 30 years experience in the K–12 public school system. She has worked extensively as a teacher of students with visual impairments and as a learning support teacher for complex learners. Educated in Ontario and British Columbia, she has spent most of her teaching career in the pursuit of, and as an advocate for, inclusion of all learners in our classrooms.

Dr. Jeffrey MacCormack, PhD, is an assistant professor of educational psychology and inclusion in the Faculty of Education at the University of Lethbridge, Alberta. As a former classroom teacher, his research on after-school programs, executive functions, social competence, and play-based learning is informed by 10 years of experience teaching elementary students and many years of teaching post-secondary adult learners. His work has focused on play and creating spaces where youth can thrive.

Jessica Mantel, BA, BEd, completed her bachelor of arts and bachelor of education degrees at the University of the Fraser Valley, British Columbia. She is currently an elementary teacher in the Chilliwack School District. She previously completed her diploma as a special education assistant and was an education assistant in the Surrey School District for three years. She also worked as a behaviour interventionist providing direct support to children with autism.

Susan McKay, BSW, MPA, has taught in the Education Assistant and Community Support Program at Thompson Rivers University, British Columbia, for over 25 years. Her prior practice included working with adults with disabilities and in child protective services.

Joanne Mitchell, MSW, has ancestry from the Kabeowek People of the Algonquin Nation and the Nippissing People of the Ojibway Nation and settler ancestry from Italy and France. She was raised in North Bay, Ontario, but now lives in Victoria, British Columbia, the ancestral lands of the Songhees and Esquimalt Nations. Joanne works as an Indigenous student counsellor for the Greater Victoria School District and holds a master's in social work from the University of Victoria, British Columbia.

Dr. Lindsay Morcom, DPhil, is an interdisciplinary researcher with experience in education, Aboriginal languages, language revitalization, and linguistics. She earned her master's in linguistics at First Nations University through the University of Regina in 2006. She then completed her doctorate in general linguistics and comparative philology as a Rhodes Scholar at Oxford University in 2010. She now works as an assistant professor and coordinator of the Aboriginal Teacher Education Program at Queen's University in Kingston, Ontario. She is of Algonquin, French Canadian, and German ancestry.

Dr. Nancy Norman, PhD, is a university teaching fellow (K–12 Transformation) and faculty in the Education Assistant Program at Kwantlen Polytechnic University, and the Teacher Education Department at the University of the Fraser Valley, where she both teaches and researches in the areas of social and emotional development and inclusive practices in K–12 schools. Previously, she was a specialist teacher of the deaf and hard of hearing in the Richmond School District.

Dr. Greg Ogilvie, PhD, is an assistant professor in the Faculty of Education at the University of Lethbridge, Alberta. He has worked as a language teacher and teacher educator in Canada, Ethiopia, and Ukraine. His scholarly interests include task-based language teaching, critical interculturality, restorative justice pedagogy, culturally and linguistically responsive teaching, and supervision practices to foster professional growth.

Michelle Pozin, MEd, has worked with individuals with differences as a coach, teacher, author, and consultant since 1985. She has coordinated, trained, and guided educational staff to enable individuals with differences to reach their full potential in all aspects of their lives, especially in the school setting. She continues to empower educational staff in her current role as a high school learning support teacher and as content specialist and co-author of the Spectrum ASD course at Selkirk College.

Dr. Cornelia Schneider, PhD, is associate professor at Mount Saint Vincent University in Halifax, Nova Scotia. Her main research interests focus on children and youth with disabilities and inclusive education. Originally from Germany, where she obtained her degree in special education at Universität Würzburg, she completed her PhD at Université Paris Descartes (Sorbonne), investigating peer relationships of children with and without disabilities. In her research, she combines sociology of childhood, sociology of education, and disability studies.

Dr. Nan Stevens, EdD, teaches undergraduate and graduate courses in inclusive and special education at Thompson Rivers University, British Columbia. When her first son was born with a severe developmental disability, her personal and professional career trajectory aligned, and she committed her life's work to supporting her son and advocating for those with diverse needs. In 2017, she completed a doctor of education degree in leadership and disability studies. Her research interests include the lived experiences of families with loved ones with neurodiverse needs, teacher preparation, and school choice.

Alison Taplay, MA, is a professor at Vancouver Island University, British Columbia, where she creates learning environments that are student-centred, inclusive, relational, and process-oriented. Her 30-year career in the community living sector providing direct support and leading the development of community-based services informs her practice. She sees advocacy, innovation, and engagement as essential tools for advancing the well-being of our public schools, organizations, and communities, and for the full inclusion of all citizens.

Heather Wik, MET, taught in the K–12 system for 18 years, teaching both at the high school and elementary levels. She has been an instructor in the Education Assistant Specialty at the College of the Rockies, British Columbia, since 2003 and has been the coordinator of the Child, Youth, and Family Studies Program since 2012. She has a passion for creating dynamic interactive classrooms for online learning, which foster skills in critical thinking, collaboration, and authentic knowledge building.